ALFRED HITCHCOCK'S FRENZY

The Last Masterpiece

RAYMOND FOERY

Mark —
fellow Hitchcockian —

Raymond

ROWMAN & LITTLEFIELD
Lanham • Boulder • New York • London

Published by Rowman & Littlefield
A wholly owned subsidiary of The Rowman & Littlefield Publishing Group, Inc.
4501 Forbes Boulevard, Suite 200, Lanham, Maryland 20706
www.rowman.com

Unit A, Whitacre Mews, 26-34 Stannary Street, London SE11 4AB

British Library Cataloguing in Publication Information Available

Library of Congress Cataloging-in-Publication Data

The hardback edition of this book was previously catalogued by the Library of Congress
as follows:

Foery, Raymond, 1945–
  Alfred Hitchcock's Frenzy : the last masterpiece / Raymond Foery.
     p. cm.
  Includes bibliographical references and index.
  1. Frenzy (Motion picture) I. Title. II. Title: Hitchcock's Frenzy : the last masterpiece.
  PN1997.F7442F64 2012
  791.43'72—dc23   2012000153

ISBN 978-0-8108-7755-9 (hardback : alk. paper)
ISBN 978-1-4422-4181-7 (pbk. : alk. paper)
ISBN 978-0-8108-7756-6 (ebook)

♾™ The paper used in this publication meets the minimum requirements of American
National Standard for Information Sciences—Permanence of Paper for Printed Library
Materials, ANSI/NISO Z39.48-1992.

Printed in the United States of America

To the memory of Stefan Sharff,
whose legendary Columbia University
course in film analysis started it all.

And to my son Emmanuel,
a young film lover who will, I feel certain,
continue to think deeply about cinema,
which means he will of necessity explore Hitchcock.

Contents

Acknowledgments

A S WITH ANY PROJECT requiring a good deal of research and analysis, there are many people to thank for assistance with this one. Before mentioning anyone I actually know, I wish to acknowledge all of the contributions of the small army of Hitchcock scholars upon whose virtual shoulders I now virtually stand. It is not, of course, that I put myself above them, only that I acknowledge their importance to my own climb. On a more personal level, I wish to thank, first, my mentors at Columbia's graduate film division who are always in my thoughts as I proceed to examine nuances of cinema. These would be Andrew Sarris, Annette Insdorf, and Stefan Sharff. The faculty research committee at Quinnipiac University supported my visits to the Hitchcock archives, and faculty colleagues gave me helpful hints and encouragement over the past few years. I thank Michael Calia, Ed Alwood, John Gourlie, Len Engel, Becky Abbott, Ewa Callahan, Liam O'Brien, and many others. I thank Mark Thompson and Angela Skyers for administrative support and Charles Getchell and Janet Valeski for help from the Arnold Bernhard Library at Quinnipiac. From the Sterling Memorial Library at Yale, I wish to thank Bill Massa and Tobin Nellhaus for their assistance, and Mary Beth Radigan for her encouragement.

While in California doing the research, I stayed with my dear cousin Linda, and I wish to thank her and her housemate Joy for their warm hospitality.

Everyone at the Margaret Herrick Library in Beverly Hills was gracious and helpful; they all deserve my thanks. Most especially appreciated, however, was the professional assistance of Barbara Hall, archivist for the

Alfred Hitchcock papers. She was instrumental in guiding my research to the proper documents. Many thanks as well to my editor at Scarecrow Press, Stephen Ryan, for his patience.

Finally, I wish to thank my wife, Jan: an ideal second reader and a best first friend.

Prologue
Over the Atlantic and Down the Thames

THE OPENING OF ALFRED HITCHCOCK'S *Frenzy* is described in the
final version of the script (under "Exterior, Aerial View—London—
Day") as follows:

> Part of a printed map FILLS THE SCREEN. At the top right hand cor-
> ner the word London is written in elaborate scrollwork in a white inset
> together with its scale. The CAMERA FAVOURS the curving blue snake
> line space which indicates the course of the River Thames. As we follow
> the route of the Thames, the printed map gradually changes into the real
> thing. We follow the course of the river with the helicopter, from which
> the scene is being shot, which gradually lowers until it is a couple of hun-
> dred feet above the Thames—ahead of us we see Tower Bridge. As we
> approach the bridge, the bascules open as though welcoming us. With the
> help of a zoom, the CAMERA goes through and under the upper part
> of the bridge. We are now on the opposite side of the bridge, having just
> gone through.[1]

The film itself commences with this scene, replete with the addition of a
rather heraldic score by composer Ron Goodwin. This opening can be seen
as not only a grandiloquently melodramatic way of beginning the film but
as a metaphor for Alfred Hitchcock's triumphant return to London, city of
his birth and source of his early success as a filmmaker. Certainly no commercial airliner could have taken this particular route—soaring low over the
Thames—and so there is a quality of personal fantasy about the shot. It can
stand for Hitchcock's own imagining of how he might have orchestrated his
return to the city of his origins. It can also remind us of Hitchcock's lifelong appreciation of the grand cinematic gesture, exemplified often by the

sweep of the moving camera. Hitchcock was always experimenting, always looking for new ways to expand his cinematic grammar, always enamored of the moving camera perhaps because it so clearly exemplifies the language of the medium.

In his carefully researched monograph on the making of *Psycho*, Stephen Rebello notes Hitchcock's disappointment that what he had envisioned for the opening shot of that film—an overhead shot taken by helicopter into the window of a hotel room—was simply not able to be executed within the technical limitations in place in November of 1959, when shooting commenced on *Psycho*.[2] Now twelve years later, in the summer of 1971, Hitchcock was able to achieve that kind of shot. And as he embarked on this project, his fifty-second feature film—and the first one to be fully filmed in London since his departure for the United States three decades earlier—he was about to enjoy the technical support that would allow virtually all of his script ideas to be fully realized. Hitchcock's voyage to London, then, can be seen as a triumphant return to his artistic and professional base, although, as we shall see, it hardly began as such.

Alfred Hitchcock had left London for New York on the luxury liner *Queen Mary* in March of 1939. He was not quite forty years old at the time. He was to begin his Hollywood period under the notoriously punctilious David O. Selznick, a relationship that proved satisfactory to neither party.[3] At the time of his departure, Hitchcock was easily the most successful and probably the best-known movie director in England. His recent films had been critically acclaimed as well as box-office successes. Several Hollywood companies had joined Selznick in expressing an interest in signing him to an American contract. Perhaps most significantly, the New York Film Critics had named Hitchcock the "best director of 1938," largely on the basis of their appreciation of *The Lady Vanishes*, making that film a hit on both sides of the Atlantic.[4] Hitchcock, then, was already a celebrity director when he left England, and many in the British press acknowledged that he was leaving his homeland at the height of his powers. "Any day now," lamented one journalist, "our most celebrated director, Alfred Hitchcock, will be off to Hollywood."[5]

An early biography of Hitchcock was written by his friend and collaborator, John Russell Taylor. In describing this particular period of Hitchcock's life, Taylor speculates on the reasons for such a successful artist to be seeking a new venue. "He was beginning to feel just a trifle restless," wrote Taylor in 1978.[6] In addition, Taylor notes, Hitchcock was beginning to feel a bit pigeonholed: "By now critics and public alike knew, or thought they knew, much too exactly what a Hitchcock film would and should be."[7] Taylor observes that Hitchcock had gone as far as he could go within the confines of the British film industry and that he was therefore "in danger of becoming the prisoner of his own success."[8]

Of course, Alfred Hitchcock was to have a splendid career in the United States. By the time of his death in 1980, he had become recognized as one of the few true auteurs of cinema, his work studied by scholars, his persona appreciated by commentators. Indeed, by the 1970s, it seemed as if the name "Alfred Hitchcock" guaranteed both success at the box office and appreciation by the scholarly community. His string of Hollywood films of the 1950s remains today one of the crowning achievements of the medium: a dozen films in just over a decade, including such internationally acknowledged masterpieces as *Rear Window*, *Vertigo*, and *Psycho*. He is recognized as both a master of the moving camera and a genius at montage. His films have been examined and analyzed by more scholars than have those of any other director, and his work continues to be a staple of university film courses across the globe. To give but one example, *Vertigo* is regarded by the acclaimed film journal *Sight and Sound* as the second "greatest film ever made," just behind the perennial standard bearer, *Citizen Kane*.[9]

Ironically, it was the project that brought Hitchcock to America that was recognized by the Academy of Motion Picture Arts and Sciences as the "best film of the year," the only time in his entire career that a Hitchcock film was so chosen. *Rebecca* was given the award in 1941 (as the best picture of 1940), but it was the producer, David O. Selznick, who actually walked away with the statuette (the Oscar). Hitchcock had never before encountered the kind of production oversight that defined a David O. Selznick enterprise, and by all accounts, he was none too pleased about it. The ubiquitous Selznick memo would remind Hitchcock—almost on a daily basis—that, for example, the rushes seemed too slow or that the budget was growing because of the time Hitchcock was taking to shoot each scene.[10] Hitchcock parried by utilizing his carefully crafted approach to on-set production: so much would be storyboarded in advance that there would be very few choices to be made in the editing room. As Taylor puts it, Hitchcock's approach to shooting resulted in "a strict limit to what Selznick could do afterwards."[11] Years later, in his series of interviews with French director François Truffaut, Hitchcock simply labeled *Rebecca* as "not a Hitchcock picture."[12]

Many authentic "Hitchcock pictures" followed this initial association with Selznick, however. By the 1950s, Hitchcock was able to operate more or less independently (certainly without daily memos from a studio head), and the results were impressive. In addition to the obvious masterpieces already mentioned here, Hitchcock contributed a full range of great works to the cinematic canon during this extraordinarily productive decade: *Strangers on a Train* (1951), *Dial M for Murder* (1954), *To Catch a Thief* (1955), *The Man Who Knew Too Much* and *The Wrong Man* (both 1956), and *North by Northwest* (1959). These and others—not to mention his extremely successful television series (*Alfred Hitchcock Presents*)—made him perhaps the wealthiest director in Hollywood and certainly the most recognizable. His weekly introductions to the TV series, delivered in his droll London accent, made Hitchcock the only Hollywood director who would be recognized on the street by tourists, this in an age well before the French "auteur theory" had led to a lionizing of the director. Hitchcock became, according to one writer, "the first universally acknowledged star director in . . . Hollywood."[13] In the 1950s it was far more often the stars whose faces were universally identifiable. While the players in these great films of the era—Cary Grant, James Stewart, Grace Kelly—would be immediately recognized by the average movie fan, most of these same fans had never seen an image of John Ford, Howard Hawks, or Vincente Minnelli, for example. On the other hand, the adjective "Hitchcockian" had begun to appear during the decade of the '50s, and it continues to be used extensively today. Patricia Hitchcock O'Connell, Hitchcock's only child, recently commented on its omnipresence. Writing a foreword to Laurent Bouzereau's 2010 appreciation, *Hitchcock: Piece by Piece*, O'Connell claims, certainly not without reason, that we encounter the phrase "It's so Hitchcockian" on an almost daily basis.[14]

If life were indeed to have imitated art, Alfred Hitchcock's return to London in the spring of 1971 would have clearly been as triumphant a one as his opening shot suggested. He might even have been returning as "Sir Alfred" had his name ever appeared on the annual year-end list of "Queen's Honours." Alas, that hadn't (yet) happened, and Hitchcock's return to his native England was hardly the equivalent of the entry into Rome of a victorious general after a series of noble victories. Hitchcock was, rather, returning to London after a string of disappointments. That majestic entry, then, that gliding over the Thames and under the bridge, remains a part of the master's (always lively) fantasy life.

Alfred Hitchcock with his wife, Alma Reville, and daughter, Pat, at home in Hollywood in the 1940s. *Photofest*

Notes

1. See *Frenzy* Folder #261 of the Alfred Hitchcock papers at the Margaret Herrick Library, Beverly Hills, California. The script being referred to here is the "final" script dated July 21, 1971.

2. Stephen Rebello, *Alfred Hitchcock and the Making of* Psycho (New York: St. Martin's, 1990), 129.

3. The standard (and most recent) biography of Hitchcock, which includes considerable material on the relationship between Hitch and Selznick, is Patrick McGilligan's *Alfred Hitchcock: A Life in Darkness and Light* (New York: Harper-Collins, 2003). There is also Leonard J. Leff, *Hitchcock with Selznick: The Rich and Strange Collaboration of Alfred Hitchcock and David O. Selznick in Hollywood* (New York: Weidenfeld & Nicholson, 1987).

4. McGilligan, *Alfred Hitchcock*, 230.

5. J. Danvers Williams, "What I'd Do to the Stars: An Interview with Alfred Hitchcock," *Film Weekly*, 4 March 1939, 12.

6. John Russell Taylor, *Hitch: The Life and Times of Alfred Hitchcock* (London: Faber and Faber, 1978), 147.

7. Taylor, *Hitch*, 147.

8. Taylor, *Hitch*, 147.

9. The most recent *Sight and Sound* poll took place in 2002. Another is expected in 2012.

10. Taylor, *Hitch*, 157.

11. Taylor, *Hitch*, 158.

12. François Truffaut, *Hitchcock*, rev. ed. (New York: Simon & Schuster/Touchstone, 1985), 127.

13. Dennis McDougal, *The Last Mogul: Lew Wasserman, MCA, and the Hidden History of Hollywood* (New York: Crown, 1998), 253.

14. See Laurent Bouzereau, *Hitchcock: Piece by Piece* (New York: Abrams, 2010), 8.

Hitchcock in 1970   1
The Lion in Waiting

ALFRED HITCHCOCK, BORN IN AUGUST and thus a "lion" according to his astrological sun sign, had something to prove by 1971. Based on virtually all the accounts from what Thomas Leitch calls the "Hitchcock industry" (referring to the ever-growing community of Hitchcock scholars, biographers, and commentators), that period of the artist's life immediately preceding his embarking on the film that came to be known as *Frenzy* had not been his most professionally satisfying.[1] The critical and financial failure of both the 1966 *Torn Curtain* and the 1969 *Topaz* found Hitchcock to be at the lowest ebb in his career, according to one biographer (and friend), John Russell Taylor.[2] Donald Spoto, in a considerably more sensationalized examination of Hitchcock's life, characterized this period as a time when the often-despondent director "seemed to have lost faith in his own ability to make good motion pictures."[3] The more recent (and more balanced) biography—Patrick McGilligan's 2003 *A Life in Darkness and Light*—describes a disappointed but not defeated Hitchcock spending most of 1970 resting and reading properties, keenly aware that "failure had made it all the more important for him to try again."[4] McGilligan noted that everyone around Hitchcock had "witnessed the depths of the director's despair after *Topaz*" and that the studio executives at Universal (especially his longtime friend and financial adviser, Lew Wasserman) were eager to give the master at least one more project, certainly if it could be a relatively low-budget one.[5] The subsequent idea of making a modest film in London was therefore generated as much out of a sense of economy on the part of Universal Studios as from any desire on Hitchcock's part to return to his homeland.[6]

The situation was seen by those around Hitchcock in 1970 to be somewhat desperate. After all, the reviews *had* been bad. Indeed, Hitchcock had not had a "blockbuster" commercial success since *The Birds* in 1963. By 1970, then, he had realized three commercial failures in a row, something that had never before happened in his career. (*Marnie*, to be fair, had not actually lost money for the studio; it merely had not made anywhere near as much as had been expected.) While scholars (most notably Robin Wood) have come to think of *Marnie* (1964) as an exceptionally complex and sophisticated work, it was hardly received in that manner at the time of its release. In fact, it was almost universally panned. Even the reviewer for the usually sympathetic local paper, the *Los Angeles Times*, called *Marnie* "naggingly improbable."[7] Perhaps the cruelest comment can be attributed to Judith Crist of the *New York Herald Tribune*; she called *Marnie* "pathetically old-fashioned."[8] Reading this in his bungalow on the grounds of Universal Studios could hardly have amused the director, the review having been published but a few weeks shy of his sixty-fifth birthday.

While *Marnie* has its defenders among contemporary scholars and critics, the same cannot be said of either *Torn Curtain* or *Topaz*. Neither received any truly stellar reviews and both were counted by the studio's arcane bookkeeping methods as box-office failures. *Topaz*, in fact, lost more money than any other Hitchcock film, in part because it was the most expensive movie he had ever shot. *Torn Curtain* had been viewed by at least one observer as "a profound failure that indicated a more chronic condition—a malaise."[9] Hitchcock was not happy with the results of either project, feeling in both cases that there had been too much interference by the studio resulting in too many compromises. He was especially unhappy with *Topaz*, concluding that "it just didn't work on any level."[10]

Topaz had been released in December of 1969, so it was certainly clear to Hitchcock by the beginning of the succeeding year that his by now legendary powers were suspected by many around him to be in decline. He therefore spent most of 1970 searching for a project that might prove them wrong. It was not to be easy. First of all, there was the paradoxical problem of his cozy relationship with the power structure at Universal Studios. His former agent, Lew Wasserman, was now the head of Universal, and while this had led originally to a quite generous contract, it also had the ironic effect of causing Hitchcock to answer to the very man who had represented him to other studio chieftains in the past. Secondly, Hitchcock had been looking for the "right property" for years now. Neither *Torn Curtain* nor *Topaz* had been a proper fit for his talents. Yet it was the studio, not Hitchcock himself, that controlled the flow of material to the director and his readers. *Topaz* had come to him, for example, because Universal had purchased the rights to the novel when it had become a best-seller.

Hitchcock directing *Topaz* in 1969. Just behind him is his longtime assistant, Peggy Robertson. *Photofest*

Finally, by 1970, Hitchcock had lost many members of his trusted entourage, a small group of associates who had worked with him on his various projects for almost two decades. Over the past few years, George Tomasini, his chief editor, and Robert Burks, his director of photography, had both died. He had severed his relationship with the masterly composer

Bernard Herrmann over a disagreement on the score for *Torn Curtain.*
His television associates, most notably Norman Lloyd and Joan Harrison
(she had come with the Hitchcocks from England in 1939), had little to
do once *Alfred Hitchcock Presents* ceased operations in 1968. In short, what
had until very recently been a bustling office staff of professionals, each of
whom engaged in either the present project or the next one, had by the
end of 1969 been reduced to a very small number. A visitor during this
period commented that Hitchcock had not only aged but that he seemed
unhappy and distant.[11] (Only adding to the melodrama, Hitchcock's personal physician of the previous thirty years had also recently passed away.)

The delicate situation that characterized Hitchcock's relationship
with Lew Wasserman calls for some explication. (Hitchcock biographer
McGilligan identified Wasserman as "a man as important as any other in
Hitchcock's life story.")[12] He, too, was one of those larger-than-life figures
who so often seem to gravitate toward Hollywood, California. Indeed, the
title of one of the biographies of Wasserman is "When Hollywood Had a
King."[13] He was a former theatrical agent (he had actually begun his fascination with the movies as a young theater usher) who rose through the
ranks of his company (MCA, the former Music Corporation of America)
to become its president in 1946.[14] By this time, MCA had less to do with
music than with representing actors as their business agents, and Wasserman had an enviable client list: Fred Astaire, Jack Benny, Bette Davis,
Henry Fonda, Judy Garland, Gregory Peck, and James Stewart, to name
but a few. He also represented several directors, especially those not already under long-term studio contracts. In 1945, the agency that had been
representing Hitchcock was sold to MCA, and Lew Wasserman thereby
became Hitchcock's agent.

They seemed to have hit if off immediately, in part, suggest several
biographers, because Wasserman did not dress nor act like a typical Hollywood agent of the 1940s. He was restrained and proper, dressed in dark
suits and conservative ties, a man, then, of taste, perhaps even elegance; a
man, one might observe, very much like Hitchcock himself. Wasserman
was younger than Hitchcock by some dozen years or so, but they had
each arrived in Hollywood at roughly the same time (Wasserman in 1938,
Hitchcock in 1939), and they each seem to have recognized the fact that
the old studio system was in decline and that a new age was upon them,
one that required flexibility and professional mobility. Wasserman was to
build his empire on that very combination, and he viewed Hitchcock, he
admitted later in his life, as a true genius.[15] Hitchcock, in turn, thought of
Wasserman as one of his closest personal friends. The two of them, with

their spouses, socialized at each other's houses and at Chasen's, Hitchcock's favorite Beverly Hills restaurant, and they even vacationed together from time to time. A Universal executive recalled that "the Hitchcocks were the only ones that the Wassermans really vacationed with."[16] One of Hitchcock's extremely rare appearances as part of the annual Academy Awards ceremony (after all, he had been nominated for Best Director five times and never won) was to introduce Wasserman when he was awarded the Jean Hersholt Humanitarian Award in 1974. In short, this was far more than a mere professional relationship of agent to client or, later, of director to studio head. Alfred Hitchcock and Lew Wasserman were friends, and it was Wasserman who was able to successfully provide continued support for Hitchcock's career after these recent disappointments. At the same time, the project that Hitchcock chose would have to be approved by Wasserman.

This proviso had caused some conflict between the two in the past. It was Wasserman, for example, who had insisted on the casting of Paul Newman in *Torn Curtain*, a casting situation that was an unhappy one from the perspective of either party. ("As you know, he's a 'Method' actor," Hitchcock complained to Truffaut.)[17] It was Wasserman who had insisted that a part of Hitchcock's long-term contract with Universal would clearly state that Hitchcock could under no circumstances make *Mary Rose* while at the studio; this had been a pet project of Hitchcock's for many years, but Wasserman found it to be not to his liking and probably not commercially viable. Wasserman was a diplomat; he tended to offer persuasion rather than coercion. In addition, Hitchcock knew that Wasserman had very fine instincts. For one, it was Wasserman who had persuaded Hitchcock to enter the realm of television in 1955, and it was Wasserman who had crafted that contract. It was to make Hitchcock extremely wealthy: he made far more money from his TV series than he ever had as a film director. And it was Wasserman who had convinced Hitchcock to cast Kim Novak in *Vertigo*, thus contributing significantly to the aura surrounding that film. Hitchcock thereby trusted Wasserman while at the same time recognizing that by 1970, the balance of power between the two had shifted significantly and that Wasserman was now diligently overseeing Hitchcock's choices of future projects.

Hitchcock spent most of 1970 doing just that: searching for a project that Wasserman might approve. It was hardly his most fruitful period. He spent a lot of time looking at other films. He lunched with Wasserman and other Universal executives. (By this time, Alfred Hitchcock was the third largest shareholder of Universal's corporate entity.) He went to the theater.

He read. According to one biographer, his schedule had never been more open ended.[18] He never considered retiring; rather, he wrote to Truffaut: "I am looking for a new film project, but it is very difficult."[19] By the end of the year, he had found one.

Notes

1. Thomas Leitch, *The Encyclopedia of Alfred Hitchcock* (New York: Checkmark, 2002), xxv–xxvii.

2. John Russell Taylor, *Hitch: The Life and Times of Alfred Hitchcock* (London: Faber and Faber, 1978), 281.

3. Donald Spoto, *The Dark Side of Genius: The Life of Alfred Hitchcock* (Boston: Little, Brown, 1983), 503.

4. Patrick McGilligan, *Alfred Hitchcock: A Life in Darkness and Light* (New York: HarperCollins, 2003), 697.

5. McGilligan, *Alfred Hitchcock*, 698.

6. Of course, all Hitchcock biographers agree that the director was himself extremely proud of his budgeting prowess. See, for example, McGilligan, *Alfred Hitchcock*, 698.

7. Quoted in McGilligan, *Alfred Hitchcock*, 655.

8. Quoted in Spoto, *The Dark Side of Genius*, 478.

9. McGilligan, *Alfred Hitchcock*, 676.

10. Spoto, *The Dark Side of Genius*, 503.

11. Spoto, *The Dark Side of Genius*, 502.

12. McGilligan, *Alfred Hitchcock*, 406.

13. See Connie Bruck, *When Hollywood Had a King* (New York: Random House, 2003).

14. In addition to Bruck's text, there are two other sources of biographical information on Wasserman: Dennis McDougal, *The Last Mogul: Lew Wasserman, MCA, and the Hidden History of Hollywood* (New York: Crown, 1998) and Kathleen Sharp, *Mr. and Mrs. Hollywood: Edie and Lew Wasserman and Their Entertainment Empire* (New York: Carroll and Graf, 2003).

15. Bruck, *When Hollywood Had a King*, 467.

16. Sharp, *Mr. and Mrs. Hollywood*, 221.

17. François Truffaut, *Hitchcock*, rev. ed. (New York: Simon & Schuster/Touchstone, 1985), 313.

18. McGilligan, *Alfred Hitchcock*, 697.

19. Truffaut, *Hitchcock*, 333.

Property Values   2
The Hitchcock Standards and the
First "*Frenzy*"

T HE PATH TOWARD what was to become *Frenzy* was hardly direct.
Hitchcock was being sent "properties" all the time, each one accompanied by the sentiment that the particular piece enclosed
would make an ideal Hitchcock film. As he complained to Truffaut, "The
story department [at Universal] sends me all kinds of properties which
they claim are likely to make a good Hitchcock picture. Naturally, when
I read them, they don't measure up to the Hitchcock standards."[1] In fact,
the studio was to later put out the story that Hitchcock had worked his
way through fourteen hundred properties before settling on what would
become *Frenzy*.[2]

What, then, were the "Hitchcock standards" that so many of the suggested properties failed to satisfy? Certainly by 1970, it was clear enough
to Hitchcock himself what he was *not* looking for. He often complained
that people thought of him as a mere crime writer who happened to
direct films. He would be sent any number of murder mysteries, for example, almost none of them ever suitable for his needs. He told Truffaut,
"I don't really approve of whodunits because they're rather like a jigsaw
or crossword puzzle. . . . You simply wait to find out who committed
the murder."[3] In several interviews over his career, he had described the
process by which he chose a property. Foremost, of course, was that the
story must be able to be told visually. "I visualize my story in my mind
as a series of smudges moving over a variety of backgrounds," he claimed
as early as 1936.[4] Then, of course, the project must provide the opportunity for one of the Hitchcock "moments" for which he had come to be
celebrated. As he put it in an early interview, his formula was to find a

"single problem which is sufficiently enthralling to hold the attention" of the audience (and, of course, of Hitchcock).[5] In an article for the *Hitchcock Annual*, Thomas Leitch enumerates many of these "problems" or "moments," from the scene in *Blackmail* when the young woman who has just stabbed her assailant has to sit through a conversation during which the word "knife" seems to leap out at her to the moment in *Psycho* when Norman Bates submerges the car with the body in the trunk—and the $40,000.[6] Finally, Hitchcock had to be convinced that he would be able to fully participate in the preparation of the shooting script; that is, that the subject and setting could be tailored to his expertise. He had no interest in elaborate costume dramas, for example, and never delved into totally unrealistic settings, such as those that appear in the science fiction genre. "In a costume drama, I always wonder how they go to the bathroom," he quipped on more than one occasion.[7]

What he was looking for can be summed up to some extent by the word "thriller," but that is hardly definitive. It had to be a thriller, as one scholar has put it, of "a certain type and style" so that the resulting project would indeed become a "Hitchcock picture."[8] The process may have been no more complicated than the approach recalled by Hitchcock's daughter, Patricia Hitchcock O'Connell: "Father would bring home the story or the novel and if Mother didn't like it, then he wouldn't do it. It was that simple."[9] Mother, of course, was Alma Reville, Hitchcock's lifelong helpmate and as much a part of the preproduction process as anyone; indeed, her opinion was easily the equivalent of the Selznicks or even the Wassermans within Hitchcock's universe. Alma had been with Hitchcock from the earliest days of his career. They were unusually close, a marriage based certainly more on their intellectual connections than on their romantic ones. (Hitchcock once famously told author Leon Uris that he "hadn't been laid" in twenty-five years.)[10] This cerebral association, coupled with their shared avidity for reading, provided a solid grounding for the decision-making process. Mrs. O'Connell's recollection is no doubt accurate: the next project probably always had to have the approval of Mrs. Hitchcock.

The challenge of finding the right property after *Topaz* was exacerbated by the fact that Hitchcock himself had by all accounts begun to have fewer ideas that might lead into one of those classic "moments" that would provide his signature to a film. He was seventy-one years old by August of 1970, and while, as biographer John Russell Taylor points out, he hated not working, both his support system and his own creative capacity seemed to be on the wane.[11] He had also had some disappointments in recently unrealized projects, one of which had been tentatively entitled "Frenzy."

It began after his completion of *Torn Curtain*, when he decided that he would rather return to a modest film like *Psycho* than take on another large budget international project. (With *Topaz*, he was to do just that, of course.) According to his biographers, the project was to involve the story of "a necrophiliac serial killer."[12] Working with Benn Levy, a writer he had used during his British period films (on *Blackmail*, for one), the tentative idea involved a psychotic killer who tries to make an undercover policewoman one of his victims. Levy arrived in Los Angeles in February of 1967, and he and Hitchcock set to work immediately on what they had decided to call "Frenzy." They worked together for two months then traveled in April to New York City where Hitchcock gave Levy a tour of the locations that he intended to use for the film. Back in California, Levy continued to refine the script, and Alma joined in with her suggestions. It was a nostalgic return to their early days, as the three of them would work through each scene together, striving for what Hitchcock would call "the maximum effect" in each one.[13] They worked through June with Hitchcock revising Levy's treatment and dictating details to his assistant, Peggy Robertson. Only then did Hitchcock feel that the treatment was ready for dialogue, and to provide that he hired novelist Howard Fast, who had written *Spartacus* and was the author as well of dozens of other highly regarded works of fiction.

Hitchcock meanwhile returned to New York for some camera tests. Over a few days in July he supervised the shooting of some forty minutes of material. He also engaged a still photographer to make some slides. Howard Fast continued to work on the dialogue, and Hitchcock turned his attention to other matters in order to give Fast time to complete his task. "Hitchcock gave me a very free hand," Fast recalled.[14] Since Hitchcock often worked on more than one potential project at a time, he set "Frenzy" aside for a few months, this in part because Lew Wasserman—who had been kept informed of the progress of the treatment—was less than enthusiastic about "Frenzy" and urged Hitchcock toward what would become *Topaz*.

What followed was one of Hitchcock's more unfortunate encounters with a screenwriter. He met with Leon Uris, author of the novel. They did not hit it off. In fact, Uris came to feel that "Hitchcock tried to lord over him, making it clear who was the boss and who was the underdog."[15] Hitchcock's usual charming approach to his screenwriters failed to reach Uris, and the two, according to biographer McGilligan, simply became enemies.[16] Hitchcock concluded that the film could not be made—at least not with this particular writer—and he turned his attention again to "Frenzy," a project that had also become known as "Kaleidoscope," although none of the biographers seem to know quite when and why. (It remains identified as "Frenzy" throughout McGilligan's text. Dan Auiler, in his *Hitchcock's Notebooks*, prefers "Kaleidoscope.")[17]

Unfortunately, Lew Wasserman and the other powers that were at Universal had developed no affection for "Frenzy." Wasserman strongly objected to the "inelegance" of the story; he felt it wasn't up to Universal's standards. Donald Spoto describes a meeting with the MCA/Universal studio chiefs that was so dismissive of Hitchcock's proposal that the great and once more powerful director "broke into tears."[18] Hitchcock was not able to persuade them to change their minds, and "Frenzy/Kaleidoscope" was to become, in the words of Patrick McGilligan, "the greatest film Hitchcock never made."[19]

Now Hitchcock had no choice but to complete the project that Universal obviously wanted: *Topaz*. At the conclusion of that ordeal, he was once again back to searching for a story that might measure up to "the Hitchcock standards." In early December, he received a small package with a book tucked inside. Through one of his usual channels—in this case the literary agents Curtis Brown Ltd.—Hitchcock had been sent Arthur La Bern's 1966 novel *Goodbye Piccadilly, Farewell Leicester Square*. La Bern was not a great novelist, and this was not a great novel. It did have, however, some elements that appealed immediately to Hitchcock. It was the story of a psycho-killer who raped and murdered young women in London, a kind of contemporary version of Jack the Ripper. It even had a favorite Hitchcockian element: the innocent man wrongly accused of the gruesome crime. It was, in short, just the sort of story that Hitchcock might be able to build upon, to turn into one of his mélanges of cinematic verve and compelling melodrama. Hitchcock remarked in a memo to one of the Universal executives (Edd Henry) that the book "contains what I've been looking for for so long now and that is a light touch."[20] It seemed so right for Hitchcock that one biographer has speculated that "La Bern could be accused of having written it with the director in mind."[21] There were, of course, two people who had to be convinced of the project's value. The first was Alma; she had often said that she never wanted to return to England for any length of time (short visits were fine), and it was clear from Hitchcock's initial analysis that the project must be shot in London for the sort of verisimilitude that it would demand. Second, of course, was Lew Wasserman; his agreement would be absolutely essential. Interestingly, Alma came to feel that London provided "a better chance of making a film cheaper, quicker, and with less interference than in Hollywood."[22]

At a lunch on December 10, Hitchcock presented his case to Wasserman and his associate, Universal vice president Edd Henry. Wasserman was won over by a realization that this was a project that was less offensive (to him and to his cadre of executives) than the previous "Frenzy" had been, and he cleverly realized that a Hitchcock return to London would provide great publicity for the studio. His only concern was the budget. *Topaz* had been a financial disaster, in his view; he strongly felt that it had been over-budgeted at $4 million. He offered $2.8 million for *Frenzy*; Hitchcock accepted, and Edd Henry set about acquiring the rights from the author. By December 21, 1970, he had succeeded: Universal now owned the rights to *Goodbye Piccadilly, Farewell Leicester Square*. The price was $25,000.[23] (Interestingly, author La Bern had wanted $35,000 if Hitchcock were to direct. Apparently he had heard rumors that this was to be the case. Universal closed the deal without naming a director.)

The process of writing a treatment could then begin. Of course, first Hitchcock had to engage a writer. According to biographer Spoto, the initial overture—a rather unlikely one, it might seem—went to Vladimir Nabokov. Hitchcock had apparently long been an admirer of Nabokov, seeing in him, according to Spoto, a kindred spirit in terms of wry, dark humor.[24] The two artists happened to be exactly the same age, the sort of serendipitous detail that could very well have attracted Hitchcock's attention. The piece of work that might have resulted from this peculiar collaboration between the author of *Lolita* and the director of *Psycho* is fascinating to contemplate, but alas, Nabokov politely declined Hitchcock's offer, pleading that he was far too busy at the moment with his own writing schedule.

On New Year's Eve, 1970, Hitchcock called British playwright Anthony Shaffer.

Notes

1. François Truffaut, *Hitchcock*, rev. ed. (New York: Simon & Schuster/Touchstone, 1985), 333.

2. Marilyn Beck, "'Frenzy' to Continue Hitchcock Tradition," *Hartford Courant*, 24 March 1971, 18.

3. Truffaut, *Hitchcock*, 74.

4. Alfred Hitchcock, "Close Your Eyes and Visualize!," *Stage* 13 (July 1936): 52–53.

5. Alfred Hitchcock, "Life among the Stars," *News Chronicle*, 1–5 March 1937; quoted in Sidney Gottlieb, *Hitchcock on Hitchcock* (Berkeley: University of California Press, 1995), 46.

6. Thomas M. Leitch, "The Hitchcock Moment," *Hitchcock Annual* 6 (1997–1998): 19–39.

7. See, for example, Peter Bogdanovich, "Period Piece," *New York Magazine*, 25 February 1974, 64.

8. See Dan Auiler, *Hitchcock's Notebooks: An Authorized and Illustrated Look inside the Creative Mind of Alfred Hitchcock* (New York: Avon, 1999), 25.

9. Auiler, *Hitchcock's Notebooks*, 22.

10. Patrick McGilligan, *Alfred Hitchcock: A Life in Darkness and Light* (New York: HarperCollins, 2003), 685.

11. John Russell Taylor, *Hitch: The Life and Times of Alfred Hitchcock* (London: Faber and Faber, 1978), 279.

12. McGilligan, *Alfred Hitchcock*, 676.

13. McGilligan, *Alfred Hitchcock*, 679.

14. McGilligan, *Alfred Hitchcock*, 682.

15. McGilligan, *Alfred Hitchcock*, 684.

16. McGilligan, *Alfred Hitchcock*, 686.

17. Auiler, *Hitchcock's Notebooks*, 443.

18. Donald Spoto, *The Dark Side of Genius: The Life of Alfred Hitchcock* (Boston: Little, Brown, 1983), 496.

19. McGilligan, *Alfred Hitchcock*, 682.

20. See *Frenzy* Folder #296 of the Alfred Hitchcock papers at the Margaret Herrick Library, Beverly Hills, California.

21. McGilligan, *Alfred Hitchcock*, 698.

22. Spoto, *The Dark Side of Genius*, 508.

23. See *Frenzy* Folder #333 of the Alfred Hitchcock papers.

24. Spoto, *The Dark Side of Genius*, 508.

Working with Writers **3**
Hitchcock and the
Preparation of the Scenario

As Anthony Shaffer recalls in his 2001 autobiography, the New Year's Eve phone call to his temporary Manhattan apartment (his hit play, *Sleuth*, had opened on Broadway the previous month) must have been the work of a "hoaxing friend."[1] The person on the other end of the line was inviting him to write the screenplay for the director's next project. Shaffer was naturally suspicious, and yet the book itself—La Bern's *Goodbye Piccadilly, Farewell Leicester Square*—had been delivered to him during the previous week. Indeed, Shaffer was being just a bit disingenuous; he had, after all, called Hitchcock's office after reading the novel and left the message that he "likes the story."[2] As the conversation progressed, Shaffer surmised that he was indeed talking to the "legendary master of suspense," as the playwright identified his caller. He realized after hanging up that he was about to join a distinguished group of previous screenwriters, and he recalled the names of several: Raymond Chandler, Maxwell Anderson, Ben Hecht, and James Bridie. Of course, not every screenwriting experience with Hitchcock proceeded swimmingly. They varied greatly and remain a continued source of bemusement for Hitchcock commentators.

Hitchcock's occasionally strained but just as often felicitous relationships with his various screenwriters have been the subject of many of the chapters of many of the Hitchcock biographies. As an example of the latter situation, we can cite John Russell Taylor's description of the director's association with playwright Thornton Wilder on *Shadow of a Doubt* as "one of the most harmonious collaborations of [Hitchcock's] working life."[3] On the other hand, Donald Spoto, always attentive to acerbic backstories, describes the tension between Hitchcock and detective writer Raymond Chandler on *Strangers on a Train* as deriving "not from confrontation between complementary talents,

Story conference for *Lifeboat* in 1944. Hitchcock looking toward Alma, with producer Kenneth MacGowan on left,

but from a smoldering suspicion that each knew the other's soul rather more fully than either desired."[4] How Spoto arrived at this particular insight into two discrete souls remains a mystery; nevertheless, Hitchcock very soon fired Chandler and went on to engage other writers to complete the script for *Strangers on a Train*.

Hitchcock's professional arrangements with his writers are not among Patrick McGilligan's major concerns, but his 2003 biography does provide some interesting insights into the working methodologies of the writers themselves. We find, for example, that Ernest Lehman, in researching what was to become *North by Northwest*, "visited the United Nations, underwent a mock arrest in Long Island . . . and toured Mount Rushmore with a forest ranger."[5] Hitchcock, McGilligan reports, was pleased by these efforts. Lehman remained a Hitchcock favorite throughout the rest of the director's career; he is the screenwriter of record, for example, on Hitchcock's final film, *Family Plot*.

An interesting illustration of the complexities of the writer-director relationship can be found in the production history of *Vertigo*. No Hitchcock film presently rests on a higher pedestal in the scholarly pantheon of the master's work. A film that received only a mediocre reception upon its 1958 release—*Time* magazine, for example, called it just "another Hitchcock and bull story"—it is now regarded by most serious critics as the quintessential Hitchcock film.[6] Perhaps the scholarly community's present appreciation of the work is best summarized by Robin Wood's poetic assertion regarding its singular achievement: "*Vertigo* seems to me of all Hitchcock's films the one nearest to perfection. Indeed, its profundity is inseparable from the perfection of form. . . ."[7] *Vertigo* was based upon a rather lackluster "policier" written by two French authors who, some say, had Hitchcock in mind when they wrote it.[8] According to British critic Charles Barr, Hitchcock needed to make but three—admittedly significant—changes when he converted *D'entre les Morts* into *Vertigo*: he needed to shift place from Paris to San Francisco and time from the World War II era to the present; thirdly, Hitchcock required a "formal shift from novel to film narrative."[9] Barr's third significant change covers a lot of ground, and indeed it took no fewer than four screenwriters (Hitchcock himself not included) to produce the shooting script that guided the director when the production commenced in February of 1957. Those familiar with Hitchcock's modus operandi cannot be surprised by this; after all, he went through literally dozens of screenwriters during his long career. While it is virtually impossible to now sort out the specific individual contributions of each screenwriter (of course, their own reminiscences, some published, tend to be self-serving), there seems to be no doubt that the major change between the original novel and the completed film is one upon which Hitchcock himself insisted. This would be the melodramatic confession that reveals to the audience—two-thirds of the way through the film—the truth about the murder. This rather bold stroke changes the tone of the work and the very nature of the narrative. (In the book, the truth is revealed on the last several pages.)

Hitchcock described the decision-making process to François Truffaut: "At the beginning of the second part, when Stewart meets the brunette, the truth about Judy's identity is disclosed, but only to the viewer. . . . Everyone around me was against this change. . . ."[10] What must be recognized is that this change was clearly in keeping with virtually everything that Hitchcock had ever said about his insistence upon the primacy of suspense over surprise. He articulated this view to Truffaut in his famous comparison of the two. Speaking of a hypothetical film during which a bomb explodes, Hitchcock cites two choices: surprising the audience with the explosion or letting them in on the fact that a bomb is about to explode. "In the first case," Hitchcock explained, "we have given the public fifteen seconds of surprise at the moment of the explosion. In the second we have provided them with fifteen minutes of suspense."[11] The original ending of the novel provided a surprise twist to the plot of the narrative. Hitchcock's *Vertigo* provides the viewer with forty minutes of suspense after the "secret" of the plot is revealed. It is a masterly stroke, and one that is philosophically consistent with Hitchcock's approach to cinema throughout his entire career.

What the *Vertigo* experience suggests is that Hitchcock, at the height of his powers, was able to work harmoniously with a number of different writers and marshal their talents toward his own creative goal. This suggests, too, that the French critics have been right about Hitchcock all this time, that indeed he is the author—the auteur—of any given Hitchcock film. Recent scholarship, much of it serving to counter the auteur theory, has suggested that it is a bit more complicated than that; for while *Vertigo* is clearly one of Hitchcock's masterpieces, it happens to be one of his darkest visions, and it lacks the biting wit and truculent sense of humor that so often characterizes his other master works, like *Rear Window*, for example. And it is to that film—and the three that immediately followed it—that we might turn our attention in order to probe more deeply into Hitchcock's relationships with his writers. In fact, for an example of his working relationship with but one writer over time, no production history is more poignant than that of the four films created together by Hitchcock and screenwriter John Michael Hayes.

In 1954, Hayes was a young radio writer whose agent happened to work at MCA, the organization that also represented Hitchcock at the time. The agency thought that the young Hayes might have something to offer Hitchcock and suggested a meeting between the two. As later recalled by Hayes, the meeting was to be a Friday night dinner at the Polo Lounge of the Beverly Hills Hotel.[12] Hitchcock arrived quite late; Hayes had by that time had quite a bit to drink, yet he nevertheless managed to impress Hitchcock with his analysis of *Shadow of a Doubt*. Nothing was said about any specific collaboration between the two, but on the following Monday morning, Hayes received a call from his agent announcing that he was to meet the next day with Hitchcock to start work on what was to become *Rear Window*.[13] The result of their collaboration was to be the only other film that often vies with *Vertigo* for that top spot in the Hitchcock pantheon. *Rear Window* was an enormous financial success, and it was critically acclaimed as well. It is now simply acknowledged as one of the masterpieces attributed to master Hitchcock. Hayes managed to continue to work for Hitchcock on his next three projects, despite the predilection on Hitchcock's part for turning to a variety of screenwriters. (It has been suggested that Hitchcock felt that after two pictures with the same writer, he would have gotten all he could from that particular collaborator. One commentator suggests that this may be true if only because after two projects, "a writer may have gotten to know the director's methods so well that any spontaneity of collaboration is not longer possible.")[14] The films that followed—*To Catch a Thief*, *The Trouble with Harry*, and *The Man Who Knew Too Much*—while not as highly regarded by contemporary scholars as *Rear Window*—are nevertheless classic examples of the adroit, intelligent, elegant work that Hitchcock became known for in the 1950s.

By all accounts, Hitchcock and Hayes worked well together. John Russell Taylor notes that Hitchcock's collaboration with Hayes provided the exception to the rule that the process of preparing the scenario was always arduous and difficult.[15] Hayes later claimed that Hitchcock was, in general, "very easy to work with."[16] Hayes seemed to have effortlessly and gracefully accommodated himself to the Hitchcock approach to scenario preparation, an idiosyncratic method by now well known. Indeed, Hitchcock quite often acknowledged his own preference for preproduction:

> The most enjoyable part of making a picture is in the little office, with the writer, when we are discussing the story-lines and what we're going to put on the screen. The big difference is that I do not let the writer go off on his own and just write a script that I will interpret. I stay involved with him and get him involved in the direction of the picture. So he becomes more than a writer; he becomes part maker of the picture.[17]

But only part maker. Hitchcock never let anyone forget who was finally responsible for the Hitchcock touch on a Hitchcock project, and it was not the hired screenwriter. This fruitful collaboration was to end, in fact, when Hayes had what Hitchcock perceived to be the audacity to challenge him on screenplay credit for *The Man Who Knew Too Much*. (Hitchcock had wanted to give partial credit to an old friend who had sketched out a few plot ideas; Hayes complained to the Writers' Guild, which then awarded him sole credit.) For Hayes it was a matter of principle; for Hitchcock it was a case of ingratitude. Hayes won the arbitration, but "the partnership of Alfred Hitchcock and John Michael Hayes had been forever severed."[18] They were never to work together again, and Hitchcock was never again to engage a writer for more than one project at a time. After *The Man Who Knew Too Much*, Hitchcock completed ten more films; official screenplay credit was awarded to nine different writers.

Notes

1. Anthony Shaffer, *So What Did You Expect?* (London: Picador, 2001), 67.

2. See *Frenzy* Folder #333 of the Alfred Hitchcock papers at the Margaret Herrick Library, Beverly Hills, California.

3. John Russell Taylor, *Hitch: The Life and Times of Alfred Hitchcock* (London: Faber and Faber, 1978), 185.

4. Donald Spoto, *The Dark Side of Genius: The Life of Alfred Hitchcock* (Boston: Little, Brown, 1983), 322.

5. Patrick McGilligan, *Alfred Hitchcock: A Life in Darkness and Light* (New York: HarperCollins, 2003), 557.

6. Quoted in, among other sources, Ken Mogg, *The Alfred Hitchcock Story*, rev. ed. (London: Titan, 2008), 171.

7. Robin Wood, *Hitchcock's Films Revisited*, rev.ed. (New York: Columbia University Press, 2002), 129.

8. François Truffaut, *Hitchcock*, rev. ed. (New York: Simon & Schuster/Touchstone, 1985), 243.

9. Charles Barr, *Vertigo* (London: British Film Institute, 2002), 25.

10. Truffaut, *Hitchcock*, 243.

11. Truffaut, *Hitchcock*, 73.

12. See Steven DeRosa, *Writing with Hitchcock: The Collaboration of Alfred Hitchcock and John Michael Hayes* (New York: Faber and Faber, 2001), 7.

13. DeRosa, *Writing with Hitchcock*, 7–10.

14. DeRosa, *Writing with Hitchcock*, 144.

15. Taylor, *Hitch*, 275.

16. DeRosa, *Writing with Hitchcock*, 94.

17. DeRosa, *Writing with Hitchcock*, ix (quoting *Take One* 1, no. 1: 14–17).

18. DeRosa, *Writing with Hitchcock*, 201.

Working with Another Sleuth   **4**
Hitchcock and Anthony Shaffer

JOINING THE LEGION OF HITCHCOCK COLLABORATORS would now be Anthony Shaffer. He was somewhat of a prodigy. His first major play, *Sleuth*, ran for a remarkable eight years in London and another four on Broadway, having opened in London in January of 1970 and then in November of the same year in New York; indeed, it was an enormous hit in both venues. Hitchcock had seen the play, and he recognized its wit and its sharply defined structure. Hitchcock knew the world of the theater, of course, and in general he appreciated the craftsmanship of a solid playwright. He once commented to Truffaut that "a playwright will tend to make a better screenwriter than a novelist because he is used to the building of successive climaxes."[1] In any event, Shaffer accepted Hitchcock's telephoned New Year's Eve overtures to the extent that he at least agreed in principle to collaborate with the director at his studio offices in California. First, though, the two of them met briefly (over four days) in London to discuss the novel and to scout locations. (They were joined by Mrs. Hitchcock.) The two partners-to-be gathered again in California in late January; a studio car delivered Mr. Shaffer to the Hitchcock offices at Universal at 10:30 on the morning of January 22, 1971.[2]

Interestingly, the collaboration seemed at first less than promising. Unlike the young John Michael Hayes, the forty-four-year-old Anthony Shaffer felt no compulsion to flatter Hitchcock with a fawning analysis of a favorite work. In fact, Shaffer began their association by doing just the opposite; he offered to point out the weak moments in some of Hitchcock's most celebrated films. "There are huge holes in a number of your films that logically make no sense," he claims, citing a sequence in *North by Northwest* as an example.[3] After watching *North by Northwest* together and then lunching in what Shaffer describes as "wintry silence," Hitchcock then commenced to offer his defense of the plot twists in the film, after which, Shaffer recalls, the two set about working on *Frenzy*. Apparently, Shaffer had earned the grudging respect of the aging master, and their collaboration then proceeded with remarkable efficiency.

They met each morning at Hitchcock's "bungalow" on the Universal lot. Labeling the space a bungalow is a not unlike the American captains of industry calling their mansions in Newport, Rhode Island, "cottages." Hitchcock's suite was the largest at Universal and included "offices for his design staff and a writer; adjoining rooms with editing equipment; a separate office for his assistant, Peggy Robertson; a kitchen, cocktail lounge, and bathroom attached to his spacious private office; a dining room; and a projection room seating eight."[4] By the time Shaffer arrived for their first meeting, Hitchcock had been occupying this space for over eight years, and his routine was by then well established. He liked to keep regular hours. He would arrive sometime between 9:30 and 10 each morning, break for lunch shortly after noon, and leave for his home in Bel Air (adjacent to Beverly Hills) no later than 5 P.M. His interaction with his scenario writers had by now also become well entrenched. Many of Shaffer's predecessors recalled their experiences with Hitchcock either in their memoirs or through interviews with one of the biographers.[5] There is a pattern that emerges from a synthesis of all of these recollections. For when Hitchcock described the most enjoyable part of making a film as being those sessions with the writer as they discussed story lines and plot details (see previous chapter), he was revealing a part of himself that was to become only too familiar to his collaborators. Hitchcock was a great raconteur, and he loved to regale his guests with tales of his career, telling and retelling stories that made their way into all the biographies. Most of the stories seem to have been told after lunch. The mornings were generally reserved for the serious work of creating the treatment that would lead eventually to a finished script.

Shaffer claims in his memoirs that he indulged Hitchcock in his storytelling role, and it seems clear from all sources that the collaboration proceeded quite smoothly.[6] Donald Spoto calls it "the smoothest since *Psycho*," so smooth in fact that neither participant chose to comment much about it.[7] The only anecdote to appear in Shaffer's memoirs, for example, is the delightful one about lunch. As a man of regular habits, Hitchcock tended to stop work each day at the same time and have a lunch brought to his office complex. Each day the lunch was the same: steak and salad.

After quite a few of these, Shaffer gently suggested that they might have something different once in a while. The next day, Shaffer recalled, "a fifteen-course dinner arrived, catered by Chasen's, and was laid at my tableside. Hitch, of course, had his small steak and salad."[8] Shaffer summarizes his experience on the *Frenzy* script as a positive one: Hitchcock was "extremely kind and considerate to me," he relates in his memoirs. "He even called me up on one occasion to ask if he could change a single word in the script."[9] As for Hitchcock, he later proclaimed that he had had "a happy time with the writer."[10] Indeed they must have; Hitchcock soon took to ending their sessions at 4 P.M. rather than at 5 and to offer a pitcher of daiquiris for the two to share.[11]

An examination of the production records housed at the Herrick Library in Beverly Hills coupled with what Hitchcock outlined in numerous published interviews reveals quite a bit about the workmanlike approach that each artist brought to the project. We know from several of the interviews, for example, that Hitchcock claimed to read his source material only once. He would then proceed to "ruthlessly" (his word) adapt the story itself to the screen. "I never soak myself in a book before starting to adapt it," he asserted on more than one occasion.[12] The source material for this project was, in that sense, a perfect vehicle for Hitchcock. Arthur La Bern's *Goodbye Piccadilly, Farewell Leicester Square* is hardly the sort of novel that anyone need peruse more than once, and yet it is obvious upon reflection what must have attracted Hitchcock to it. The "wrong man" motif, the gruesome murders, the interplay between the police and the real criminal; all of these elements must have seemed quite familiar to Hitchcock. He needed merely to transfer them through his idiosyncratic vision into a film that echoed so many of his familiar themes, a film, one might say, that lived up to the Hitchcock standards.

The first step was to ask one of the readers at Universal to prepare a detailed synopsis of the novel. This forty-two-page chapter-by-chapter breakdown was provided by staff writer Estelle Conde and forwarded to Hitchcock on December 22, 1970. A much more concise three-page précis of the plot and characters that were to eventually become *Frenzy* was completed by Conde on December 30. Working from these summaries, Hitchcock and Shaffer moved toward the treatment, the essential document in any Hitchcock production. It is the treatment, really, that contains most of the Hitchcock magic, for it is within the treatment that Hitchcock generally placed his visual approach to the material. This has often been understated by even the most judicious of the Hitchcock biographers—and misunderstood entirely by some. For Hitchcock, the words "scenario" and "script" were more or less synonymous. During his career in England, he worked with scenarists; in Hollywood, they were called screenwriters. As far as Hitchcock was concerned, these often-talented collaborators were there to write the dialogue, an aspect of his work that interested him very little. His concern, as he so often reiterated, was with those things that could be shown, not with those that must be told to an audience. "Dialogue," he pointed out to Truffaut, "should simply be a sound among other sounds, just something that comes out of the mouths of people whose eyes tell the story in visual terms."[13] The writers, on the other hand, almost universally accepted Hitchcock's concern with the visual but felt—many of them quite strongly—that they were doing far more than merely coming up with lines for the characters to speak. Most of them felt that at the very least, they were developing the characters themselves.[14]

Hitchcock and Shaffer met every morning, lunched each day, and shared cocktails each afternoon for the next month. By February 24—just about four and a half weeks after their first session together—they had produced a fifty-five-page treatment. Interestingly, on the title page, above the date, are the words "Dictated by Mr. Hitchcock with Mr. Shaffer."[15] The magisterial opening of the film appears on this treatment, although in an early stage of its development:

> At the outset, the screen should be filled with part of a printed map. At the top right-hand corner of the screen we see in a white inset with its scale, the word: "LONDON." Nearby on the actual map itself we see in blue the lines indicating a canal. Along this we read the words: "REGENTS CANAL." The CAMERA now begins to follow the route of the canal— as it does so, the printed map dissolves in exactly the same precise proportions to the real landscape that coincides with this particular part of the map. The CAMERA now follows the course of the canal. At some points we lose it—and then it reappears—finally, as we reach our destination, we zoom down low enough to see a group gathered by the side of the canal.
>
> During all this, the lettering of the Main Title and Credit Titles has been appearing. The last title goes just as we stop our zoom down to the large crowd of people.[16]

This is followed by a scene during which the minister of health is making a speech while someone in the crowd spots what appears to be a body floating down the river. The scene would later be expanded to include Hitchcock's cameo appearance. Interestingly, the scene as written in this treatment describes the discovery of the body as follows: "a red open-knit stocking tied around her neck. The ends of the stocking are floating in the water. One of her legs is still covered with the other stocking."[17] (The idea to use a necktie obviously came later.)

No part of this sequence is in the original novel. The novel opens with a scene not too dissimilar to what occurs on the third page of this first treatment: "We immediately cut to a man whose name is RICHARD BLAMEY, standing at a mirror in a small bedroom putting on his tie." This is indeed how the completed film itself introduces the protagonist (after the title sequence and the Hitchcock cameo), with the distinction that the main character's family name has been changed to "Blaney" from the original "Blamey" in the novel.[18] What is noteworthy is indeed how "ruthlessly" Hitchcock and his latest collaborator have managed to tear down the narrative of the novel and build it back up again into the sort of coherent whole that even at this early stage begins to transform itself into a proper Hitchcock project. Many of the scenes in the novel have simply been eliminated; the collaborators found them to be irrelevant. For example, La Bern implied that the seemingly ongoing depression afflicting his protagonist was caused by his morose response to the suicide of one of his mates from the war years. In La Bern's view, the poor bloke's fate—he was found hanging in his cell—provided impetus to Blamey in his quest to avoid the authorities at all cost. Hitchcock and Shaffer simply dropped this questionable source of motivation. For them, the protagonist's often-acerbic view of the world was something that they could use to lead the audience down the wrong (man's) path. La Bern had concocted an ancillary love story between Blamey and a friend of a friend who was living in Paris; this too disappeared from the February 24 treatment. Finally, an entire trial, which occupies page after page of the La Bern novel, was reduced in the Hitchcock/Shaffer treatment to a single scene of a bailiff outside a courtroom door he happens to swing open at just the right moment; the audience hears the verdict and need not be bothered with the details of the trial itself.

What remained among the fifty-five pages was the basic structure of the projected film. Remarkable for its directness and its concision, the treatment included many of the scenes that were to become celebrated as "signature moments" in the completed film. For example, the scene that described the killing of Babs Milligan has been carefully transposed from rather pedestrian prose to a compelling piece of cinema. In the novel, Babs is dispatched with rather inelegantly. Indeed, La Bern's description can be used as a fine example of "purple prose":

Suddenly, he had pulled her down on the divan and had reversed positions with her. She shook her head frantically.

"No, no, no. Please."

"You're my kind of girl."

"Please no, not now. I told you I was off colour."

"It doesn't matter, you're lovely."

She opened her mouth to scream but as she did so, he pulled the handkerchief from his pocket and stuffed it into her mouth. Soon, she ceased to struggle.[19]

The Hitchcock/Shaffer version of this scene can be found on page 32 of the treatment, and it is a fine example of the "ruthless" cutting that Hitchcock and Shaffer have by this time done to the novel. In their version, the killing itself is not shown, and the moment sets up one of the most celebrated camera movements of Hitchcock's mature era, although the treatment itself hardly hints at the visualization that Hitchcock will bring to the scene when he actually films it:

They finally arrive outside the house in Henrietta Street. Rusk ushers her through the door and the last we see of them, they mount the stairs and turn on the landing towards the apartment. Without going any further, we hear him unlock the door and we hear the voice faintly coming through when he says to Babs, in quite a nice way: "You now, Babs, you're my sort of girl." We hear the door close with a click.

My own appreciation of the film has been greatly enhanced by my admiration for what I have come to call "the blank brick wall scene."[20] This is the moment when the secretary, returning from lunch, discovers the dead body of her employer. In the original novel, the scene is presented quite straightforwardly:

Monica opened the door, just a few inches, peeping in. Then she flung the door wide open. She clapped one hand to her mouth, then turned and ran down the stairs. She did not start screaming until she reached the street level.[21]

In the treatment, we do not see any of this. Hitchcock and Shaffer instead created a moment that engages the audience's imagination as they watch the secretary enter the building:

We return to Monica, and this time the CAMERA becomes objective because it pans her over to the entrance of the matrimonial agency. We wait. Imperceptibly, the CAMERA retreats, giving us a wide view of the back end of the courtyard. There are people going about their various business. We wait a second or two and then we hear the throat-piercing scream which tells us that Monica has discovered her dead employer. One or two people stop and look around. Others ignore the scream. Those who look around cannot tell where the scream is coming from and after a pause they also move and go about their business.[22]

In the final film, the wait before the scream seems agonizingly long and provides one of those moments of "pure cinema" with which the work of Hitchcock is so often associated.

One of the elements that Shaffer presumably brought to the collaboration was his finely tuned sense of humor, something that Hitchcock came to admire—and had found so lacking in other collaborators, like Leon Uris, for example. Peggy Robertson, in an interview for the Oral History program at the Margaret Herrick Library, recalled that Hitchcock's appreciation of Shaffer's sense of humor, as expressed in his writing, was "one of the reasons he picked Tony."[23] This initial treatment is full of those comic touches that characterize the best Hitchcock screenplays. Indeed, the resulting *Frenzy* came to be seen by many as the wittiest Hitchcock film script since Ernest Lehman's contributions to *North by Northwest*. In the novel, for example, there is absolutely no interplay between the police inspector and his wife. Hitchcock and Shaffer created an entire subtext to the plot by having the inspector discuss the details of the case with his spouse, a would-be gourmet cook. This allowed for some macabre touches that in retrospect seem so "Hitchcockian," like the following detail from page 51 of the treatment:

"Obviously he was looking for something," Oxford replies. "How do you know that?" "Because he broke the fingers of the right hand," Oxford says. At this moment, Mrs. Oxford is in the act of breaking the sticks of Italian bread. Oxford frowns at the timing of the bread breaking and asks why they can't have normal bread.[24]

As might have been expected, Hitchcock and Shaffer had done their homework on even this gruesome bit of business: one note in the file from Peggy Robertson indicated that the county morgue had advised the Hitchcock team that "rigor mortis would set in from 10 to 12 hours in a temperature of around 60 degrees."[25] In addition to the bits of dark humor injected into the narrative at this point, there was an example in this treatment (on page 37) of a bit of humor that did not make it into the final film:

We go to the driver who is happily steering his truck along the outer sub-
urbs of London. We see this from his viewpoint. He is singing heartily—
but his voice is not heard too loudly because of the engine noise although
we are permitted to hear some of the words of his song which seems to be
a request to "take me in your arms, etc., etc." Back in the truck, Rusk is
groping inside for the other hand.[26]

In addition to the treatment, a document labeled "Character Description" was completed on February 25 and logged into the office the next
day. On these pages, the protagonist is described as "being somewhat of
a little boy, readily confused by economic realities, and ashamed of his
downward path from Squadron Leader to barman." He is, the description
continues, "the born loser—the natural target for fate."[27] This certainly
seems like an approximation of a classic Hitchcockian "wrong man."

Hitchcock was pleased enough with the treatment to let Shaffer return
to New York to complete work on a finished script, one that would contain the lines of dialogue. Shaffer's contract with Universal included a paragraph that allowed him to work out of New York in order to complete
the "first-draft screenplay with dialogue."[28] The Hitchcock office log lists
Shaffer as being on an 11 P.M. flight to New York on Saturday, February
27, a mere three days after the completion of the treatment.

Shaffer continued to be quite productive. He called Hitchcock's assistant Peggy Robertson on March 23 and told her that Hitchcock could
expect a first draft of the completed script sometime around April 9. Hitchcock, meanwhile, was working on the storyboards and on solving some of
the problems with the narrative that had come up during their collaboration. He sent Shaffer a telegram on March 18 that indicated how involved
he remained in the process:

> Dear Tony:
> While eating a baked potato yesterday it suddenly occurred to me that
> our reason for returning a load of potatoes to Lincolnshire seemed rather
> flimsy. We talked of a quote glut unquote. I fear the mass audience won't
> appreciate this word. Would you like to consider the possibility of a mi-
> nor strike against a Covent Garden potato company whose porters refuse
> to unload. This could be the complaint of the potato man in the bar of
> the Spotted Wonder when he is talking with Blamey. Whether this will
> necessitate having a couple of pickets walking near the truck during the
> day time I don't know. Personally I would prefer to avoid this. I will now
> have another baked potato.
>
> Hitch.[29]

Robert Lantz, Shaffer's agent, notified Hitchcock in a letter of April 7 that three copies of the "completed First Draft Screenplay of FRENZY" were on the way via airmail special delivery; two copies to the studio address, one directly to Hitchcock at home. According to the office log, the copies arrived on Friday, April 9. Hitchcock read the script over the weekend and summoned Shaffer to return to Los Angeles, suggesting an arrival date of the following Tuesday (April 13). Shaffer, however, had sustained an attack of food poisoning and had to delay his return. He flew out from New York on Sunday, April 18, and met with Hitchcock the next morning (April 19) at 10:15 A.M.[30] Their immediate project was script revision, something about which Hitchcock was extremely assiduous. Indeed, Hitchcock had already begun the process, having sent to Shaffer over a dozen suggestions that he expected his collaborator to execute. The office log includes a series of suggestions dictated to the file by Hitchcock between March 22 and April 15. Many of the suggestions call for minor revisions; for example, a general note reminded the writers to avoid such "British" dialogue as "lorry"; the word "truck" should be employed instead. "Monica should wear glasses (nearsighted)," one note reads; another that "Blamey expects to eventually get back together with Brenda." Other suggestions call for a far more ambitious revision; one, for example, asks that Shaffer "characterize Hetty more," while another poses the rather tall order of revising the hospital ward scene.[31] Hitchcock continued to think about the filming of the "blank brick wall" scene. On April 1, he added this question to the file: "Should we delay Monica's screaming by having her take off gloves, etc.; going to the desk; sitting down and going through some papers?" It is that delay that will eventually give the scene its power. One of the most significant notes is dated March 31. On that day, Hitchcock added to the file the following description of the closing moments of the film:

> As Rusk comes right into the room and closes the door behind him, Oxford immediately switches the light on and says something like:
> "Mr. Rusk, you haven't got your tie on."[32]

The importance of this, of course, is that Hitchcock was dictating dialogue to the master script—and authoring one of the more famous lines of the film at that. This is significant, too, as it relates to Hitchcock's level of collaboration with his screenwriter, a topic to which we shall return.

By the time Shaffer arrived back in Los Angeles, the fifty-five-page treatment had by then become his 160-page screenplay, complete with dialogue. The cover page of this bound folder lists the title as "Frenzy" with "Necktie" in parentheses next to it; apparently, an alternate title was still being considered. The author is listed clearly: "A screenplay by Anthony Shaffer."[33] By all reports, this first full draft was solid. The two collaborators worked each day for the next two weeks, and Shaffer left Los Angeles for New York—he was to receive an award from the "Mystery Writers Association for *Sleuth*—on the afternoon of April 29, after, of course, having had lunch with Hitchcock. On the morning of that day, the two of them had gone rather quickly through the script, making minor changes. Hitchcock was not satisfied that the script was as yet ready, and he instructed the legal department at Universal to inform Shaffer that these small modifications did not constitute "second revisions." (Shaffer's contract with Universal called for full payment to be made—in this case $75,000 with a "bonus" of $25,000 if Shaffer were to receive solo screenplay credit [which he did]—only after second revisions had been completed.) Shaffer responded through his agent, Robert Lantz, that he fully agreed that this was the case and that he would make himself available to Hitchcock in London for any further revisions.[34] Shaffer was to leave for London on May 5.

Meanwhile, small revisions continued to be made, including some suggestions by Mrs. Hitchcock, listed in the file on April 30. Her handful of questions give us some idea of the role she played throughout Hitchcock's career. For example, she asks "Where does Rusk's mother go to? Is she on a visit?" (A very fine question, by the way, which is not, as it turned out, answered in the film.) "Wouldn't Blamey tell his defense lawyer about Rusk?" she queried. "Does Rusk know Blamey's wife?" These questions were dutifully posted by Peggy Robertson to Shaffer on April 30.[35]

The script was by then at least ready for Hitchcock to begin preparations for transferring his operations to London. The biographers who summarized this period are unanimous in their appraisal of the success of this particular collaboration. "Because Shaffer was so professional," reports Patrick McGilligan, the script advanced with remarkable ease."[36] "A rare Hitchcock film without multiple writers," McGilligan notes, *Frenzy* could be ready for preproduction in London by May 23.[37] Upon its eventual release, of course, *Frenzy* was to prove to many that Hitchcock had not lost his celebrated touch, but how much of its success is owed to the playwright-turned-script-collaborator Anthony Shaffer? Unlike the situation with those many contributors to *Vertigo*, here the single contributor seemed quite content to minimize his role. His only stated quibbles regarding the *Frenzy* scenario had to do with what he took to be Hitchcock's odd insistence on dialogue that seemed quaint by contemporary standards. "He was intractable about not modernizing the dialogue of the picture," Shaffer recalls, "and he kept inserting antique phrases I knew would cause the British public a hearty laugh or even some annoyance."[38] If this turned out to be so, the British public was not very demonstrative on the subject. *Frenzy* was a success in London as it had been in New York and as it was to be in Paris. Biographer McGilligan suggests that "Hitchcock was determined to make the film deliberately archaic—as, at the twilight of his career, he consciously sought to replicate his beginnings."[39] Peggy Robertson recalled in a later interview that it was Hitchcock's intention to have the main character speak in "an outdated language" because he "was living in the past." "A lot of people didn't realize that it was deliberate," she continued.[40] Ironically, perhaps, the only person who was clearly unhappy with the project turned out to be the author of the original novel, Arthur La Bern. He denounced the film as "distasteful," among other things, in a scornfully written letter to the editor of the *Times* of London.[41] This many years later, of course, one can pretty well rest assured that very few people are going to criticize Alfred Hitchcock's last masterwork for any failure on its part to adhere to the standards of Arthur La Bern's quite forgettable *Goodbye Piccadilly, Farewell Leicester Square.*

The question, then, of the level of contribution of this particular screenwriter to this particular project remains somewhat moot, as it does, I should point out, in most successful Hitchcock pictures. For when that idiosyncratic Hitchcock modus operandi worked as intended, the resulting collaboration between director and hired writer was seamless. Just as it would be quite difficult to presently ascertain the precise textual contributions of Ben Hecht to *Notorious* or Ernie Lehman to *North by Northwest,* Anthony Shaffer's participation on *Frenzy* is by now virtually impossible to quantify. It can, of course, be qualified, and perhaps the most succinct summary has been made by Spoto: Shaffer, he insists, "kept the tone of their work light."[42] Since the film "was to be about a betrayal of friendship," writes Spoto, "about the cross-matched relationship between a psychotic and any angry non-hero . . . there would have to be some humor in the dialogue."[43] And indeed there is. The dinner scenes between the detective and his charmingly wacky wife, a woman who has decided to test all of her new French recipes on her meat-and-potatoes husband, are witty, well written, and add a warm glow to an otherwise dark film. We know enough of Hitchcock to know of his obsession with food and his fascination with food-related tropes. We know from *Sleuth* of Shaffer's adroit ability to handle sophisticated exchanges between two characters in a room. The scenes between the detective and his wife sparkle with wit and charm, as do so many scenes in *Sleuth*, but they are leavened by that touch of mischievous irony that is so characteristic of Hitchcock. We shall perhaps never know who wrote each word. What we do know is that the collaboration served the project extremely well. The dinner scenes alone can stand as a monument to the success of this particular partnership between writer and director.

The fact is that the real scenario writer on a Hitchcock project was the master himself, even though he virtually never took actual screen credit. Some writers, as we now know, chafed at this; most—Anthony Shaffer being one—were simply delighted with the opportunity to work with him.[44]

Notes

1. François Truffaut, *Hitchcock*, rev. ed. (New York: Simon & Schuster/ Touchstone, 1985), 72.

2. Shaffer's daily schedule was kept by the Hitchcock staff. See *Frenzy* Folder #333 of the Alfred Hitchcock papers at the Margaret Herrick Library, Beverly Hills, California.

3. Anthony Shaffer, *So What Did You Expect?* (London: Picador, 2001), 68.

4. Patrick McGilligan, *Alfred Hitchcock: A Life in Darkness and Light* (New York: HarperCollins, 2003), 608.

5. See, for example, Charles Bennett's reminiscences as quoted in Steven DeRosa, *Writing with Hitchcock: The Collaboration of Alfred Hitchcock and John Michael Hayes* (New York: Faber and Faber, 2001), 65.

6. Shaffer, *So What Did You Expect?*, 70.

7. Donald Spoto, *The Dark Side of Genius: The Life of Alfred Hitchcock* (Boston: Little, Brown, 1983), 510.

8. Spoto, *The Dark Side of Genius*, 509; McGilligan, *Alfred Hitchcock*, 700.

9. Shaffer, *So What Did You Expect?*, 71.

10. Spoto, *The Dark Side of Genius*, 510.

11. Spoto, *The Dark Side of Genius*, 509.

12. See Sidney Gottlieb, *Hitchcock on Hitchcock* (Berkeley: University of California Press, 1995), 18.

13. Truffaut, *Hitchcock*, 222.

14. See, for example, author DeRosa's exposition of John Michael Hayes's contributions to Hitchcock's films in DeRosa, *Writing with Hitchcock*, xiv.

15. See *Frenzy* Folder #247 of the Alfred Hitchcock papers.

16. *Frenzy* Folder #247 of the Alfred Hitchcock papers.

17. *Frenzy* Folder #247 of the Alfred Hitchcock papers.

18. Personal note: I have always been bemused by the notion that had they kept the original name, the wife's business would have been the Blamey—that is, "Blame Me"—Matrimonial Agency.

19. Arthur La Bern, *Goodbye Piccadilly, Farewell, Leicester Square* (New York: Stein and Day, 1967), 122–23.

20. This scene is examined in some detail in chapter 9.

21. La Bern, *Goodbye Piccadilly, Farewell Leicester Square*, 56.

22. *Frenzy* Folder #247 of the Alfred Hitchcock papers.

23. *An Oral History with Peggy Robertson*. Interviewed by Barbara Hall. (Academy of Motion Picture Arts and Sciences, Oral History Program, 2002), 331.

24. *Frenzy* Folder #247 of the Alfred Hitchcock papers.

25. *Frenzy* Folder #296 of the Alfred Hitchcock papers.

26. *Frenzy* Folder #247 of the Alfred Hitchcock papers.

27. See *Frenzy* Folder #248 of the Alfred Hitchcock papers.

28. *Frenzy* Folder #333 of the Alfred Hitchcock papers.

29. *Frenzy* Folder #251 of the Alfred Hitchcock papers.

30. *Frenzy* Folder #333 of the Alfred Hitchcock papers.

31. *Frenzy* Folder #251 of the Alfred Hitchcock papers.

32. *Frenzy* Folder #251 of the Alfred Hitchcock papers.

33. *Frenzy* Folder #250 of the Alfred Hitchcock papers.

34. *Frenzy* Folder #333 of the Alfred Hitchcock papers.

35. *Frenzy* Folder #265 of the Alfred Hitchcock papers.

36. McGilligan, *Alfred Hitchcock*, 701.

37. McGilligan, *Alfred Hitchcock*, 702.

38. Spoto, *The Dark Side of Genius*, 510.

39. McGilligan, *Alfred Hitchcock*, 701.

40. *An Oral History with Peggy Robertson*, 359.

41. John Russell Taylor, *Hitch: The Life and Times of Alfred Hitchcock* (London: Faber and Faber, 1978), 283.

42. Spoto, *The Dark Side of Genius*, 509.

43. Spoto, *The Dark Side of Genius*, 509–10.

44. The script that was used on the set is referenced in appendix B in this volume. The script itself is copyrighted, but the appendix includes a listing of the scenes from the final "approved" script of June 3 (with changes through July 9), 1971.

Brief Intertitle   5
Looking for a Lost London

THE LONDON THAT ALFRED HITCHCOCK was to find in 1971 was certainly not the London he had left in 1939. The ravages of World War II alone had been enough to alter the face of the old city; the architectural fad called "modernism" did the rest. It was not, of course, the case that Hitchcock was entirely unfamiliar with contemporary London. He certainly had returned many times to visit—almost yearly in fact—often stopping there on his way to Paris or to St. Moritz, where he and Alma had honeymooned and to which they frequently returned. He had, in addition, filmed major portions of both *Under Capricorn* and *Stage Fright* in the city. Interestingly, while Shaffer was back in New York working on the first draft of the screenplay, Hitchcock had to interrupt his own preparations in order to pop over in March to his native city to receive honors from the British Society for Film and Television Arts; the presentation in front of fourteen hundred guests took place at a familiar venue—the Royal Albert Hall—and was presided over by Princess Anne.[1] This visit, coupled with his brief journey in January with Alma and Shaffer, served as the location scouting for the project. It was a bit more nostalgic than that; what Hitchcock was looking for was the London of his memories. Biographer John Russell Taylor notes the paradox: "There is no denying a certain anachronistic quality to Hitch's 1971 view of London life and character—though physically it is the London of today, the atmosphere is really that of thirty or more years ago, when Hitch last lived in London and knew it as a native."[2] As one reviewer of the completed film noted, "Hitchcock carries us at once to his own London, the scene of *The Lodger*, *Sabotage*, *The Man Who Knew Too Much*, a once-upon-a-time city of narrow alleys and dark stairways."[3]

Hitchcock's father had been a greengrocer and as such was intimately acquainted with the great open-air market at Covent Garden. This historic area was scheduled to be demolished by 1974, and Hitchcock wanted to make sure that it would be included in the film. While Covent Garden had been a principal setting in the original La Bern novel, for Hitchcock

Hitchcock showing Ingrid Bergman around London during the production of *Under Capricorn,* 1949. *Photofest*

it represented far more: not merely London itself but his considerable love affair with food and with the preparation of good food. "To everyone who would listen," reports Donald Spoto, "Hitchcock spoke of his childhood in old London, and of the Moroccan tomatoes available at Covent Garden in both 1901 and 1971, and of the citrus fruits from Israel, the grapes from Spain, the vegetables from California, and the special produce from all over the world."[4] Rejecting suggestions from Shaffer and others that he should shoot the film in "modern" London, Hitchcock instead returned to the Old Bailey Court and to the narrow alleys around Bow Street, Oxford Street, and County Hall. The upstairs apartment dwelling of the killer would be on Henrietta Street, an address already made noteworthy (at least to British audiences) because it had once been the residence of the playwright and novelist Clemence Dane, who had written a popular history of Covent Garden. Hitchcock even had trouble finding a good old-fashioned English pub as a location for many of the important scenes in the film. He complained to reporters about the "psychedelic nature" of the modern ones. One needed dark wood in a good pub, he would claim.[5]

Shaffer managed at least two concessions. Hitchcock agreed to a scene at the "new" Scotland Yard and to one at the recently completed Hilton Hotel. The irony is that, with the benefit of hindsight, it is clear that Hitchcock should have stayed with his original vision. Those two locations seem oddly out of place in the film. The forty years that have passed since the heyday of "mod" London have only made the Hilton and other "contemporary" structures seem far more dated than does the Old Bailey. What Shaffer failed to realize is that the landscape in a Hitchcock film is part of the director's canvas, part of his creative energy. As biographer Taylor put it, "Hitch's landscape always has been a landscape of fantasy. All that counts is the intensity and conviction of the fantasy. And no doubt about it, Hitch's London in *Frenzy* exists, whether or not it has much to do with the London anyone else sees today."[6] The fact is that Hitchcock searched for and found—or created—a place that might simply be labeled "classic" London, the London not just of his youth and early career, but the London that tourists seek and that film audiences appreciate. For Hitchcock, the inclusion of Covent Garden was not only nostalgic; it was emblematic. It was meant to stand as a classic image of London in the same way that his colleague Truffaut might use the Eiffel Tower to signify Paris.

After all, this would hardly be a novel approach for Hitchcock, this construction of a "cinematic" London to stand for the geographic one. He did this sort of thing throughout his career, especially during his "golden era" of the 1950s. The London in *Dial M for Murder* is one where gentlemen gather at their private clubs for a night of cards; the New York City in

Rear Window is a neighborhood courtyard on a summer's day; the Vermont of *The Trouble with Harry* is a small town where everyone knows everyone else; the Riviera of *To Catch a Thief* is represented by the flower market in Nice; the Manhattan of *North by Northwest* is seen through the windows of the Oak Bar at the Plaza Hotel; the San Francisco of *The Birds* opens with a shot of Union Square and stages a crucial scene under the Golden Gate Bridge. This is the universe that Hitchcock loved to create: he would incorporate his imagined world into a world with which the audience was already familiar. The result would be a kind of verisimilitude that would play against the macabre fantasy of whatever tale he was telling.

And so it is with *Frenzy*. Does Covent Garden represent the "real" London or does it represent a tourist's idealized view of London? In the case of the actual Covent Garden, of course, the question touches a poignant and ironic nerve, for Covent Garden no longer exists, a victim of the sort of "modernization" that Hitchcock must have deplored. Yet even if it remained, as the Eiffel Tower remains—no longer used for the purpose for which it was constructed but now a tourist destination—would it not still be an ideal locale for a Hitchcock scenario that was to have as its principal locale the city of London? Hitchcock was himself an inveterate traveler, a tourist par excellence, one might say. His construction of mythical tourist settings as the central geographical motif is not, finally, unlike his summation to Truffaut about his central artistic mission: "Some directors film slices of life, I film pieces of cake."[7] The London that Hitchcock created in *Frenzy*—a London indeed lost to us now and even to those who watched the filming in 1971— is, nevertheless, a London that is cinematically real, if less geographically so. It is a slice of the London cake that Hitchcock created as a testament to a place and a time of both his memory and his imagination. A lost London, perhaps, but one recovered by him through the power of his cinematic inventiveness.

Notes

1. Donald Spoto, *The Dark Side of Genius: The Life of Alfred Hitchcock* (Boston: Little, Brown, 1983), 510.

2. John Russell Taylor, *Hitch: The Life and Times of Alfred Hitchcock* (London: Faber and Faber, 1978), 283.

3. David Robinson, "Old Master," *Financial Times*, 26 May 1972, 3.

4. Spoto, *The Dark Side of Genius*, 511–12.

5. Patrick McGilligan, *Alfred Hitchcock: A Life in Darkness and Light* (New York: HarperCollins, 2003), 699.

6. Taylor, *Hitch*, 283.

7. François Truffaut, *Hitchcock*, rev. ed. (New York: Simon & Schuster/Touchstone, 1985), 339.

Cattle Calls
Ruminating over a Cast

6

A MONG THE MANY OFT-REPEATED STORIES surrounding the persona of Alfred Hitchcock, perhaps the most persistent was his supposed remark that "all actors are cattle." His rejoinder was even more widely reported: "I didn't say actors are cattle. What I said was, actors should be treated like cattle."[1] Carole Lombard, whom Hitchcock adored, once famously poked fun at the director's purported attitude by constructing a little corral on the set of *Mr. and Mrs. Smith* (1941); in the corral were three calves, each garlanded with the name of one of the main actors in the film, Lombard's included. That stunt, of course, merely added to the notoriety of Hitchcock's remark. It might well have also contributed to the ongoing dilemma regarding casting that Hitchcock had experienced throughout his Hollywood period; he often complained that the A-list actors were reluctant to work with him because they felt he was making B-list pictures.[2] In addition, Hitchcock had developed a reputation for being a somewhat aloof director. In the age of the "Method" actor, this could cause anxiety, as it quite obviously did on the set of *Torn Curtain*, to cite the most notorious example. "Hitch's impatience with the affectations of the Method actors was well-known," claims John Russell Taylor, but apparently the exchanges between the director and his expensive—and studio-chosen—star, Paul Newman, proved to be even more disastrous than either one could have expected.[3] This was not the first time that Hitchcock had developed frustration over the "method" employed by some of his performers. In her memoir about her mother, Hitchcock's daughter Pat recounts a story that took place on the set of *I Confess* (1953), starring Method-trained Montgomery Clift. Apparently, he was lost in thought—for a Method actor, "preparation"—when Pat and her mother visited the set. "The next shot," she writes, "required Monty Clift to simply walk across a large ballroom—and he just sat there to think and think about it. He was holding everybody up, and Daddy became very impatient."[4]

Even as professional (and conventionally trained) a performer as Doris Day confessed to having had quite a bit of apprehension while working with Hitchcock on *The Man Who Knew Too Much*. In a meeting that she called to discuss their professional relationship, Day asked Hitchcock whether her work was pleasing him. Hitchcock replied that he was perfectly satisfied. He had, however, never commented on her performance, and Day felt "insecure." Hitchcock claimed that all of us are insecure and that he tended to react to actors only when he wished to change something about their particular delivery of a line or to enact a shift in the blocking of a scene. Day, reassured, went on to demonstrate that Hitchcock had indeed been correct in casting her. The performance she gave as Jo McKenna met with almost universal praise.[5]

This was often the case. Hitchcock's attitude was that he would choose the best possible actor he could find for the part, and he would then expect the actor to do the job competently and well, in the same way he expected such participation from the cinematographer and the costume designer. His directing methodology was straightforward and trusting; he expected professionalism from his actors without accompanying histrionics. While some performers found themselves without the guidance they might have received from other directors, the reality is that Hitchcock managed to elicit some quite profound performances from his actors. He was, in fact, one of the finest directors of acting talent that we have in the history of cinema. Is there, for example, a better performance by Cary Grant than the one he gives in either *Notorious* or *North by Northwest*? Is Grace Kelly ever more luminous and yet at the same time more believable than she is in *Rear Window*? (Hitchcock assistant Peggy Robertson went even further in a 1995 interview: "Grace Kelly has never been so great as she was in the Hitchcock pictures.")[6] Is James Stewart ever more nuanced than he is in *Vertigo*? (To add an example from the end of his career: Is Barbara Harris ever any better than she was for Hitchcock in *Family Plot*?) These observations apply not only to the heroes and heroines of Hitchcock films, but—perhaps more importantly—to the villains as well. As François Truffaut notes during the recorded interviews, "the better the villain, the better the picture."[7] He gives as examples Claude Rains in *Notorious*, Joseph Cotten in *Shadow of a Doubt*, and Robert Walker in *Strangers on a Train*. One could easily add James Mason in *North by Northwest* and the incomparable Anthony Perkins in *Psycho*.

Anticipating his sojourn to England to cast *Frenzy*, Hitchcock would not expect to encounter any difficulties in recruiting A-list actors for his latest production. In fact, as biographer Donald Spoto points out—suggesting that the thought originated with Alma—"the actors could be handpicked from the London theater, where training was substantial, where attention to detail was taken for granted, and where—unlike Hollywood—famous actors do not think it unworthy to accept small, well-written roles."[8] Indeed, Hitchcock found that the London theater actors were only too happy to be a part of the project. He was able to draw upon list after list of performers from the British theatrical world, and the cast he eventually assembled was full of names that would have been known to anyone familiar with recent London stage productions, although not too many of them would seem quite as familiar to American audiences. The point is that Hitchcock had been granted complete freedom in assembling his cast, and he was able to do so without any resistance from those on either an A-list or a B-list. Perhaps more importantly, the studio executives were now five thousand miles away.

By early May of 1971, Hitchcock was ready to move his operations to London. The office log indicates that his staff had booked a suite at Claridge's in Mayfair from May 14 through September 28. A car and driver had been booked as well, although Peggy Robertson noted in a May 6 memo that Hitchcock wanted a different driver from the one he had had on his previous visit in March; that particular driver had tended to be late. Robertson was to arrive in London on Sunday, May 9, and was expected to have set up an office by Monday. Mr. and Mrs. Hitchcock were scheduled to arrive on the following Saturday.[9]

The immediate challenge was to cast the picture. While a great deal of preliminary speculation had taken place in California regarding who might play which role, nothing definitive had as yet been concluded. Hitchcock, for example, had lunched with Michael Caine on March 17, after which he entered a note into the file that listed casting suggestions: Caine as Bob Rusk, Nicol Williamson as Inspector Oxford, and—imagine what a film might have resulted—Richard Burton as Blamey (Blaney). Caine was eventually to decline, and it seems that Hitchcock never forgave him for turning down the role.[10] Many other suggestions were to make their way into one of the office file folders over the next two months. On March 22, Hitchcock added to the file the possibilities of John Mills as Inspector Oxford and Elsie Randolph as the receptionist at the Hilton Hotel. On April 7, Hitchcock noted the potential of Ralph Richardson as Oxford. After a lunch with two Universal executives on April 9, Hitchcock added the names of Richard Harris as Blamey, and Glenda Jackson, Lynn Redgrave, or Geneviève Bujold as Babs.[11] How much of this was serious consideration and how much might have been idle speculation over lunch is impossible to determine. Studio casting director Bill Batliner added his suggestions for Inspector Oxford on May 5. Among his list of eleven names were Trevor Howard, Michael Redgrave, Paul Scofield, Laurence Olivier, and Peter Ustinov.[12] On May 7, Hitchcock added two more: James Mason and Christopher Plummer. John Gaines of the International Famous Agency, in preparation for Hitchcock's impending voyage to London, sent a list of British actors and actresses who might be suitable. Among the forty-seven names were some that had not yet appeared: Robert Shaw, Albert Finney, Michael York, Julie Christie, Marianne Faithful, Irene Worth.[13]

Of course, once word leaked out in the Hollywood community that Hitchcock was planning another film, the office was inundated with letters and photos of potential cast members. An especially poignant one arrived the very day Hitchcock was lunching with Michael Caine on March 17; a young unknown named Dixon Adams announced that "this is yet another letter from an actor who would give his eye teeth to appear in your film, 'Frenzy.'" Another was just as direct if a bit more clever; Sandra Rudkin sent this simple plea:

> Dear Mr. Hitchcock:
>   This face might be right for some moment in FRENZY. It is mine. Height 5'4", build proportionate. I know where to put my feet before the camera.

It was among Peggy Robertson's duties to respond to such material. The standard reply would usually include the following: "At present Mr. Hitchcock's next film is still in the preliminary stages, but we will certainly keep your pictures and letter on file."[14]

Even old hands who had been involved with Hitchcock for years expressed interest in being part of the new project. One letter came from Hume Cronyn, an old friend who had actually helped Hitchcock with the preliminary treatment for *Rope*. In a March 15 letter, he, too, was direct:

> Dear Hitch,
>   If there's something I can do in your new film please consider me.
>   There it is, blunt and to the point. You'll say that any such nudge is unnecessary. Perhaps, but I've been professionally idle—with a good many other people—for nine months and as you know that's painful.

This is not an "auld lang syne" request. Either there is somewhere I can make a contribution or quite possibly none. You will have to deal with my suggestion professionally and you will. No reply is called for.

Love,
Hume

PS. As a Canadian of British descent I don't believe there's any problem about my working in England.

This letter was answered directly and swiftly by Hitchcock himself, on March 19:

Dear Hume,
    As you well know, if the right part was there you'd be on the top of my list.
    Unfortunately, the yarn I'm going to do provides no opportunity for a part of any size that would be up your alley. Apart from the two leading men, the rest of the cast consists of two women, and the rest are just bits except for one Scotland Yard superintendent.
    All the bits are just two or three days work and none of any stature.
    It leaves me a little unhappy that there is nothing in this picture for you, because, as I said above, you'd certainly be at the top if there were the right character in the story.

Love,
Hitch[15]

In the weeks before leaving for London, Hitchcock screened literally dozens of films, in whole or in part, as he scanned them for potential actors and actresses. He would add his notes on their performances or their suitability for a role in *Frenzy* to the files. About one, he wrote "too lightweight"; about another "no, too mean looking."[16] As the process continued, his list of possibilities continued to grow as well. By May 15 he had whittled the master list down to eleven names for Rusk, ten for Blaney (name changed from Blamey), twelve for Mrs. Blaney, and eighteen for Inspector Oxford. The list for Babs continued to be a work in progress.

Alma and Alfred Hitchcock arrived in London on May 15, 1971. After resting on Sunday at the hotel, Hitchcock was ready to venture on Monday morning to the temporary office in central London that Peggy Robertson had set up the previous week (she had arrived in London on the morning of May 9). At this point, the only order of business was to hire the cast and crew. As far as the crew was concerned, things were a bit easier. Hitchcock was able to draw upon connections he had made years before and to take the recommendations of former associates as to which technicians might be best suited to work under Hitchcock's meticulous approach to filmmaking. For his "lighting cameraman" (what Hollywood would call the "director of photography"), for example, he chose veteran Gil Taylor from a list of twenty possibilities; he had come highly recommended by the executive staff at Pinewood Studios, the well-equipped facility just outside London that would serve as the base for his studio (interior) work. Taylor also happened to have been a young crew member on one of Hitchcock's most forgettable films, the 1930 *Elstree Calling*. Colin Brewer was appointed to the extremely important position of assistant director. He, too, came highly recommended by the veteran technicians whose opinions Hitchcock had come to trust during his years in London. In order to prepare each of them for the "look" of the film, he ordered a volume of color reproductions of the great Dutch painter, Johannes Vermeer, for them to consult—and to absorb.[17]

Casting the actors proved to be not so fortuitous. Hitchcock was very concerned that he find properly trained actors who could move easily into their roles with little direction from him. "I hired you because you're an actress," he told Vivien Merchant, whom he had chosen to play Inspector Oxford's wife. "You do your business, and you just let me play with my camera."[18] In order to familiarize himself with those performers whom he did not already know, he spent hours in the screening room looking at films—or, again, parts of films—in order to evaluate performances. In the evening, he and Alma would often go to the theater, in part, of course, because he had nurtured a lifelong affection for the London stage, and in part to continue looking at players. By the end of the first week in London, no decision had yet been made about casting. Mr. and Mrs. Hitchcock were guests for dinner at the home of Mr. and Mrs. Anthony Shaffer on Sunday evening, May 23. He and Shaffer agreed to meet during the following week for lunch in order to talk about the casting. They in fact met three times that week. In addition to casting, they needed to discuss changes that Shaffer could incorporate into the revised screenplay. They proceeded to meet several times each week for the next two weeks; Hitchcock continued screening films and dictating notes to the file.

The "first revised" screenplay is dated June 3 and contains all of the changes—most of them minor—that Hitchcock and Shaffer had been working on over the previous two months. Indeed, there are very few major changes.[19] A comparison of the June 3 script with the previous one (dated April 9) indicates that the revisions have not substantially altered the approach that the two of them had been taking since they had begun in January. The 166 scenes of the April 29 script have been reduced to 163.[20] Some new shots have been inserted, and some dialogue rewritten. One scene involving a girl running from Rusk's apartment has been added; it was later dropped. The single most important change, at least in terms of how the finished film would be affected, involved a small instruction added by Hitchcock to scene #83. In this script, this would be the scene that takes place just after the murder of Babs. The shot that makes it into the film itself will eventually be hailed as one of the finest in the picture. In this script, Hitchcock has added just these words: "The CAMERA continues its retreat across the street outside Rusk's house and comes to rest holding the whole building in a longish shot." This is a very sharp example of how detailed Hitchcock wanted his script to be in terms of what the camera sees. It is an exemplar of his commanding visual style. The shot when completed will be the concluding moment of one of the signature sequences in *Frenzy*. Hitchcock was always thinking of the camera, of where it was to be placed, of how it was to be moved, of what its lens was to capture. This sentence added to the latest version of the script is a fine example of his thought process as he prepared the work.

Hitchcock was ready then to return to casting the picture, but his methodical approach was suddenly interrupted by the sort of event that escapes even the most meticulous planning. Alma had a stroke on the morning of June 9. As life would have it, her granddaughter was arriving that very morning from Los Angeles to join her and her mother, Patricia Hitchcock (Hitch and Alma's daughter), on a sightseeing tour of Europe. Hitchcock himself rushed to the airport to pick up Mary and to tell her of her grandmother's situation. Characteristically, Alma refused to leave Claridge's and insisted on being treated by the hotel physician and by Hitchcock's personal physician, who had made the trip to attend to the director during what looked to be an arduous period of preproduction and production. The stroke was serious but not life threatening; certainly by this time in her life, Alma Reville must have known how much she was needed by her partner and husband. She stayed on, at least until filming was well under way. She had twenty-four-hour care, with a day nurse and a night nurse always on duty. Hitchcock was disheartened but managed to continue. According to Donald Spoto, Hitchcock was at first "almost incapacitated himself."[21] Alma insisted that her daughter and granddaughter leave London on the trip they had planned to take together, and this decision perhaps allowed Hitchcock to return his intensity to the challenge of casting. Alma would be there—assisted by the round-the-clock nursing care—to assume her customary role of essential adviser as he made his way through the dozens and dozens of names that continued to be presented to him. More and more of the meetings, though, were now to take place at Claridge's so that Hitchcock would not have to leave the hotel.

By Tuesday, June 15, though, Hitchcock resumed going to the office in the afternoons to interview potential performers. By Wednesday the sixteenth he had met with four different actresses for the role of Babs; none seemed quite right. On Thursday morning, he met with several candidates for the role of Rusk; again, none seemed to fit the part.[22]

By the following week, the interviewing schedule intensified. The film was scheduled to begin shooting in mid-July, and the cast had not yet been assembled. On Monday the twenty-first, Hitchcock began interviewing at 10:30 in the morning. Breaking for lunch at 12:30, he returned to the process at 2:30, with the last interview scheduled for 5 P.M. The same sort of schedule continued for the rest of the week. (On the twenty-first, Peggy Robertson had sent a note to the Los Angeles office answering a query about the cast: "No, no cast has been set yet. Suspenseful, isn't it: but true. Mr. Hitchcock spends all day interviewing & screening film.")[23] The log of these interviews records a meeting at 3 P.M. on Wednesday, June 23, with Barry Foster, but no comments appear next to the entry. The following day, Hitchcock looked at more film clips and took a tour of the new Scotland Yard facility during the afternoon. On the twenty-fifth, he had Robertson send the script to Glenda Jackson for her to consider the part of Brenda and to Lynn Redgrave for Babs. The week of the twenty-eighth continued with more or less the same schedule. In addition to casting interviews, Hitchcock would meet most mornings with Shaffer to further modify the script. He would also try to include some location scouting. On Monday the twenty-eighth, for example, he made a trip to Covent Garden.[24]

On Thursday, July 1, Hitchcock met with Jon Finch at 11 A.M. and noted that he was interviewing him for the part of Bob Rusk. The office log also indicates that Hitchcock began to intensify the pace of viewing film clips; each afternoon would now be devoted to looking at the work of one artist or another, usually several film sequences each day. On Friday afternoon, July 2, for example, he screened parts of *Lock Up Your Daughters, 30 Is a Dangerous Age, Cynthia,* and *Wake in Fright.* What he might have thought of any of these is not recorded.

The preparation for production had to continue, of course, even without a cast. On Monday, July 5, Hitchcock met with Dulcie Midwinter, the wardrobe mistress. What they could have decided without actors to dress remains a mystery. What we do know about Hitchcock is that he tended to have very clear ideas about every detail of the set, including the costuming. With production scheduled to begin in a matter of weeks, the necessity of having a cast to costume became increasingly obvious. By July 6, he had compiled a preliminary cast list. It included many names of artists who had not yet committed to the project, but it clearly renders an idea of the sort of ensemble for which he was hoping:[25]

"FRENZY" CAST

Blaney	Jon Finch (providing he is not too young)
Forsythe	Bernard Cribbins
Babs	Lynn Redgrave [Judy Cornwall handwritten in]
Rusk	Barry Foster
Monica	Jill Bennett
Mrs. Blaney	Glenda Jackson
Inspector Oxford	Max Bygraves
Sgt. Spearman	Michael Bates
Porter	Clive Swift
Hetty Porter	Billie Whitelaw
Mrs. Oxford	Vivien Merchant

On the morning of July 7, Hitchcock met with Alec McCowen and that afternoon at 3 P.M. took a second meeting with Jon Finch. The next day he met with Anna Massey, who expressed interest but asked to see the full script. By Monday, July 12, the press had concluded that at least part of the cast was now solidly in place. The *London Evening Standard* published a photograph with the following caption: "Alfred Hitchcock, now in London preparing his first British film for 35 years, has signed two fast-rising young actors for leading roles in the film, *Frenzy*. They are Jon Finch (left), taken from comparative obscurity by Roman Polanski to play the title role in his recently-completed film of *Macbeth*, and Barry Foster (right), an established stage actor."[26] Universal then had no choice but to release at least a preliminary cast list that included the names of Finch, Foster, Massey, Vivien Merchant, Alec McCowen, and Bernard Cribbins; this they did on July 19. Meanwhile, Hitchcock's interviews continued: another ten on July 15, nine on July 16, and lunch at Claridge's with Vivien Merchant on Saturday, July 17. By the end of the following week, only the role of Monica remained to be cast, for on Thursday the twenty-second, Hitchcock noted "OK" next to the name of Barbara Leigh-Hunt for the role of Brenda Blaney.[27] While perhaps not his "dream" cast—with such well-known performers as Laurence Olivier, Glenda Jackson, or Lynn

Redgrave—it was indeed a solid cast. As John Russell Taylor comments, this cast "combined demonstrated talent with a pleasing unfamiliarity for picturegoers, and gave a richness of characterization sadly lacking in Hitch's two previous films."[28]

Production on *Frenzy* was therefore scheduled to begin at Covent Garden on Monday, July 26, with the following cast:

Blaney	Jon Finch
Forsythe	Bernard Cribbins
Babs	Anna Massey
Rusk	Barry Foster
Monica	as yet uncast
Mrs. Blaney	Barbara Leigh-Hunt
Inspector Oxford	Alec McCowen
Sgt. Spearman	Michael Bates
Porter	Clive Swift
Hetty Porter	Billie Whitelaw
Mrs. Oxford	Vivien Merchant

Peggy Robertson later wrote to the Los Angeles office that "the cast is just great—best we've had for years."[29]

Notes

1. François Truffaut, *Hitchcock*, rev. ed. (New York: Simon & Schuster/ Touchstone, 1985), 140.

2. Truffaut, *Hitchcock*, 133.

3. John Russell Taylor, *Hitch: The Life and Times of Alfred Hitchcock* (London: Faber and Faber, 1978), 276.

4. Pat Hitchcock O'Connell and Laurent Bouzereau, *Alma Hitchcock: The Woman behind the Man* (New York: Berkley, 2003), 161.

5. Patrick McGilligan, *Alfred Hitchcock: A Life in Darkness and Light* (New York: HarperCollins, 2003), 517–19. The full story can be found in A. E. Hotchner, *Doris Day: Her Own Story* (New York: William Morrow, 1975).

6. *An Oral History with Peggy Robertson*. Interviewed by Barbara Hall. (Academy of Motion Picture Arts and Sciences, Oral History Program, 2002), 354.

7. Truffaut, *Hitchcock*, 191.

8. Donald Spoto, *The Dark Side of Genius: The Life of Alfred Hitchcock* (Boston: Little, Brown, 1983), 508.

9. See *Frenzy* Folder #344 of the Alfred Hitchcock papers at the Margaret Herrick Library, Beverly Hills, California.

10. *Frenzy* Folder #275 of the Alfred Hitchcock papers.

11. *Frenzy* Folder #275 of the Alfred Hitchcock papers.

12. *Frenzy* Folder #276 of the Alfred Hitchcock papers.

13. *Frenzy* Folder #275 of the Alfred Hitchcock papers.

14. *Frenzy* Folder #275 of the Alfred Hitchcock papers.

15. *Frenzy* Folder #296 of the Alfred Hitchcock papers.

16. *Frenzy* Folder #276 of the Alfred Hitchcock papers.

17. *Frenzy* Folder #302 of the Alfred Hitchcock papers.

18. Spoto, *The Dark Side of Genius*, 511.

19. See *Frenzy* Folder #259 of the Alfred Hitchcock papers.

20. For the April 29 script, see *Frenzy* Folder #256 of the Alfred Hitchcock papers.

21. Spoto, *The Dark Side of Genius*, 512.

22. *Frenzy* Folder #276 of the Alfred Hitchcock papers.

23. *Frenzy* Folder #327 of the Alfred Hitchcock papers.

24. *Frenzy* Folder #276 of the Alfred Hitchcock papers.

25. *Frenzy* Folder #276 of the Alfred Hitchcock papers.

26. *Evening Standard*, 12 July 1971, 8. Photo itself with caption in *Frenzy* Folder #276 of the Alfred Hitchcock papers.

27. *Frenzy* Folder #276 of the Alfred Hitchcock papers.

28. Taylor, *Hitch*, 284.

29. *Frenzy* Folder #327 of the Alfred Hitchcock papers. The full cast and crew list can be found in appendix A in this volume.

The Thirteen-Week Production   7
Mornings and Afternoons on the Set

P ART OF THE MYTHOS OF THE Alfred Hitchcock legend is that the master spent so much time and attention to detail in preproduction that there was actually very little for him to do once he arrived on set. This aspect of the Hitchcock persona was only enhanced by his often being quoted as feeling that whichever project he happened to be working on was essentially finished once the storyboards had been completed. Hitchcock seemed to have thoroughly enjoyed embellishing this particular myth throughout his career, even going so far as claiming in a 1966 article that he usually wished he didn't have to actually shoot the film, his ultimate satisfaction instead having been derived from the completion of one of his elaborate and detailed shooting scripts.[1] The implication, of course, is that he really would prefer not to have to actually film the very scenes he had so laboriously created with his screenwriter. Indeed, the suggestion is that the shooting script was so tightly woven that all that would be left for any director to do was to, in the words of the old Hollywood injunction from the early days of the industry: "shoot as written." "I wish I didn't have to shoot the picture," Hitchcock claimed in an interview for the journal *Take One*; "when I've gone through the script and created the picture on paper, for me the creative job is done and the rest is just a bore."[2] While shooting *Topaz* in Paris, he confided to a reporter for *L'Express* that he had often dreamed of an IBM machine "in which I'd insert the screenplay at one end and the film would emerge at the other end, completed, and in color."[3]

A concomitant part of the mythology had to do with Hitchcock's insistence that his films were essentially preedited, that there was very little to do in postproduction since the preproduction process had been so meticulous.

In the same *Take One* piece, Hitchcock dismissed any "creative" editing on his projects because the film is, as he put it, "designed ahead of time—precut, which it should be."[4] The impression that Hitchcock liked to leave with his interviewers was of an artist who arrived on the set with such a detailed shooting script that the actual filming could take place with a minimum of effort on his part. It was another aspect of his personal mythology that he spent a great deal of his career in promulgating. Hitchcock would have his admirers believe that most of his work on set could be summarized by a "one take and print" approach; that is, that since so much effort had gone into the preparation, most of the shots on set could be captured by the crew in one take.[5] It was a reputation for on-set efficiency that he nurtured and embellished over time.

The myth remained largely unchallenged through decades of scholarship on Hitchcock's working methodology until the publication of Bill Krohn's *Hitchcock at Work* in 2000.[6] By carefully examining production records and camera reports, Krohn was able to establish that indeed Hitchcock often strayed from his shooting script and in fact did not rely on storyboards as much as he had led his commentators and biographers to believe. By closely comparing source material now housed at the Margaret Herrick Library in Beverly Hills with the actual film as produced, Krohn was able, for example, to reveal significant departures from the published scripts of both *Psycho* and *North by Northwest*. Regarding the latter film, Krohn was able to ascertain that the famous crop-duster sequence had not actually been made into storyboards until after the shooting; Hitchcock instead had worked from an elaborate set of drawings as he planned the airplane attack on Cary Grant.[7]

Krohn had very little to say about *Frenzy*. (He provides detailed analyses of ten Hitchcock classics, ranging from *Saboteur* to *The Birds*, while touching briefly on several others, *Frenzy* among them.) Nevertheless, the same approach to the material can be brought to bear on the making of this film, and an examination of the documents catalogued into the Alfred Hitchcock papers at the Herrick Library sheds a significant amount of light on the actual production details of *Frenzy*.

Day one of a scheduled thirteen-week production period was July 26, 1971, and for a project that had begun with a phone call from Hitchcock to his screenwriter on the previous New Year's Eve, it was quite remarkable that all of the script writing, all of the casting (or at least most of it), and all of the meticulous preproduction could have been completed in such a short amount of time. From inception of the project to the first day of shooting, not seven full months had passed. Most of Hitchcock's previous projects had consumed far more time in preproduction.

While Hitch himself continued with casting decisions and production-planning lunches at Claridge's—his film was not completely cast until the week of the actual shooting—his team of professionals met with the executives of Pinewood Studios on July 15 to complete all the necessary arrangements for the commencement of shooting. According to the minutes of the meeting, the executives of Pinewood, including J. E. Fennell, chairman, and Roy Goddard, studio productions manager, were joined by Brian Burgess, production manager for *Frenzy*, and Bill Hill, associate producer for the project. In addition, the chief stewards of the professional craft unions were in attendance. After agreeing to a closed set throughout the shooting period and offering an acknowledgment of the importance of the project to London ("It was accepted by all concerned that this was a film which could have been staged against any background but Mr. Hitchcock preferred to give it a London setting") as well as to Pinewood Studios, it was recorded in the minutes that "this was a film to be made by 'The Master'; that he looked for quiet efficiency in all his team" and that "great care had been taken by both the Production Company and the Studio to provide people to form a unit which should be compatible with the way Mr. Hitchcock always worked." If any problems were to arrive, "it would be better if the Unit Stewards refer them to the Production Manager, or, in matters of interpretation of Agreements, the Chief Steward, in order that any difficulties can be dealt with away from the set."[8] This last part of the memorandum of agreement would prove to be quite important and would be called upon during the very first day of shooting.

The call sheets for Monday, July 26, indicate that the cast and crew reported to the studio at 7 A.M. and were transported to the Covent Garden area for an 8 A.M. setup. (The second unit team had done some preliminary background plates the previous week.)[9] The arrival of the director onto the shooting location on that first day can easily stand for the "triumphal return" that Hitchcock might have envisioned, and for which the helicopter shot that would eventually open the film might stand. Nevertheless, while most of the biographers have commented upon Hitchcock's magisterial entry onto the Covent Garden set—in his chauffeur-driven Rolls Royce—none seem to have noted that the commencement of shooting had been accompanied by an inauspicious omen.[10] Indeed the daily progress report for that first day includes this "medical note": "After a fall in his hotel room on Friday night the 23rd, Mr. Hitchcock hurt his back and had to remain in bed for the weekend. Dr. Southward was called through Claridge's. Mr. Hitchcock was able to work on Monday. . . ."[11]

The progress report noted that the first setup was not completed until 12:05 and that the crew was dismissed at 6:15 P.M. By all indications, it was an uneventful opening day: eight setups completed, all of them exteriors within the Covent Garden neighborhood. If Hitchcock had been suffering any further complications from his hotel room fall, none are revealed in any of the official studio records. There was, however, one potentially serious problem, as recalled by Hitchcock's personal assistant, Peggy Robertson. In a 1995 interview for the Margaret Herrick Library archives, Robertson spoke of a union official on set the first day interrupting a take because the hour was approaching 6 P.M. Hitchcock claimed that he had been given to understand by studio management that he would be allowed to finish whichever take he was on, and he adamantly insisted that, as a director, he would never break in the middle of a take: "It's not good for the actors." Hitchcock threatened to leave the set and finish the picture in Hollywood. "So the studio held a hurried meeting," Robertson recalled, "and decided that we could finish the shot."[12] Hitchcock had made his point, and, according to Robertson, there was no further interference from the union representatives regarding either the start or end of a shooting day.

The continuity sheets for that first day are revealing.[13] Hitchcock seems to have dispatched two exterior shots with ease, capturing each of them in one take. A longer scene—#8 on the master script—took more effort. It seems to have taken six full takes before Hitchcock was satisfied that this scene had been properly recorded, and takes #5, 6, and 7 are merely listed as "same" on the continuity sheets, suggesting that the director wanted to leave himself a few choices in the editing room, something he of course had led his commentators to believe he rarely needed to do. Scene #8 was, however, the first dialogue scene of the day—it is between Babs and Blaney, with one line by Forsythe—and as such presented the possibility of more complications than the two scenes just completed; they were mere single shots of the Covent Garden neighborhood. Interestingly, Hitchcock's schedule notes that he found time during this busy first day of shooting to interview two candidates for the one remaining role in the film; he met at 2:30 with Patsy Byrne and then immediately afterward with Jean Marsh. The interviews took place right there at the Covent Garden location, and shortly thereafter, Ms. Marsh was announced as having been awarded the role of Monica in the production.

The next day, Tuesday, July 27, could be seen, by contrast, as an example of the "one take and print" approach that is suggested by the Hitchcock mythology. According to the production reports, Hitchcock managed to shoot scenes #12, 122, 132, and 133 in one take each. They are all individual exterior shots, without dialogue. Scene #134 took two takes, and this only because Hitchcock decided to use two different lenses, one on each take. He finished the day by recording one take of scene #11, a rather long dialogue scene—mainly between Blaney and Rusk—that he would return to on both Wednesday and Thursday of that first week. The day's shooting was concluded at 5:45, the first take having been completed at 9:20 that morning. (The crew call had once again been for 7 A.M. at the studio.) No problems were reported on any of the official records.

The next day, the crew dispatched with scene #14—Rusk introduces his mother to Blaney—with four takes, and #15—Blaney crushing the box of grapes in frustration—in but three takes. The rest of the day was spent on scene #11: three more takes. Eight more takes were devoted to scene #11 the next day (Thursday, July 29); two more rather straightforward exterior shots were also captured that day.

Aside, then, from the rather melodramatic incident involving the brief skirmish with the union representative, the first week seems to have gone smoothly, with Hitchcock operating in the quietly efficient style for which he had by now become well known. The crew responded to his obvious professionalism, and the cast hit their marks as expected. The progress reports list a total of forty-two setups for the week, an average of just over eight per day, with but one particular problem mentioned. The progress report for Wednesday, July 28, notes that the exteriors were "difficult" and that the production was therefore already "one day behind schedule." As noted, the exteriors shot on that Wednesday had not included any of the more difficult shots. The call sheet mentions "the weather" as a factor, and this is no doubt what slowed down production. Only three scenes were shot that day, and none of them were completed in a single take. What is perhaps most remarkable about the first week's shooting is that Hitchcock moved quickly from these rather straightforward opening scenes to one of the most complex sequences in the entire film. By Friday the thirtieth he was ready to begin work on scene #82, a shot that sets up the much-admired and complicated reverse track out of Rusk's apartment after he entices Babs to join him there. It is instructive to quote from the script to illustrate the complexity of the scene:

82. INT. THE STAIRS LEADING UP TO RUSK'S APARTMENT—DAY
THE CAMERA goes upstairs ahead of Rusk and Babs, with the latter in the lead. Rusk wears an enigmatic expression. The CAMERA turns a corner at the top of the stairs and follows them down to the door of Rusk's

apartment. Rusk moves forward and opens the door standing aside for her to enter. He follows, and the door starts to close behind him. Before it does so however we have time to hear one sentence.

RUSK

    I don't know if you know it, Babs, but you're my type of woman.
The door closes with a click.
THE CAMERA, as if saying goodbye to Babs, retreats down the stairs and out through the front door.[14]

Hitchcock decided to shoot the scene two ways, with two different lenses. Beginning with a 32-millimeter lens on the camera, he ordered six takes, printing three of them (even though take #1—listed as a "Print"—was "too fast," according to the continuity sheets). Three more takes followed with a 25-millimeter lens, and only take #3 was printed. Hitchcock now had four takes from which to choose in editing one of the most celebrated shots in the entire film. The complicated shooting of this scene is more closely examined—along with the other "signature" sequences—in the following two chapters.

There was more to do on that Friday, however. Hitchcock decided to proceed with the rest of that sequence, shot #83. This was the completion of the backward movement of the camera as it returns to the busy street in front of Rusk's apartment. The actual cut between the studio section of the shot and the location section is cleverly hidden by a man with a sack of potatoes crossing in front of the doorway at an opportune moment. The shot itself took eight takes, with only two printed. The first two were unsuccessful due to "crowd action," and three others had to be cut before the action was completed.

Perhaps most remarkable about this particular day is that Hitchcock was not through yet. He decided to film the long walk from the pub to Rusk's apartment, a complicated moving camera shot that included a long conversation between Babs and Rusk as they stroll through the busy fruit and vegetable market, threading their way among the workers while maintaining a civil conversation. Hitchcock's mastery of the moving camera is one of his trademarks. Indeed, it can be argued that very few directors are his peer in this regard. This particular shot, while not as elegant or emotionally rewarding as the famous crane movement in *Notorious* or as cinematically revealing as the opening of *Rear Window*, nevertheless demonstrates Hitchcock's ability to make the complex look easy.

The market is full of people. They all needed to be orchestrated through the scene. It was important to do this without distracting the

Hitchcock between takes while shooting *Frenzy,* 1971. *Photofest*

audience from the central characters. After nine takes, Hitchcock called it a day, and the cast and crew were released at 6:30 P.M. He had gotten his shots. And it had been a remarkably productive day: twenty-eight takes in all, and the undertaking of several of the more complicated moments in the film. (To be completely accurate, it should be noted that Hitchcock returned to scene #79—Babs leaving the pub—on August 5; he had decided to use a zoom lens on the shot and recorded six more takes with this particular setup.)

The first full week of shooting on *Frenzy* had been a remarkably productive one, but no one there at the time would have characterized Hitchcock's method as "one take and print." It should be clear from an examination of the progress reports and the continuity sheets that despite the fact that Hitchcock was working from a script that he had deemed entirely satisfactory, there was far more to translating the word to the screen than merely to "shoot as written." Yet a simple totaling of the week's efforts reveals that all or part of twenty scenes were shot and that this required sixty-seven takes. That works out to just over three takes per shot, a level of efficiency quite rare in the annals of Hollywood productions. Perhaps a more indicative way of looking at the "machine" that Hitchcock was guiding is to count the number of individual camera setups. During that first week, there were a total of forty-two, working out to just over eight per day. This was indeed efficient filmmaking.

The following week's schedule produced the next logistical challenge: the helicopter shot of Tower Bridge and the crowd listening to a politician giving a speech at County Hall. It is the opening of the film, and it sets the darkly humorous tone of the work. Just as the politician is celebrating the fact that the Thames River is now cleaner than it has been in generations, a dead body washes ashore. (Hitchcock is seen in the audience listening to the speech; by this point in his career, he had learned to get his de rigueur cameo out of the way very early in the film.) Monday, August 2, was spent shooting all of this. The helicopter shot alone took five takes, but the shooting of the scene of the minister's speech proved to be much more tedious: twenty-seven takes. Apparently, all of this effort was for naught, because when Hitchcock saw the rushes that evening, he decided that everything had to be reshot. According to the progress report, he was unhappy with four of the actors, and they would have to be recast. He also felt that the crowd number (in this case, sixty) was insufficient and would have to be increased before the reshooting. It should be clear from this example that Hitchcock was fully in charge on the set: the fact that he found four members of a crowd of sixty to be not performing to his standards should give some indication of his attention to detail.

The crew was unable to accomplish the retakes the next day. The progress report for Tuesday, August 3, indicated that there was very heavy rain at the location that morning "and it was decided to return to the studios to shoot the weather cover," in this case one of the scenes at Inspector

Oxford's flat. The rain continued all day, so Hitchcock turned his attention to scenes #86 through 89, during which Inspector Oxford discusses the case with his wife. Two of the four shots are without dialogue, and despite the fact that it was not until 4:20 in the afternoon that the first of these was properly lit and ready to be shot, they were easily dispatched with one take each. Scene #89 is a long dialogue exchange, and Hitchcock broke it up into sections, took three takes of one part of the conversation, and called it a day at 5:35 P.M. The crew would return to these scenes later in the month.

The weather the next day was not much better: "rain and bad light held up shooting at various times during the day," reads the progress report for Wednesday, August 4. The schedule called for exteriors, specifically scenes #16 and 17, which are simple shots in the alleyway near the Blaney Matrimonial Agency; these were followed by a single shot of Rusk leaving the agency. Despite the weather, one take was sufficient for each of these. More time was taken with scene #34, the one that I have previously labeled the "blank brick wall scene" (see chapter 4). We have seen how this sequence is described in the script; here is what appears on the continuity sheet:

> Camera shooting from courtyard outside matrimonial agency onto Monica Barling as she walks thru alley from Oxford Street on her way back after lunch . . . camera tracks back in front of her . . . she looks ahead right . . . reacts as she sees Blaney O.S. [offscreen] leave the agency . . . walks on passes close to camera looks off at Blaney walking away down narrow alley close to agency . . . camera pans her to entrance of matrimonial agency . . . she goes in . . . disappears . . . camera runs on . . . people walking towards camera react as Monica screams on finding Brenda's body . . .

Hitchcock took five takes of the establishing shot then two more of the shot that indicates Monica's point of view. The day closed with three fairly simple shots of Blaney in a phone booth. The crew was dismissed precisely at 6 P.M. They would be returning to this sequence at a later date as well.

The weather was better on Thursday, August 5, and Hitchcock wanted to complete as much of the exterior work as he could while the fickle London weather held. The first setup was ready at 9:05 that morning and involved a simple shot of Blaney jumping into a cab with Babs. Three takes proved sufficient. This was followed by an exterior shot of the Coburg Hotel as the taxi pulls up to it, and Blaney and Babs descend from the cab and enter the hotel; again, three takes. The crew then returned to scene #11, which they had shot in part on Tuesday and Wednesday of the previous week;

two takes were added to the long conversation scene this time. Especially important in this scene was a close-up of Rusk's tiepin. According to the script, "WE SEE the pin in sufficiently big CLOSE UP to be able to recognize it again." Hitchcock had to make sure that the camera crew got this shot, since the tiepin plays such a significant role in the story. (This particular shot was so important, in fact, that Hitchcock returned for a retake of it on September 24.)

The day concluded with Hitchcock's decision to work on scene #79 at the end of the afternoon. This is a key moment in the final film that opens with Rusk seeming to appear out of nowhere as Babs leaves the pub; he casually offers her "a place to stay." It is a complicated shot in that there is a clever zoom movement that makes Rusk's sudden appearance credible. Hitchcock directed six takes, printing the last three. He dismissed the crew at 5:50 P.M.

Friday, August 6, was devoted to interiors shot on stage D at Pinewood. A bedroom set had been constructed, and Hitchcock shot five parts of a scene that takes place within the Coburg Hotel, where Blaney and Babs have rented a room for the night. The day went quite smoothly, with no problems reported. They even shot a scene—#51, a brief exchange between Blaney and Babs—that was later cut from the final film. The first take had been at 10:35 in the morning, and the crew was dismissed early—at 5:20 P.M. It was Friday night, after all, and a rare Saturday camera rehearsal for an even more rare Sunday shoot was scheduled for the next day. The second week of filming was now complete, and the totals for this period suggest a continuation of what seemed to be becoming the usual efficiency: twenty-three scenes in whole or in part, seventy-six takes, forty-three setups.

Scenes #136 and 139 were rehearsed at the Old Bailey on Saturday, August 7, and shot on Sunday. It was a full day, with twelve setups. By the afternoon, while two more scenes in the Old Bailey sequence were being shot, part of the crew returned to the Tower Bridge area to try again with the helicopter shot that would open the film. The shoot ended at 5:30 P.M. By Monday, August 9, Hitchcock had seen enough of the rushes to have decided upon some retakes.[15] He returned to the long dialogue scenes between Inspector Oxford and his wife, beginning with retakes of scenes #86 through 89. (The only concession to what must have been an exhausted crew—after all, they had worked the entire weekend—was that the morning call was at 8:30 rather than at 8 A.M.) This very witty dialogue sequence covers six full pages of the script and turned out to be one of the highlights of the film, at least in the eyes of many of the critics. Hitchcock's perseverance in the casting paid off; his veterans from the London stage—Alec McCowen and Vivien Merchant—demonstrated their professionalism and their practiced ability to establish their characters and to maintain them throughout the shooting. Hitchcock was delighted with their performances, even commenting to his old friend—and frequent collaborator—Samuel Taylor that he had "forgotten what actors could do for me; they're not only prepared, they have ideas of their own—marvelous little bits of business."[16] McCowen and Merchant had worked on their scenes before appearing for the camera rehearsals; this was precisely the kind of professionalism that Hitchcock so appreciated. (He did not share this sort of admiration for Jon Finch, as we shall see.) Nevertheless, even with the most assiduous preparation, such scenes depend to a great extent on timing, and it turned out that quite a few takes were necessary before Hitchcock felt he had captured what he was seeking. In one part of the scene, Mrs. Oxford is presenting a fish soup to her husband and listing the ingredients for him: "smelts, ling, conger eel . . ." On the first take, one of the ingredients dropped on the table; in take #2, the candle had not been lit, and in take #3 the action and the dialogue were not properly paced. Take #4 was acceptable and was the only one printed. In all, ten setups were needed for the shooting of this scene; the crew was dismissed at 5:28 in the afternoon.

Tuesday was more of the same. Hitchcock seemed determined to record as much of the repartee between the inspector and his wife as possible. He set about filming these very important dialogue scenes that serve two purposes in the film: providing the light entertainment that Hitchcock liked to include as a counterpoint to the weightier matters of his scenarios, and, in this case, giving the audience the information it needed to follow the course of the inspector's investigation. Parts of scenes #147 through 151 (back at Inspector Oxford's flat) were shot on Tuesday, and parts of scenes #149 and 151 on Wednesday. He finished the day by returning to scene #89—the earlier conversation about the fish soup—and took six takes of close-ups so that he would have some choices in the editing. By the end of the day on August 11, then, Hitchcock had managed to film virtually the entire dinner sequence at the Oxford flat: in all, sixteen full pages of the script. A small pickup shot was scheduled weeks later (October 4) but this involved only a close-up of Inspector Oxford's hand as he ladled out some of the soup his wife had prepared.

What Hitchcock had accomplished—with the able assistance, of course, of actors who knew their lines and understood their roles—was nothing short of the addition to the fabric of the film one of its most popular sequences.

Virtually all of the reviews of the film—even the negative ones—were to mention the counterpoint achieved by the integrating of these witty dialogue scenes with the gruesome aspects of the plot.

This obviously successful aspect of the scenario, then, should be attributed to whom? Returning once again to the question of who contributed what to the final project, we begin with the fact that there were no such scenes in the original La Bern novel. We know that one of the aspects of Anthony Shaffer's work that appealed to Hitchcock was his ability to craft sharp and witty dialogue, as evidenced within his hit play, *Sleuth*. But whose idea was it to add these scenes in the first place? According to Peggy Robertson (Hitchcock's assistant since 1948), it was the director's idea. In her interview with Barbara Hall of the Margaret Herrick Library, Robertson states clearly that "Hitch added that. He got the idea of a woman who cooks exquisite dinners and feeds them to her hungry husband who only wants meat and potatoes, and then goes on from there."[17] Given Hitchcock's lifelong fascination with food and its preparation, this seems quite plausible. Indeed, Hitchcock spoke at length on the subject to Truffaut as they were winding down their marathon interview process: "I'd like to try to do an anthology on food, showing its arrival in the city, its distribution, the selling, buying by people, the cooking, the various ways in which it's consumed. What happens to it in various hotels; how it's fixed up and absorbed. And, gradually, the end of the film would show the sewers, and the garbage being dumped out into the ocean."[18] Shaffer, one must recall, was hired—as were so many of Hitchcock's collaborators—to write the dialogue, so we must assume that many if not most of the actual words exchanged by the inspector and his wife were written by Shaffer. What emerged after the shooting and the careful editing that was to come is an excellent example of the sort of seamless collaboration that characterizes the best of Hitchcock. These dialogue scenes are among the most memorable of Hitchcock's late work, and they stand as a tribute to his successful collaboration with this particular screenwriter.

In contrast to the wit and sparkle of the work captured by Hitchcock's crew on these previous few days, Thursday, August 12, was a fairly routine day at the studio. Nine setups were needed to film scenes #3, 4, and 5. This sequence introduces the audience to the protagonist, Richard Blaney, as he puts on his tie and prepares to go to work at the pub. The only significant note in the records regarding this day refers to the fact that the lunch break must have been longer than usual, because Mr. Hitchcock was scheduled to screen rushes at 1 P.M. Dismissal was at 5:10. The third week then ended on Hitchcock's seventy-second birthday, ironically a Friday the thirteenth. It was, though, a day like any other: eight setups covering parts of twelve scenes, ranging from several short background shots at the pub to a brief dialogue scene between Rusk and another pub customer. Hitchcock celebrated his birthday and that of his wife (she was born a day after he) the next evening at Carrier's in Cheshire. The crew was given the weekend off. There were ten weeks left to go.

The challenge for week four was the shooting of the interiors at the pub. Most of these scenes involved Blaney, played by Jon Finch, and this particular relationship between director and actor evolved in stark contrast to what Hitchcock had just experienced with his veterans, McCowen and Merchant. Jon Finch had not been Hitchcock's first choice for the role. He would have preferred Michael Caine, and he had even speculated at one time about the possibility of Richard Harris or even Richard Burton.[19] Finch somewhat resembled Caine, and Hitchcock had taken the time to look at some of his previous roles (most especially his "Macbeth" for Roman Polanski); he decided to take a chance with him. Finch came to the role with enthusiasm, even going so far as to offer suggested script revisions to Hitchcock. Apparently, these offerings were not welcomed by the director. According to Gil Taylor, the lighting cameraman for the project, Hitchcock was actually "very angry and he was thinking about recasting."[20] Instead, he simply made his irritation obvious: when Finch next suggested a minor change in dialogue, Hitchcock quite ceremoniously halted the shooting until Anthony Shaffer could be summoned to the set for a consultation. One biographer noted that "Hitchcock gave Finch no warmth or support on the set," causing the actor to seem off balanced or ill at ease.[21] This may very well have contributed to Finch's edgy, seemingly nervous performance.

Much has been made of this, in fact. Critics have called Blaney, among other things, "the least sympathetic, most irascible innocent man in any of Hitchcock's films."[22] We are introduced to him very early in the film— scene #3 in fact—and our first encounter with this particular protagonist does indeed startle us. He is not Cary Grant. He is not Jimmy Stewart. He is not Robert Donat. Nor even Farley Granger. He is not, in short, a typical clean-cut hero who has so often found himself to be either the wrong man within this Hitchcockian universe or at least the man who happens to be in the wrong place at this moment. He is instead a rather ordinary-looking bloke named Blaney. In this early scene (still within the final film's first five minutes), we are introduced not to the sophistication of a Grant or to the earnest Boy Scout attitudes of a Stewart, but to the hotheaded and mercurial bartender who looks and acts like the guilty party. Within the first six minutes of the film, Blaney has been fired from his job, and the way the scene is eventually orchestrated by Hitchcock suggests to us that the action on the part of the pub owner is probably justified. As Stefan Sharff suggests in his study of the film, "The viewer, always on the lookout for hints and signs, here picks up a veiled suspicion that perhaps Blaney is the killer."[23] And so we have from the very beginning of the film an unnerving intuitive misgiving about the main character, the protagonist around whom the entire plot will be built. As Thomas Leitch puts it in his ever-useful *Hitchcock Encyclopedia*, "Unlike all Hitchcock's other men on the run, Blaney is clearly capable of murder, of *this* murder in particular."[24]

It now seems entirely possible, of course, that Hitchcock knew precisely what he was doing and that he achieved exactly what he wanted from the Jon Finch character. After all, in his complaints to Truffaut about dealing with the Hollywood establishment, he noted that in addition to often not being able to enlist the best actors for his films, he had the parallel problem of once having landed a Cary Grant or a Jimmy Stewart, he could hardly be expected to cast them as villains. It is well known how *Suspicion should* have ended, for example, but the Hollywood studio system would never have stood for Cary Grant as the murderer.[25] For in cinema, it might be said that casting is character. The characters, especially if they are known actors whose previous performances have registered with the mass audience, are already developed, but it is up to the director to reveal those aspects of the players' personalities that best suit the needs of the scenario. In Jon Finch's Blaney, Hitchcock is able to develop a character around a whole parcel of negative qualities: Blaney is coarse, short tempered, irrational, unsophisticated, and not very photogenic to boot. But, he is also innocent. He really *is* the wrong man. Hitchcock's development of this character, then, becomes the ultimate extension of his lifelong examination of the philosophical premise that things are not always as they seem and that appearances can indeed distort reality. In *Frenzy*, we have an almost Voltaire-like statement: we may not find anything at all to like about this character Blaney, but we ought to defend to the death his right to be as innocent as is Cary Grant when he is called away from his martini by some thugs lurking just outside the Oak Bar at the Plaza Hotel. Blaney, to underscore, is "the wrong man." Blaney is, to again make the point, innocent.

Back on the set, the fourth week of the shooting schedule turned out to be not the most felicitous one. After spending most of Monday and Tuesday on the pub scenes, the perhaps more complicated prison hospital ward sequence was taken up on Wednesday, August 18, and continued through all of Thursday, August 19. Scene #152 alone—Blaney making his escape from the hospital—took an entire day and fourteen setups. The next day—Friday, August 20—was even more frustrating. Heavy rain caused the canceling of the scheduled shoot on the street outside the inspector's apartment, and only four setups were completed during the afternoon session back at the studio. The totals for the week, while not as impressive as some of the earlier ones, nevertheless continued to suggest a kind of relentless efficiency: twelve scenes, fifty-four takes, forty-one setups.

On Monday, August 23—the beginning of the fifth week of the production—it was back to the prison hospital ward to shoot retakes of some of what had been shot the previous week. The tensions between the director and his main actor now emerged even in comments on the camera reports: "Blaney slow" is written after the first two takes of one shot. No such explanation accompanies the report for Wednesday, August 25. Nevertheless, on this date, the entire day—from an 8:30 A.M. call to the dismissal at 6:50 that evening—was devoted to one scene—#163—the closing shots of the film. In all, fourteen setups were arranged that day, and the crew was to return to the same scene at a later date. It is not clear from the progress reports what was causing this particular scene to be taking so long to record. We are in this case left to imagine the director and his least favorite actor working out the blocking.

By this point in the process, Hitchcock was, of course, seeing all the rushes. He liked to claim that he never had to watch rushes—since he was so sure of what he had managed to get on any given day—but in fact, while he tended not to watch them each day, as do most directors, he would catch up with all of the material by the end of any given week. This in turn would lead to decisions about reshooting, and all of Thursday, August 26, was devoted to reshooting the opening scenes at the Tower Bridge that had displeased him on August 3. The call was at 8 A.M., dismissal at 6 P.M., and fifteen setups were necessary to compete the sequence. More retakes took up virtually all of the next day, Friday the twenty-seventh, including several more takes on scene #163, the closing scene of the film. This sequence was complicated by the fact that some extra shots were necessary as coverage for the television version of the film. Generally, films that are expected to be later released on television would go through redubbing in postproduction, so that, for example, "dirty rat" could be substituted for "bastard." (This was one of the changes that had to be made for the TV version of the film.) This sort of alteration typically required no additional shooting; however, many films, especially since the 1970s, have included material that continues to be deemed inappropriate for television. In this case, it was the image of the last murder victim found in Rusk's apartment. When Blaney pulls back the bedcovers, she is seen with her breasts exposed. A separate version had to be shot as coverage for the TV version, noted in the production report as "Take 1: Print; not showing breasts." Eight setups proved sufficient, and the crew was dismissed at 5:30 P.M. Monday, August 30, was the national bank holiday, so the following week would be a four-day workweek; Mr. and Mrs. Hitchcock spent the long weekend in Scotland. The production schedule was by this point nearly half-completed.

Tuesday and Wednesday were devoted to a number of "pickup shots," individual shots that were part of already completed scenes. Wednesday afternoon, however, also included an alternative ending for the film (as well as more shots of the model labeled "breasts covered; breasts uncovered"). The sequence not used in the final film was to have been a comedic touch that would have returned us to the dinner table at the Oxford apartment. Alec McCowen and Vivien Merchant were brought into the studio once again for a brief period. The production report of the scene that was shot gives a clear idea of how the film might have ended:

> Camera starts on Blaney and Oxford sitting at table toasting each other while sitting at table. . . . Blaney has a Margarita. . . . Oxford has whiskey. . . Track back as Mrs. Oxford comes from kitchen carrying silver covered dish . . . she puts it on the table . . . removes lid and we see it is duck with cherry sauce . . . as she starts to carve camera tracks in to CS of duck and camera runs on for over 100 feet (titles b.g.) as she carves puts pieces of duck on plates and hands out plates. . . .

It is a charming and even witty ending, but hardly as riveting as the one that Hitchcock did use to close the film.

After a few more pickup shots, Thursday and Friday were devoted to interiors at the matrimonial agency. The four scenes involved Blaney's visit to his ex-wife's office and their conversation; she remained calm and civilized throughout, while his bitterness erupted into some shouting that could be heard by the secretary sitting in the outer office. It is a crucial scene in that it planted in the secretary's mind the clear notion that Mr. Blaney was mercurial and could indeed be thought of as a violent man. Twelve setups were completed on Thursday, and another eight on Friday. The crew was dismissed at 5:30 P.M. Hitchcock, in addition to overseeing the shooting, scheduled four different times throughout the day for rushes to be screened, a sure sign that he was concerned about the progress of the shoot. This was extremely unusual for him; the result was that he scheduled additional retakes for the following Monday, September 6. On Tuesday, September 7, he began the undertaking of one of the most difficult sections of the film, the gruesome rape and murder of Mrs. Blaney. This was to become the most controversial scene of the film and perhaps the most notorious scene of his career, but the filming of it was in itself tortuous. Almost the entire rest of the week was devoted to this scene. It is examined in more detail in the following chapter.

When Hitchcock was satisfied that scene #30—the rape/murder—had been adequately choreographed, he turned on Friday afternoon, September 10, to scenes #41 through 43; these also took place at the matrimonial agency and involved Inspector Oxford's investigation of the crime. This involved ten setups. Hitchcock then decided to return to scene #82—the leading by Rusk of Babs up the stairs and into his flat—and he recorded nine more takes of this important moment. This scene, too—another of the signature passages in the completed *Frenzy*—is examined more completely in the following chapter. Here it must suffice to note that only two of the nine takes were printed. A very difficult day ended with crew dismissal at 6:25 P.M. A note in Hitchcock's office diary reminded him to order flowers for Princess Grace (of Monaco), who was to be visiting the set the following week.[26]

This particular week was not yet over, however, for shoots were scheduled for both Saturday and Sunday. Saturday was a full day, with eight setups in the area around the Coburg Hotel. Sunday was even more challenging: a 7:30 A.M. call, ten setups, with a dismissal at 5:30. Sunday's work included two important retakes: scene #34, the blank brick wall scene, and scene #83, the continuation of the track back out of Rusk's apartment after he enters with Babs; this part of the shot brings us to the exterior in front of the flat. Hitchcock had obviously been unhappy with some aspect of these scenes and had ordered the retakes. It was the second series of retakes for scene #34, another one of the signature moments discussed in the following chapter.

Monday, September 13, began with a few shots of the scene between Blaney and Babs that takes place after their morning escape from the Coburg Hotel and ended with a return by the crew to scene #30, the rape/murder sequence. Once again, Hitchcock no doubt had discovered something in his viewing of the rushes that called for remedial action. Tuesday was a fairly uneventful day, with a few shots of the dinner scenes between Blaney and his ex-wife at her club. The crew was dismissed relatively early—at 5:20 P.M.—in part, no doubt, because Hitchcock was having dinner with Princess Grace and her husband that evening.

The production undertook a different sort of challenge on Wednesday, September 15. For the first time, the crew was called to night shooting. The first setup occurred at 7:55 that evening, and the crew was dismissed at 1:30 the next morning. The scenes scheduled were a continuation of the dinner scene between Blaney and his ex-wife and a couple of shots outside the prison hospital. There were only four completed setups, and more nighttime shooting was scheduled for the next evening. On Thursday, the dinner scene was completed at a real dinner club in Piccadilly (rendering a kind of authenticity to the scene that a studio locale—no matter how professionally decorated—could not approach). It was another long night: first setup at 8:10 P.M., dismissal at 1:40 A.M. The night ended with three brief exterior shots of Blaney making his escape from the prison hospital. The week ended with yet another nighttime shoot on Friday, September 17: first setup at 8:50 P.M. and dismissal not until 3:45 the following morning. (Fortunately for the crew—and the now seventy-two-year-old director— no Saturday shooting was scheduled.) Interestingly, what kept the crew working so late turned out to be a scene that did not make it into the final cut of the film. The script included the following scene, #52:

EXT. HENRIETTA STREET OUTSIDE RUSKS APARTMENT— NIGHT
    The front door of the building opens and a girl, fully dressed except for her blouse which she carries, rushes out and turns down the street. A young constable watches her go, speculatively. He turns as Rusk appears through the door. He is in short sleeves and his collar open with his tie loose round his neck.
                              RUSK
    I can't understand it. I'd just undone my tie, when she bolted.

The policeman and Rusk exchange a few more lines, and the scene ends with a laugh at the expense of the fleeing girl. It is the kind of scene that would have appealed to Hitchcock's sense of dark humor, and it would have also served the purpose of demonstrating to the audience that Rusk was a serial assailant who could get away with his crimes before the very eyes of the police. For whatever reason, it does not appear in any of the extant prints of *Frenzy*.

    On Monday of the following week, the crew returned to a daytime schedule. The rigors of the previous week had, however, taken a toll. A medical note attached to the call sheet for Monday, September 20, indicated that "Mr. Hitchcock . . . was suffering from a sore throat." He was treated by a doctor and given a prescription. The shooting went on as scheduled, with the first setup at 11:03 that morning. The work this day consisted of two scenes at Scotland Yard, one scene of Blaney being interrogated at the police station, and a very important shot of Inspector Oxford as he ruminates over the case after the jury has found Blaney guilty and the judge has sentenced him. Oxford sits alone in the empty courtroom at the Old Bailey. Blaney's plea that "it was Rusk" who committed the crime rings in Oxford's ear. Hitchcock printed three separate takes of the shot, one with Oxford seated throughout the scene, and two others where he stands up at the end. He used the seated one in the final film.

Hitchcock was not well the next day and was given penicillin. Most of the material was therefore shot by the second unit. It was an "extended day," which meant that the crew would be on overtime after 6 P.M. The call was at 8:30 in the morning, and the dismissal was not until 7:45 that evening. Under the supervision of assistant director Colin Brewer, eight setups were completed that included a number of straightforward exterior shots, including the Salvation Army hospital where Blaney spends a night and the Coburg Hotel as viewed from the street. Brewer and the crew completed seven more setups the next day, this time taking the necessary exteriors around the Hilton Hotel where Blaney meets up with his old pal from his flying days in World War II. The interiors at the Hilton were shot the next day, with Hitchcock again in charge. These interiors continued to occupy the crew on Friday, September 24. A somewhat revealing—given what had transpired between Jon Finch and his director—note on the call sheet for that day suggests that this ninth week on the production had not been the smoothest one: "Mr. Finch late and shooting held up from 9:45 to 10:50." Anthony Shaffer mentions in his own memoir that Hitchcock made Finch apologize to the entire cast for being persistently late.[27] Whatever the reason, the efficient Hitchcock machine was slowing a bit.

Hitchcock was still not feeling quite chipper by Monday, September 27. The call sheet indicates that he complained of a sore throat and was attended by a doctor but continued working. Only seven setups were completed, several at the Coburg Hotel and then one take at the prison. Tuesday's work involved the scene where Blaney is remanded to his cell after the trial—completed in four takes—and then a return in the afternoon—yet again—to the Tower Bridge. This was the crew's third visit to this area, and they spent the entire afternoon there. The scene ends with the minister's wonderfully ironic line: "I say. That's not my club tie, is it?" The crew was dismissed at 5:20 P.M. with Hitchcock now apparently satisfied that he had finally gotten what he was trying to achieve in the scene that would, after all, set the tone for the entire film.

Wednesday, September 29, turned out to be one of the most productive days of the entire shooting period. Beginning at 8:30 in the morning and finishing relatively early at 5:20 P.M., Hitchcock and his crew completed twenty-one setups, including two scenes that required two cameras each—one to capture Blaney's double tumbling down the stairs at the prison hospital ward, the other to cover the body floating in the river at the beginning of the film. In addition, Hitchcock filmed two more takes of part of scene #90, the important one that involves Rusk leaving his apartment with the body of Babs stuffed into a potato sack.

The production was beginning to wind down, but what was to become perhaps the most celebrated sequence of the film—the potato truck journey—had not yet been shot. It would occupy most of the remaining three weeks, and it was begun the day after this very productive Wednesday. With the exception of some pickup shots on October 4 and an important retake on October 12, the next seven shooting days would be devoted to this sequence. It, too, is examined in some detail in the following chapter.

What remained for Hitchcock after this arduous period was over were various inserts and second-unit shots that would extend the production period until Tuesday, October 26, when he departed for Los Angeles at 1 P.M. For all practical purposes, the last day of principal photography had been Thursday, October 14. A few pickup shots were then taken by the crew on the fifteenth. Poignantly, a handwritten note appears at the bottom of the call sheet for that day: "This is the last. Whoopee!! (I hope!)" It almost was.

When asked by Truffaut—who visited with Hitchcock when the director brought the completed *Frenzy* to the Cannes Film Festival in 1972—what it was like to shoot a film in London as opposed to Hollywood, Hitchcock replied that "when I enter the studios—be it in Hollywood or London—and the heavy doors close behind me, there is no difference. A coal mine is always a coal mine."[28] Hitchcock was extremely well treated by his cast and his crew in London during the shooting of *Frenzy*, but a detailed examination of the day-to-day routine that defined a thirteen-week production period can certainly suggest what Hitchcock was referring to with this metaphor. Arriving on set in a chauffeur-driven Rolls Royce cannot really be compared to descending into a coal mine, of course, but the accumulation of routine might be somewhat similar. In any case, the seventy-two-year-old Hitchcock was exhausted by the end of the shooting of *Frenzy*; he had, though, produced some of his signature moments of pure cinema.

Notes

1. "Hitch," *Take One* 1, no. 1 (September/October 1966): 14–17.

2. Quoted in Albert LaValley, ed., *Focus on Hitchcock* (Englewood Cliffs, N.J.: Prentice-Hall, 1972), 25.

3. Recounted in François Truffaut, *Hitchcock*, rev. ed. (New York: Simon & Schuster/Touchstone, 1985), 330–31.

4. LaValley, *Focus on Hitchcock*, 24.

5. A word about "printing" as it applies to filmmaking. In order to save money, all productions shot on film (as opposed to video) keep a log of all shots taken. Not every "take" is "printed," that is, sent to the lab to be developed and copied for editing. The director, usually in consultation with the cinematographer (or lighting cameraman, in this case) decides which takes to print.

6. Bill Krohn, *Hitchcock at Work* (London: Phaidon, 2000).

7. Krohn, *Hitchcock at Work*, 206–7.

8. See *Frenzy* Folder #312 of the Alfred Hitchcock papers at the Margaret Herrick Library, Beverly Hills, California.

9. See the "call sheets," *Frenzy* Folders #270 and 271 of the Alfred Hitchcock papers at the Margaret Herrick Library, Beverly Hills, California. All further references to the call sheets in this chapter will be to these folders.

10. Patrick McGilligan, *Alfred Hitchcock: A Life in Darkness and Light* (New York: HarperCollins, 2003), 705, for example.

11. See the "daily progress reports," *Frenzy* Folder #283 of the Alfred Hitchcock papers at the Margaret Herrick Library, Beverly Hills, California. All further references to the progress reports in this chapter will be to this folder.

12. *An Oral History with Peggy Robertson.* Interviewed by Barbara Hall. (Academy of Motion Picture Arts and Sciences, Oral History Program, 2002), 127, 331.

13. See the "continuity sheets," *Frenzy* Folders #277, 278, and 279 of the Alfred Hitchcock papers at the Margaret Herrick Library, Beverly Hills, California. All further references to the continuity sheets in this chapter will be to these folders.

14. *Frenzy* Script, June 3, 1971, with changes through July 9, 1971, *Frenzy* Folder #260 of the Alfred Hitchcock papers, Margaret Herrick Library, Beverly Hills, California. All further references to the script in this chapter will be to the one in this folder.

15. A word about "rushes." The use of the word comes from the early days of cinema when material that had just been shot would be "rushed" to the lab for processing. This material would then be screened by the director and camera crew so that any mistakes might be immediately corrected. Rushes are also sometimes called "dailies," as in the material completed that day. After viewing the rushes, or dailies, the director would decide whether any "retakes" would be necessary.

16. Quoted in Donald Spoto, *The Dark Side of Genius: The Life of Alfred Hitchcock* (Boston: Little, Brown, 1983), 511.

17. *An Oral History with Peggy Robertson*, 328.

18. Truffaut, *Hitchcock*, 320.

19. See *Frenzy* Folder #275 of the Alfred Hitchcock papers.

20. McGilligan, *Alfred Hitchcock*, 704.

21. McGilligan, *Alfred Hitchcock*, 704

22. Spoto, *The Dark Side of Genius*, 511.

23. Stefan Sharff, *Alfred Hitchcock's High Vernacular* (New York: Columbia University Press, 1991), 170.

24. Thomas Leitch, *The Encyclopedia of Alfred Hitchcock* (New York: Checkmark, 2002), 114.

25. Truffaut, *Hitchcock*, 142.

26. See *Frenzy* Folder #284 of the Alfred Hitchcock papers.

27. Anthony Shaffer, *So What Did You Expect?* (London: Picador, 2001), 71.

28. Truffaut, *Hitchcock*, 338.

Shooting the Signature Sequences, Part I **8**
Hitchcock as a Master of Montage

ITCHCOCK BIOGRAPHER DONALD SPOTO is hardly a fan of the completed *Frenzy*. While he claims to have appreciated its structure, its acting, and its editing, at the same time he calls it "utterly devoid of any positive human feeling."[1] Nevertheless, Spoto admires three of the sequences in the film: "the rape-murder, with Foster as the killer and Barbara Leigh-Hunt as the victim; the camera's pullback from the villain's apartment door as he enters with his next victim, Anna Massey; and the character's search later, aboard a vegetable truck, for an incriminating tiepin in a sack of potatoes containing her corpse."[2] Spoto identifies scene #30 (the rape/murder), scenes #82 and 83 (the retreat from the apartment), and scenes #98 through 120 (the potato truck). I would add to his admired sequences scene #34, the one I have labeled the "blank brick wall" scene. Each of these could be called a "signature" moment in the work, a piece of constructed cinema that is emblematic of a master craftsman. They each deserve further attention in this study, for they each clearly demonstrate that Hitchcock, while perhaps no longer at the height of his powers in 1971, was still in possession of most of them.

One of the aspects of these creative powers was Hitchcock's mastery of the art of montage. He had learned it, of course, in his early days as a director within the parameters of the silent cinema. He had apprehended not only the practice of directing; he had also steeped himself in the early theory of cinema. Even years later, he was able to relate the details of the famous "Kuleshov experiment," conducted in Russia in the 1920s, to François Truffaut during one of their interviews: "You see a close-up of the Russian actor, Ivan Mosjoukine. This is immediately followed by a shot of a dead baby. Back to Mosjoukine again and you read compassion on his face. Then you take away the dead baby and you show a plate of soup, and now, when you go back to Mosjoukine, he looks hungry. Yet in both cases, they used the same shot of the actor; his face was exactly the same."[3] Hitchcock's recall was not total; the original experiment included a third shot—a lovely young woman would make the actor seem to be leering when audiences would see the cut back to his face—but he fully understood its importance and incorporated it into much of his work.[4] Two obvious examples of his mastery of these principles can be seen in even a cursory analysis of either *Rear Window* or *Psycho*.

Indeed, *Rear Window* can be understood as a kind of dissertation by Hitchcock on the Kuleshov experiment. The entire film rests upon the triangulation of what we see, what James Stewart sees, and what Hitchcock allows us to see. In most cases, we in fact see only what Stewart sees. But during at least one crucial moment, we are privy to an event that he does not see (he is sleeping at that moment). Stewart's somewhat phlegmatic expression provides the ideal image for Hitchcock to play against; whether he is gazing at a young woman exercising or at a couple sleeping on their fire escape to avoid the blazing heat of a New York City summer, the actor's expression seems to remain the same (just as in the Kuleshov experiment). The reaction that mattered most to Hitchcock was not that of his actor; he was far more concerned with how these images might provoke a reaction by his audience. The intercutting between Stewart and what he sees allows Hitchcock to build the tempo of his montage toward a conclusion that cleverly includes the temporary blinding by flashbulbs of his protagonist while the screen we see is also temporarily obscured by this effect. The editing strategy in *Rear Window*—relying as it does on the classical principles of montage—represents perhaps Hitchcock's cleanest example of "pure cinema," and the film itself continues to be included among virtually any list of his greatest works.

Much has been written, of course, about *Psycho*, in some ways Hitchcock's most influential film if only because of so many works that have imitated it. While there are many sequences in the film that can stand as testament to Hitchcock's mastery of mise-en-scene—a subject examined in the following chapter—it is the masterly montage of the shower scene that has received the most critical and popular attention over the years. *Psycho* was made fifty years ago, and yet it remains fresh. The shower scene itself has been the object of attention from filmmakers—and indeed from film students at our universities—ever since. There have been many books on Hitchcock's work, of course, but no other filmmaker can claim to have elicited studies of one specific scene in but one particular film. Hitchcock's shower scene is the sole subject of a recent monograph, and it will probably not be the last. In *The Shower Scene in Hitchcock's* Psycho, Philip Skerry calls the shower scene "the culmination of Hitchcock's pure cinema."[5] His book includes a production history, interviews with key figures—like screenwriter Joseph Stefano and actress Janet Leigh—and a detailed analysis of the scene itself. For Skerry, the shower scene marks the epitome of Hitchcock's mastery of the art of montage. Its power is clearly in its editing, and its editing is singularly brilliant.

Understanding the theory of montage and having then had considerable practice at it, Hitchcock nevertheless faced a new intellectual challenge with each of his projects. On the set with any one of them, Hitchcock had to capture on film the elements that would become the building blocks for his use of montage in that particular context. With *Frenzy* it was no different. No doubt having anticipated how arduous might be the task of translating script scene #30 (the rape/murder) to a piece of 35-millimeter celluloid, Hitchcock did not undertake the shooting of the piece until the seventh week of production. Then he devoted three and a half full days in a row to working out the details of the structure. Commencing on Tuesday, September 7, with a crew call at 8:30, the first setup was ready at 10:15, with dismissal that afternoon at 5:20 P.M. The crew completed nine setups that day, and covered a significant part of the opening of the scene, when Rusk appears in Brenda Blaney's inner office at the matrimonial agency. There is a good deal of dialogue between Rusk and Brenda as she slowly becomes aware that she is trapped in a locked office with a violent man. What is obvious from carefully examining the continuity sheets is that these two actors, very much like Alec McCowen and Vivien Merchant, seem to have come prepared, seem to have known their lines, and seem to have performed very much professionally.[6] The first shot took only four takes, the last one printed. The next one—a closer angle on Rusk as he comes through the door—was captured in but two takes, the second one printed. The same was true of the next shot, and the one after that took only three takes, again with the last one printed. The fifth shot in the sequence—a close-up of Brenda as she makes some excuse to use the phone—was accomplished in but one take. Shot #6 (a medium shot of Brenda's desk) took four takes, the last printed, and #7—a much longer dialogue section that concludes with Rusk telling Brenda that there is no need to call the police—involved six takes, with only the last one printed. The last two shots marked the beginning of Rusk's animalistic attack and the end of the shooting day. Each took two takes, each with only the second one printed. All in all, this first day of shooting on this complicated scene had gone well. The actors proved their professional value, and Hitchcock got the shots he would need to later orchestrate the sequence in the editing room.

The next day, Wednesday, September 8, was more difficult. The call was again at 8:30 A.M., dismissal at 5:40, but in that relatively short day, the crew managed eighteen setups and covered a long section of the vicious attack. The progress report noted that a "moviola" machine was brought to the set on this day.[7] The reason for this—on this or any other production—would be so that the director and the cameraman would be able to refer often to the material from the previous day to make sure that individual shots would match in terms of lighting and camera angles.[8] The call sheet notes that the machine had to be rented; this is a rare occurrence on a Hitchcock production, and it is a clear indication of how careful the director was trying to be with this scene. Remarkably, most of the seventeen shots that were completed on this quite productive day involved only one or two takes each. The last one of the day took seven; it takes place near the climax of the scene, and its gist is perhaps best illustrated by reproducing the continuity sheet for that particular shot:

sc 30
    CS Brenda's head against back of chair . . . shoulders bare . . .
    Rusk: O.S. Lovely, . . . lovely . . . lovely . . . She turns her head . . .
Please don't deny me.
    Brenda: Deny you? His hands go round her throat . . . then he draws
back . . .
    Rusk: O.S. You bitch . . .
    Seven takes, 6 and 7 printed

"O.S." is an abbreviation for "offscreen." What we have here is Brenda's horrified face as her assailant puts his hands around her throat. The last two takes were printed, and this particularly cloying day was over.[9]

A moment of Hitchcockian irony should be included in a report of the day's shooting: Mrs. Hitchcock, feeling much better, was on set this day as an observer. The office diary for the day has this entry: "Mrs. Hitchcock lunches with Mrs. Bernstein [old friend from the pre-Hollywood days]."[10] As Hitchcock was so fond of saying—and as his wife and life partner was by her actions this day acknowledging—"it's only a movie."[11] For the Hitchcocks, the chilling rape and murder scene was all part of a day at the office (or down in the coal mine).

Thursday, September 9, was another full day devoted to scene #30. It began with a call at 8:30, concluded with crew dismissal at 5:45, and encompassed fourteen setups. Again, given the nature of the scene, it is somewhat remarkable how efficiently Hitchcock's crew captured the events laid out in the script. Of the fourteen shots successfully completed, nine were deemed acceptable by Hitchcock after no more than two takes each, and four of these required but one take. Barry Foster, who played Rusk, turned out to be another of those London-trained actors who did not need much on-set direction from Hitchcock. He played his part with the sort of professional relish that so often endeared his director to what he might have called the "properly trained actor." An example of this can be seen by examining the continuity sheet for that day and looking at one of the scenes that required only one take:

sc 30
    CS Rusk kneeling facing right . . . his hands out of shot strangling Brenda O.S. . . . he strains to tighten tie . . . heavy breathing . . . then becomes quieter . . .

"CS" here refers to "close shot" and "O.S." to "offscreen." The script note referring to "heavy breathing . . . then becomes quieter" would allow for any number of interpretations by an actor, particularly any of those trained in the "Method" approach. Foster simply performed the task as written, Hitchcock approved, and one take was sufficient. Most of this difficult scene had now been completed. The progress report noted that the moviola was returned at the completion of the day's shooting.

There was one more setup devoted to this scene on the following day, Friday, September 10. The crew was ready for the shot by 9:20 that morning, and the part of the scene that includes Brenda's attempt to stall matters by claiming that she would be happy to lunch with Rusk if only he would let her wash her hands marked the last piece of the puzzle to be shot. The rest of the morning was spent on the relatively easier sections that took place in the outer office when Inspector Oxford came to investigate the crime.

While the bulk of this difficult and complex sequence was now "in the can" (i.e., on 35-millimeter film), Hitchcock and his crew would return to the studio set on the following Monday—September 13—to conclude the work. Most of this day was devoted to close-ups, details of the shots taken during the previous week. There was, for example, a shot of Brenda's face as she struggled with the tie that Rusk was tightening around her neck. Another shot was of Rusk's hands (in this case, a double was used) as the tie was being tightened. In all, five shots were taken, all but one in a single take or two. The one shot that required three takes was the one that marked the dramatic and poignant end of the sequence, a close-up of Brenda as she stops struggling, her breathing then dramatically slowing. The scene that would become the single most controversial one of the film was now very close to completion. Just a few pickup shots remained. Two of these were achieved on Monday, October 4: a close-up of Rusk's tiepin going into the lapel of his jacket, another of the half-eaten apple on Brenda's desk. (Rusk grabs it as he leaves the office.) One more shot was picked up on Thursday, October 21, this one being three takes—all printed in this case—of Rusk leaning against the desk after the murder, picking his teeth with his tiepin, then turning to leave. The production was truly winding down by this point, with the "last day of principal photography" having been declared on the previous Thursday (October 14) and Hitchcock himself preparing to leave London, which he did on Tuesday, October 26. In total, then, parts of at least seven shooting days—often the full day—were devoted to scene #30. It would become a signature sequence when Hitchcock had completed the arrangement of all of the pieces. This he would accomplish through his mastery of montage, that element of the language of cinema that creates meaning from the artistic assembly of moments of time and space.

The second great example in *Frenzy* of Hitchcock's ability to orchestrate a scene through his application of the classic principles of montage occurs during the celebrated "potato truck" sequence. Comprised of scenes #98 through 120 in the script, it was the last full section of the film to be tackled during the long production period. It involved a total of twelve days shooting (in whole or in part), and it turned out to be the most grueling part of the production schedule, since many of the scenes had to be shot at night on the open roads around London. That meant, of course, that the production activities would once again be held hostage to the fickle weather over Southern England (in, by then, early autumn), so the crew had to have alternative studio work ready to be scheduled as needed.

The potato truck sequence is an example of pure montage; its power comes from the intercutting of dozens of individual pieces of film into a rhythmic and meaningful whole. Gathering those discrete pieces was the task that occupied Hitchcock and the crew over those twelve days, and many of them were the grueling "extended days," that is, ones during which the crew went into overtime in order to complete the scheduled work.

The first attempt at scene #98 took place at the end of the seventh week of shooting, on Friday, September 17. It was scheduled as a night shoot, and so the call was for 7 P.M.; the first setup was ready at 8:50 in the evening, and the crew was not dismissed until 3:45 the following morning. During most of that arduous night, several sequences related to scene #52 were undertaken first; ironically, this scene—a girl leaving Rusk's apartment in her underwear—did not make it into the final cut of the film. Two takes of scene #98, though, were also shot that night. The scene shows Rusk hurriedly leaving his flat and looking around "frantically" (according to the script) "to see whether or not the truck has left."[12] He has just realized that his tiepin—which would become an incriminating bit of evidence—must be still in the hands of the murdered Babs. Since the scene of the girl leaving the flat—the one eventually cut from the film—was shot as an exterior, Hitchcock had his crew make two attempts to capture this short shot of Rusk during the same shooting session. The office diary for the date simply listed "Night shooting . . . Rusk's apartment."[13]

A full week and a half would pass before Hitchcock returned to the potato truck sequence. In the intervening days, he shot various interiors, including the police station, the inspector's office at Scotland Yard, the courtroom, the Salvation Army hostel, the Coburg Hotel, the Hilton, and the prison hospital. On Wednesday, September 29, he returned to scene #98. The crew recorded but one take of the scene at the very end of the shooting day, shortly before dismissal at 5:20 P.M. (The office diary noted that Mrs. Hitchcock was to see her physician at 1 P.M. and to see the rough assembly of what had been shot so far that evening. Hitchcock's partner, then, had returned to her invaluable role as chief commentator on the work in progress.)

The real work on the truck sequence began on Thursday, September 30. The call was for 8:30 A.M., the first setup was ready at 9:45, and the crew managed—in a remarkable display of efficiency, this late in the production schedule—to complete twenty setups by dismissal time at 5:20. A summary of the continuity sheet for that day clearly illustrates this efficiency: all but four of the shots were completed in one take; three of them took two takes, and one took three takes. Most of the day was devoted to scene #99 (two takes of scene #98 were dispatched with at the beginning of the shoot), a scene that takes place inside the truck as Rusk struggles with the body that he had stuffed into a potato sack. While Rusk had hoped to accomplish his grim task before the truck would leave Covent Garden, he fails to do so, and the scene also includes his reaction to the initial movement of the truck out of the parking area and onto the local road. It is a complicated scene, with many close-ups, each one requiring a new camera setup. By the end of the day, the scene was not quite complete, and the crew returned to it on Friday, October 1. Nine setups were devoted to scene #99 on that day, marking the end of the tenth week of shooting, but by midafternoon, Hitchcock felt satisfied that scene #99 was complete, and he went on to other shots in the long sequence. As it turned out, the scene had not been quite fully captured; Hitchcock sent his crew back to the studio on October 13 to record two more takes. Only then was the difficult and essential scene #99 ready for postproduction.

Capturing the rest of the potato truck sequence involved some of the most grueling days of the entire production period. Friday, October 1, was very much like the previous day: an efficient crew systematically captured each of the required shots as called for by the director. The first setup was ready early—at 9:38 in the morning—and the dismissal was at 5:20 that afternoon. Twelve setups were undertaken, and once again, most of them required but one take. Eight setups were devoted to scene #99, completing the action from the previous day. Next on the schedule was scene #101, another complicated piece of business for both the crew and the actor, as can be ascertained by examining the description on the continuity sheet: "Camera shooting down onto Rusk with his head inside Babs's sack . . . the truck stops; Rusk comes out of sack . . . as it starts again he is thrown backwards towards rear of truck. . . ." This took five takes, with only the last one printed. The day ended with one take each of scenes #103, 104, and 105, each one a continuation of the struggle between Rusk and the dead body in the potato sack. The crew was given the weekend off. They had completed ten weeks of shooting, with only three more on the schedule.

The eleventh week began ominously. The progress report for October 4 concluded with this note:

> Mr. Hitchcock unable to work today as he is suffering from Gout. Dr. Southward was called on Sunday 3.10.71 [Oct. 3] to Claridge's to attend Mr. Hitchcock. Mr. Hill was notified at this time. The shooting that was scheduled for today (4.10.71) [Oct 4] was abandoned and all outstanding inserts were shot under the direction of Colin Brewer (1st Asst). The Insurance company were notified at 9.30 A.M. on Monday 4.10.71 by Ron Allday.

William Hill was the associate producer on the project, and Ron Allday the company accountant. The burden of continuing to make progress fell on assistant director Colin Brewer, who had proved to be an invaluable aide to Hitchcock throughout the shooting period, often having taken over for the director—overseeing the shooting of some of the "standard" material—when Hitchcock appeared fatigued. Brewer now took charge of the crew once again and spent the entire day shooting "outstanding inserts," that is, those individual pieces of celluloid, usually close-ups, that are short but essential "inserts" into a larger scene. For example, in scene #89, the long dinner scene between Inspector Oxford and his wife, there is a close-up of his hand spooning out a piece of fish from the soup. That shot was on the list for this day; it required four takes, and Brewer had three of them printed. (This immediately suggests the difference between the master and his apprentice: Hitchcock almost never printed more than one take of any particular shot. He was usually quite certain as to which one would be best suited for the final film.)

Brewer and the crew completed thirteen setups on October 4, the majority of them in one take. Dismissal was early: 4:40 in the afternoon. The crew was able to catch up on sleep the next day, Tuesday, October 5, since the schedule called for night shooting, with the call at 6:30 in the evening and the first setup at 9:05. The medical report stated that "Dr. Southward agreed that it would be alright for Mr. Hitchcock to come to the studios and he arrived at 7 P.M. to have discussions with the key technicians regarding the night shooting."[14] Perhaps most surprisingly, the report also noted that "Mr. Hitchcock stayed on location during the night." For a man who had only recently turned seventy-two, it must have been a difficult night. The dismissal was not until 5:55 in the morning, making for Hitchcock essentially a twelve-hour "day" before he could return to his hotel to rest for yet another night shoot on the following day, Wednesday, October 6. Coincidentally, it was an empty hotel suite to which Hitchcock returned at six in the morning; Mrs. Hitchcock had left London for Los Angeles the previous afternoon. Accompanied by office secretary Sue Gauthier, she headed home for more rest and recuperation.

The scenes to be shot on Tuesday night involved the truck as it makes its way along the "dual carriageway" outside London and is discovered by a pair of policemen as it roars past their cruiser. The body is hanging out of the truck, thereby arousing the curiosity of the police patrol. Many elements of the scene had to be carefully choreographed, not the least of which was the relationship of the truck to the trailing police car. An example of the complexity can be ascertained by examining the continuity sheet's description of one of the scenes to be shot (scene #118) on that night: "Camera shooting from back of camera car onto two policemen in police car driving along road . . . blue light flashing . . . head lights on . . . sound of siren to be put in . . . they are chasing after potato truck . . ." Only nine setups were undertaken, another testament to the arduous nature of the task. Most, though, were completed in one take; the crew by now was operating at its peak level of efficiency, and Hitchcock had of course had a great deal of experience shooting "chase" scenes of this type. (Note how many there are in, say, *North by Northwest*.)

The next evening's schedule began with a call at 6:30 P.M. and ended with a dismissal at 5:10 the following morning. According to the progress report, "Thick fog prevented shooting from 4 A.M. The unit continued lining up but abandoned shooting at 5:10 A.M. when the fog persisted." Nevertheless, they managed to complete five setups, all of them being additional shots related to the truck and the police car. Hitchcock himself was off the set by 2 A.M.; according to the progress report, he "left feeling unwell." The unit continued once again under Colin Brewer. Perhaps as a kind of ironic indication of the sort of thing that can occur when the master is not present, the continuity sheet notes that the last setup involved three takes because in take #1, the car's license plate fell off, and in take #2, the camera's optical wedge was not in place. (Nevertheless, all three takes were printed.)

According to the medical note for Thursday, October 7, "Mr. Hitchcock feeling much better today and after seeing rushes at Pinewood Studios went to the location and stayed until 3 A.M." The call that evening was for 6:30 P.M., and the first setup was ready at 9:05 P.M. Hitchcock had viewed rushes from the previous day's shoot from 5:30 to 6:30 in the evening at theater #3 at Pinewood. The crew dismissal was at 3:30 the following morning, so it is clear that Hitchcock was there for virtually all of the shooting that evening.

Nine setups were completed, all of them involving the scene that takes place at the roadside café. The call sheet identifies the location as "Wally's New Café on the A.41 Watford Bypass, just south of the M.1 Motorway intersection."[15] The scene involves Rusk leaving the back of the truck after he has successfully retrieved his tiepin. All of the shots were completed in one take apiece, the crew once again having performed at peak efficiency. Hitchcock, himself exhausted, was pleased with the week's progress and gave the crew a rest day on Friday, October 8. Hitchcock clearly needed the rest as well. The medical note for the following Monday (October 11) stated that "Mr. Hitchcock was not well over the weekend and Dr. Southward attended." After some consultation with another physician (a Dr. Mason), "Mr. Hitchcock was allowed to continue working."

After the ordeal of the previous week's night shooting, the schedule for Monday, October 11, was relatively straightforward. The call was for 8:30 in the morning, the first setup was ready at 10:20, and the dismissal was at 5:30 P.M. Thirteen setups were completed, virtually all of them in one or two takes. One shot required four takes. Since this particular day was devoted almost entirely to scene #105, the continued efficiency of the crew was remarkable. Scene #105 became one of the most commented-upon scenes of the film; it is the one where the gruesome powers of rigor mortis play a role. The script description is direct; Rusk is in the back of the truck dealing with the body in the potato sack:

> He now methodically starts to open the fingers. Due to the rigor mortis, each finger has to be broken, and although the truck roar is loud, we are CLOSE enough on the hand to hear the bones breaking one by one.

It is an excruciating moment in the film, the sort that makes audiences cringe, the kind that had made Hitchcock's reputation. The crew seems to have dispatched with it easily, so much so that they had to return at a later date (October 12 and 13) for but two small inserts in order to complete the entire scene.

The shooting of the potato truck sequence was by then almost finished. By the end of the extended day scheduled for Wednesday, October 13, all that would remain would be several small inserts and one retake. Wednesday, though, was a long day: call at 8:30 A.M., first take at 10 A.M., dismissal not until 9:40 that evening. Exteriors had been scheduled, but high winds and rain forced the crew back to the studio, and several scenes were shot there. A total of seventeen setups were completed, including such individual shots as "front angle onto driver in cab of potato truck driving along country road . . . chews gum . . . leaves drift thru shot."[16] This shot, too, was done in the studio on a set that was large enough to accommodate a mock-up model of the truck itself. The daily progress report noted that "Mr. Hitchcock worked throughout the day and evening."

Thursday, October 14, was listed on the progress report as the last day of principal photography. It was also another extended day, with the morning call at 9 A.M., the first take at 11:10, and the dismissal at midnight. Hitchcock had assigned assistant director Brewer the task of reshooting the scene where the body falls off the truck, but according to the progress report, there was "considerable difficulty in pushing dummy body off truck," so much so that the shot took from 9:10 P.M. until 11:55 P.M. to complete. This put the crew behind schedule, so in fact October 14 did not turn out to be the last day after all. A few more days were scheduled to accomplish all of the retakes, including one more shot for the truck sequence on Thursday, October 21: "a low angle of potato truck passing right to left along dual carriage way," according to the continuity sheets. Finally, the long and complex sequence had been fully captured and was ready, as now indeed were the others, for Hitchcock's editing strategy.

Before examining in some detail the signature scenes that are best delineated as examples of mise-en-scene rather than montage, a few summary observations about Hitchcock's level of participation in the production process are in order. The reason is that there have been various suggestions in the Hitchcock biographical literature that paint the picture of a less than fully diligent Hitchcock on the set of *Frenzy*. The often critical Donald Spoto claims that during the production, "Hitchcock was eating and drinking more than ever—and to such excess that, as the cast unanimously remembered, he quite frequently slept through the afternoon's filming."[17] My own investigation has identified only a single member of the cast who seems to have contributed to this "unanimous" memory that Spoto describes in his text. Barry Foster is quoted by Spoto as claiming that Hitchcock appeared somewhat dispirited during the period of Alma's illness (her minor stroke in June) and that on the set "he became tired and lazy."[18] Patrick McGilligan acknowledges that Hitchcock on occasion would retreat to his private caravan just off the studio floor and leave the last take of the day in the hands of the assistant director, but this rare practice hardly suggests any real abdication of directorial responsibility.[19] Indeed, as one must surely acknowledge, there were several extremely complicated sequences in the shooting of *Frenzy*, and an examination of the progress reports from any of them—several indeed have been cited in this chapter—clearly illustrates to what extent the master was still in charge. It is, of course, far from uncommon for a celebrated director to assign certain scenes—"coverage" in the jargon of the profession—to his assistant. To mention but one example, Herbert Coleman, one of Hitchcock's most trusted assistant directors over the years, wrote in his memoirs about his success in getting the scenic shots that Hitchcock wanted for *To Catch a Thief*. (Perhaps more tellingly, Hitchcock reported to Coleman that "Alma seems pleased" with the results.)[20] This sort of work by the assistant director occurs on any major large-budget film, even those directed by a perfectionist like Alfred Hitchcock. And on *Frenzy*, Hitchcock was fortunate to have the gifted Colin Brewer to assist him; Peggy Robertson found Brewer to be "excellent . . . the best for years."[21]

What is perhaps most obvious, though, from any careful inspection of the records of the production, is that Hitchcock operated in such a confident and competent manner that the shooting schedule rarely fell behind schedule, and that when it did, the old pro managed to make up the time during the next week—if not immediately on the following day. The shooting took place over some sixty-three days, and Hitchcock was on set virtually all of that time, even if by "on set" we mean the phrase to cover occasional late afternoons in his private caravan. Since he was notoriously thorough in his preproduction stage, the shooting of a Hitchcock film usually proceeded without too much incident in any case.

So then, can it be said that Hitchcock was not behind the cameras for every single moment of the shooting of *Frenzy*? Indeed it can be said—or written—if that is one's project (as it certainly seems to have been for Donald Spoto). But I would maintain that any perusal of the actual reports of the production indicates that Hitchcock's oversight was no different from that of virtually any director on any major project. There is almost always second-unit work. There are almost always street signs to be shot, for example, and many other small inserts to be recorded under the able guidance of an assistant director. That's how the system works on these large, well-budgeted productions. *Frenzy* was no exception. But no one on that set questioned who was in charge, and all of the daily progress reports—submitted by studio production manager Brian Burgess—bear this out.

Notes

1. Donald Spoto, *The Dark Side of Genius: The Life of Alfred Hitchcock* (Boston: Little, Brown, 1983), 516.

2. Spoto, *The Dark Side of Genius*, 513.

3. François Truffaut, *Hitchcock*, rev. ed. (New York: Simon & Schuster/Touchstone, 1985), 214–16.

4. The full experiment is detailed in Vsevolod Pudovkin, *Film Technique and Film Acting* (London: Vision Press, 1958).

5. Philip J. Skerry, *The Shower Scene in Hitchcock's* Psycho: *Creating Cinematic Suspense and Terror* (Lewiston, N.Y.: Edwin Mellen, 2005), 239. A revised version of the text has since been published. See Philip J. Skerry, *Psycho in the Shower: The History of Cinema's Most Famous Scene* (New York: Continuum, 2009).

6. See the "continuity sheets," *Frenzy* Folders #277, 278, and 279 of the Alfred Hitchcock papers at the Margaret Herrick Library, Beverly Hills, California. All further references to the continuity sheets in this chapter will be to these folders.

7. See the "daily progress reports," *Frenzy* Folder #283 of the Alfred Hitchcock papers at the Margaret Herrick Library, Beverly Hills, California. All further references to the progress reports in this chapter will be to this folder.

8. A moviola is a kind of portable projection system. Long a workhorse of the industry, it is no longer used.

9. The entire continuity sheet for September 8, 1971, is reproduced in appendix C.

10. See *Frenzy* Folder #284 of the Alfred Hitchcock papers.

11. This was one of his favorite expressions, often quoted. See, for example, François Truffaut, *Hitchcock*, 189.

12. All references to the "script" in this chapter are to the June 3, 1971, "first revised screenplay" in *Frenzy* Folder #260 of the Alfred Hitchcock papers.

13. *Frenzy* Folder #284 of the Alfred Hitchcock papers.

14. The medical note is part of the daily progress report.

15. See the "call sheets," *Frenzy* Folders #270 and 271 of the Alfred Hitchcock papers at the Margaret Herrick Library, Beverly Hills, California. All further references to the call sheets in this chapter will be to these folders.

16. Quoted from the continuity sheets.

17. Spoto, *The Dark Side of Genius*, 512.

18. Spoto, *The Dark Side of Genius*, 512.

19. Patrick McGilligan, *Alfred Hitchcock: A Life in Darkness and Light* (New York: HarperCollins, 2003), 709.

20. Herbert Coleman, *The Man Who Knew Hitchcock* (Lanham, Md.: Scarecrow Press, 2007), 192.

21. *Frenzy* Folder #327 of the Alfred Hitchcock papers.

Shooting the Signature Sequences, Part II   **9**
Hitchcock as *the* Master of Mise-en-Scene and the Moving Camera

Hitchcock's appellation as the "master of suspense" is so much a part of motion picture historical lore that it would indeed be quite surprising to find anyone familiar with even a modicum of the story of cinema who has not encountered this particular honorific title. How and when the title was first conferred remains a mystery to me; I have always assumed that one could ascribe it to the creative energies of some minion working in the studio publicity mill under perhaps either David O. Selznick or Lew Wasserman.[1] What I would add here is another honorific title that could easily be conferred on the legendary director: "master of space"—or master, at least, of the moving camera. For I think that as we continue to evaluate the great pioneers of the first century of cinema, we continue to marvel at the ways by which some of them managed to so comprehensively master their craft. As each year brings the sad announcement of the passing of yet another of the giants of this early period, we come more and more to appreciate the means of expression that they so fervently embraced during such a formative time. Of all of these pioneers, Alfred Hitchcock has easily received the most critical attention. While I am not, in this work, going to begin to touch upon the enormous body of scholarly work that has created a virtual cottage industry around his name, I will simply note as a signifier of Hitchcock's universally accepted importance that the superb analyst Robin Wood has famously compared Hitchcock's work to that of William Shakespeare.[2]

Like Shakespeare, Hitchcock's lasting significance is not so much in the tale that is told but in how that tale is told. The story of King Henry V, for example, was well known to Shakespeare's contemporaries; his version of it, nevertheless, has come to stand as the official portrait. So with Hitchcock: We are not so moved, it seems to me, by the actual stories he tells—of men on the run, crimes of passion, spy intrigue, domestic turmoil; rather, we are impressed by the means he engages to relay these stories to us. Hitchcock, then, will continue to be known as a "master of cinema" because he became a master at utilizing uniquely cinematic techniques to communicate his often relatively ordinary and occasionally even somewhat banal messages. Hitchcock often said—most notably in his series of interviews with François Truffaut—that what he was pursuing in his work was a kind of expressionism that he called, simply, "pure cinema."[3] What he meant by this, we can now conclude, is that there is in the nature of cinematic expression the ability to communicate without words (which would be literature) and without dramatic gesture (which would be theater).

Hitchcock wished in his work to find that particular means of communication that could not be replicated by any other artistic form; for him, there was a kind of "language" of cinema, and he was determined to write its grammar. It is for this reason that Hitchcock's reputation, now so solid among film scholars, took so long to achieve that status. At first, he was dismissed by the literary critics because his scripts—that is, in their view, the dialogue—could hardly be read as compelling text, and by the theatrical critics because his actors, under his direction, hardly seemed to emote in ways that would win them either critical notices or Academy Awards. (Indeed, almost none of the performers in a Hitchcock film ever won an acting award of any kind; now, of course, some of these very performances are called "sublime" by international scholars and critics. Thomas Leitch, to cite but one example, praises James Stewart's performance in *Vertigo*, claiming that Hitchcock was able to "draw on every aspect of the star's persona: innocence, idealism, independence, compassion, stubbornness, romantic diffidence, emotional vulnerability, and the capacity for volcanically destructive emotions.")[4]

If, then, the power of a Hitchcock film derives neither from its dialogue nor from its acting, what, precisely, is this "pure cinema" that the master was purportedly pursuing throughout his professional career? What were the aesthetic goals of these fifty-odd feature films? I would assert that one major element in Hitchcock's search for pure cinema is his exquisite use of the moving camera. It is the moving camera, after all, that most obviously separates cinema from literature and theater. Nothing like it exists in either of these elder art forms. The moving camera uses the apparatus that indeed creates the very "moving pictures" from which we derive a definition of the form and transmutes the mechanical recording device into a vehicle for pure visual escape. The grand sweep of the moving camera cannot be replicated in any other art form; it serves as a unique signal to the spectator that film has the power to transgress space and indeed time in ways peculiar to its own technological soul.

The moving camera is not an easy tool to master. Most directors don't even bother; it has always been far easier—and thus more commonplace—to link individual shots into edited sequences than to work out the details of traversing space within the confines of a film set; the problems increase exponentially on location. (Think of Orson Welles spending an entire night struggling with the opening shot of *Touch of Evil*. Less ambitious directors would have simply scrapped the complicated setup and then cut the scene together from several individual shots. Welles persisted, and the result is one of the great opening moments—three minutes, eighteen seconds—in the history of film.) The moving camera can also be overused, or used in such a pedestrian manner that its power is drained of any meaning. To move it for its own sake—as, say, Steven Spielberg often does—is to diminish its cinematic value. The moving camera, finally, must be utilized to create a consistency of vision, to punctuate an important cinematic moment, to unify space and time at key moments in a film in such a way that the spectator recognizes the power of the moment without losing the thread of the narrative. None of this is easy. The moving camera, is not, indeed, an easy tool to master.

Many of Hitchcock's camera movements have become justifiably well known to film scholars and to their students. No course on his work would fail to include commentary on the resolving crane shot in *Young and Innocent* (1937) or the magnificent revelatory crane descent in *Notorious* (1946). That shot, in particular, is certainly emblematic of Hitchcock's mastery of the moving camera. It provides a visually dramatic punctuation at a key moment in the plot, and it does so in a manner that could never be replicated in any other medium. The gliding descent into the folded hands of Ingrid Bergman—who is holding behind her back a very important key to the wine cellar, a key that Cary Grant needs for his investigation—is a masterstroke; in a few elegant seconds, Hitchcock uses pure cinema to reveal far more than could have been demonstrated by words or with gestures. Each time we see this shot, we sigh with collective appreciation.

No discussion of Hitchcock's mastery of the moving camera could be complete without acknowledging the bold cinematic experiment that was *Rope* (1948). There is virtually no editing whatsoever in this film; it is made up entirely of moving camera shots—ten of them, eleven if one counts the credit sequence (which does, by the way, include the murder itself).[5] Some of these extremely long takes work better than others, but two in particular are classic examples of Hitchcock's visual agility. In shot #3 (here excluding the title sequence and numbering the main shots 1–10), there is a fine example of Hitchcock's concise and controlled use of the moving camera to make a visual statement not only about the plot but about the main protagonist. In one elegant motion (as part of a seven-minute, eighteen-second take), Hitchcock shows us the reason the play was called what it was and reveals the indefatigable arrogance of the young murderer. Later in the same film, Jimmy Stewart comes to rescue civilization from these young fiends, and in yet another carefully orchestrated set piece, Hitchcock wraps up the gist of the plot for us.

While *Rope* is Hitchcock's most dedicated experiment in the absolute control of screen space, there are countless other examples in his major works of his continued exploration of the grammatical meaning of the moving camera. Ironically, one of the most successful exercises can be found in a masterwork that has come to be known as a textbook example of montage, the brilliantly edited *Rear Window* (1954). In its opening moments, a beautifully composed camera movement reveals the entire nature of the space into which we as spectators will be thrust, and then some of the key elements in the narrative, all without dialogue of any sort. In that one shot, we are introduced to our protagonist, we learn of his profession, we see how he managed to break his leg, and we are given an image—in photographic negative—of the woman about whom he is quite ambivalent.

Vertigo (1958) is a film known for its mise-en-scene, of course (as *Rear Window* is for montage), and a good part of the film is devoted to Jimmy Stewart's driving around Northern California following Kim Novak. These shots deserve some attention, especially because they might at first appear to be simple "car shots," which Hollywood produces in abundance. In order to understand their power in this film, it is useful to examine the original novel from which *Vertigo* was adapted, the French "policier," *D'entre les Morts*. Here is how Pierre Boileau and Thomas Narcejac, authors of the novel, account for the surveillance of the young woman by the main character (translation mine):

> Flavières sat at his desk and opened the Gévigne dossier. April 27: a walk in the forest. April 28: spent the afternoon at the Paramount. April 29: at Rambouillet, in the Chevreuse Valley. April 30: at Marignan, then tea on the terrace of the Galleries Lafayette. A malaise provoked (in me) by the height. Obliged to go back down. She laughed a lot. May 1: a walk through Versailles. She drove well, even though (my) Simca is so capri-

cious. May 2: the forest at Fountainebleau. May 3: I did not see her. May 4: a little walk through the Luxembourg gardens. May 5: a long prom-enade in Beauce; we could see, in the distance, Chartres cathedral.[6]

Is there any real way to compare this dry recitation of a date book with the exquisite, luxuriant, languorous, compelling, enticing, exuberant, mysteri-ous, and seductive sequence of Jimmy Stewart's DeSoto (yes—named after the explorer who opened up the Mississippi and beyond to the rest of us) following Kim Novak's green Jaguar down—always down, never up—the hills of San Francisco? I for one do not think so. This justly famous driving sequence is as clear an example as one could hope for of the Hitchcock principle so succinctly enunciated by Truffaut: "Whatever is *said* instead of being *shown* is lost upon the viewer."[7]

Vertigo contains many other examples of Hitchcock's mastery of the moving camera. Perhaps the most elegant one—complicated in both its design and its execution—occurs during the hypnotic moment when Stewart first sees Novak. The oneiric quality is almost tangible. Stewart sits at the bar of the well-appointed restaurant. Novak gets up to leave and must pass by him. The moving camera shot that reveals his looking at her as she looks away is yet another example of the sort of expertly controlled mise-en-scene that only a true master could produce, in this case a true master of space.

As I have suggested in the previous chapter, *Psycho*, like *Rear Window*, derives most of its visual authority from its editing; the shower scene alone has probably been studied in more film schools than any other single se-quence ever put together. (As noted, there is even a book devoted entirely to the shower scene.)[8] In a very specific way, however, the shower scene violates one of Hitchcock's favorite premises. As noted in chapter 3 of this study, Hitchcock was often quoted on the differences between surprise and suspense. His example is worth repeating here: a bomb exploding surprises the audience; a bomb that has been planted under a table keeps the audi-ence in suspense, wondering at each passing moment whether or not it is going to explode.[9] One could argue that the attack in the shower on the vulnerable Marion Crane is a bomb that explodes and startles us all. While it can be acknowledged that it continues to startle and disturb us some fifty years later, it is still a bomb; there was no audience preparation. (Indeed, why else would Hitchcock have insisted that no one could be seated after the film had begun?) It is a brilliant example of surprise but hardly one of suspense, at least as these two terms have been traditionally applied within the realm of Hitchcock scholarship. Yet, *Psycho* does provide a marvelous example of a sequence that combines both suspense and surprise, and it is orchestrated as much by its utilization of mise-en-scene as by its use of montage.

It is the sequence best labeled "the murder of Arbogast," that chilling moment when the detective is knifed to death by "the mother." Its power derives in part from Hitchcock's careful orientation of the viewer to the splendid Victorian house that is the Bates family home. The brilliance of the mise-en-scene can here be seen in Hitchcock's calculated treatment of this interior Victorian space. He shows us only what we need to see, but he does it so well that we feel confident that we understand how each piece that is revealed to us relates to every other one. For example, by the time Detective Arbogast enters the house, we have some idea of what lies beyond the front door. We have that idea due to a short (thirty-second) sequence of three shots that occurs just before the shower scene. The first of these shots is taken from the front hallway of the house toward the formal front door. Norman enters. This shot is followed by a reverse angle as Norman approaches the stairs, then turns to his left. The third shot shows him sitting in the kitchen—the only time that we see that part of the house.

It is the first of these three shots that is important here. It lasts but four seconds, yet it begins a pattern that will recur two more times in the film, when Arbogast enters the house, and later when Marion's sister, Lila, comes looking for Mrs. Bates. This short visit by Norman to the house allows Hitchcock to introduce the space to us. This introduction, brief though it is, creates what Stefan Sharff, in his brilliant tome, *The Elements of Cinema*, would call a "familiar image."[10] This kind of image, Sharff notes, becomes a "pivot" in the film, and the viewer quickly learns to associate something specific with it. In this case, the association is very soon to become a gruesome one, since this shot precedes by only a few moments the shower scene and by a few minutes the murder of Arbogast.

The murder scene itself begins as an exterior. By this point in the film, we, too, would like to know what goes on inside that house, and Hitchcock is about to show us. He does so with the sort of visual acuity that is truly emblematic of his mastery of mise-en-scene. A series of five shots gets Arbogast from the motel office to the house. Within eighteen shots and sixty-eight seconds, private detective Arbogast will be dead, stabbed, as was Marion Crane, by the "mother."

Those eighteen shots are carefully composed and masterfully orchestrated. They begin with the familiar image: shot #1 refers back to the aforementioned hallway interior seen when Norman had entered the house. This time it is Arbogast, and while the angle is different, the interior space is now known to us. The lovely hardwood staircase is familiar, too, and shots #2 through 10 lead Arbogast to it. The shots progress in a classical manner familiar to anyone acquainted with Russian formalism in general and with the Kuleshov experiment in particular. We see Arbogast and then we see what Arbogast sees. (Hitchcock himself had perfected this format in *Rear Window*, as previously noted.) Shot #7, for example, is of the staircase, from Arbogast's point of view; it seems to serve now as a kind of invitation to climb toward the second floor of the house.

And this Arbogast does; he moves forward a few steps toward the stairs (and, in this case, toward the camera, toward us). This is followed by a close-up of his legs from behind as he gingerly mounts the first few steps. What we have here is a carefully executed example of the kind of cinematic setup for which Hitchcock became so well known, a carefully constructed mise-en-scene that is about to lead to a vortex of violence.

The truly brilliant aspects of Hitchcock's construction can be seen in the remaining seven shots, comprising only thirty-two seconds of screen time. Shot #12 begins the suite. It is an overhead shot of Arbogast moving up the stairs toward us. As he climbs each step, the camera glides backward to lead him up. (The system that was built to accommodate this shot is apparently all that is left of the interior furnishings of the Bates house.)[11] It is the kind of moving camera shot that Hitchcock seemed to feel he needed as visual punctuation in virtually all of his great films, several examples of which have already been discussed here. In this one, the moving camera brings Arbogast to us—and, of course, to the "mother." His climb—and the elaborate gliding shot—continues in shot #14, but shot #13 reveals the bottom third of a door slowly opening as a stream of light from within that room spills out upon the upstairs hallway. While this shot no doubt produces anxiety in the minds of first-time viewers of *Psycho*, it is the one that follows the return to the gliding shot—shot #15—that must be regarded as one of Hitchcock's most brilliant strokes of structural mise-en-scene. Here we have an extremely high angle overhead looking down upon the rectangle that has now become Arbogast's trap. He occupies the top left quadrant of the frame, precisely the area that is occupied by the iconic house itself in so many of the earlier shots in the film. From the right comes the "mother," storming out of her room with the knife raised. Three walls constrict the frame, with the staircase—now the only way out—occupying the fourth. Our vantage point is a privileged one, far above the action as we watch the mayhem below. The last three shots (a total of nine seconds) reveal Arbogast tumbling down the stairs, the mother quickly following to dispatch him. It is that splendid overhead shot—just under four seconds—which makes the scene work, which gives it such a disturbing quality. For now we have assumed the role of the enunciator, if only for a moment. Now we are playing God, as Hitchcock so often said that he liked to do, as indeed he did with so many of his visual tropes.

The dramatic overhead, constructed high above the scene, was a favorite shot of Hitchcock's. He employed it only when he wanted to majestically break with the classical approach to mise-en-scene and thereby add a punctuation mark to his syntax. The shot has a unique power within Hitchcock's collective cinematic vocabulary because it is so unusual and because it is used so sparingly. One thinks of *North by Northwest*, when we look down from far above to see a seemingly helpless Cary Grant flee the United Nations complex. There is also that startling overhead image from *The Birds* when the term "bird's-eye view" could hardly have more meaning: the town below seems to have erupted into chaos, and our view of it occurs from far above, as if we, too, have joined the birds of prey. Hitchcock uses it, too, in *Frenzy* when the hapless Blaney is thrown into jail; as the door slams, Hitchcock cuts to an overhead to emphasize how small and how trapped he is. (And perhaps remind the audience yet again of that oft-repeated story of his childhood, and his own purported incarceration by his father.)[12]

Hitchcock's employment of mise-en-scene and the moving camera in *Frenzy* is simply exquisite. An examination of two of the sequences should clearly demonstrate his artistry. First, the gliding pullback down the stairs and out the door of Rusk's flat is a moment in the film that seems to have caught the eye of virtually every critic who saw it. Perhaps the sincerest form of flattery came from those who did not care for the film itself but recognized the power of the sequence. Donald Spoto described it as "the justly famous single shot in which the camera descends, seemingly without a cut, to the ground level, out the building's front door, and then to the opposite side of Henrietta Street."[13] That is an accurate depiction, if rather pedestrian. It somewhat underplays the "moment of pure cinema" that is illustrated by the articulation of the shot. Creating what John Russell Taylor called that "extraordinary shot" and executing it took no small effort.[14]

The shot itself is a part of scene #82 in the script.[15] In examining the total sequence, however, it is useful to look at the previous three scenes as well in order to get a sense of how Hitchcock orchestrated the progression to the dramatic climax. The first of these is scene #79, in itself a well-choreographed piece of cinema, driven by the power of the moving camera—and in this case, by a very clever use of the zoom lens. Scene #79 involves Rusk and Babs; she has just emerged from the pub after an angry conversation with her boss. Her head fills most of the screen as we hear a voice, seemingly out of nowhere, ask, "Got a place to stay?" The power of the zoom lens—with its capacity to compress distance—has hidden Rusk from our eyes; he is revealed only as Babs turns to address his question. From this point on, Rusk and Babs converse about her situation, the camera accompanying them in a fairly standard tracking movement. Scene #80 continues their conversation, and here, Hitchcock demonstrated his mastery of the moving camera as his actors threaded their way through the crowded Covent Garden market. It should perhaps be pointed out again that one of the reasons so many directors avoid long complicated moving camera shots is that so much crowd control is involved. Here, for instance, had one grocer dropped his bag or had one technician turned the wrong way, the take would have had to have been immediately terminated, and yet another would have to be set up.

This part of the sequence—Hitchcock shot both scene #79 and 80 at the same time—was undertaken on one of the busiest days of the production schedule, Friday, July 30, at the end of the first week of shooting. It required an astonishing nine takes, one of the highest number of takes for any individual sequence in the film. According to the continuity sheets, take #1 was "bumpy" (that is, the camera transport was bumpy), take #3 was cut at the very start, and take #6 was unusable because the actors were "thrown by off-screen noise."[16] Two other takes were declared unsatisfactory due to problems with the sound or with the lighting. Only take #9 was deemed acceptable and printed. For Hitchcock, this was indeed an unusual number of takes. Certainly the complexity of the shot itself made it so. In commenting upon the inherent difficulties involved in such an elaborate shot, Stefan Sharff, whose study of *Frenzy*, *Family Plot*, and *Notorious* is a model of rigorous analysis, noted that the shot "is accomplished with extraordinary technical skill and precision (the camera has to pass through two narrow doorways that most likely needed to be taken apart during the movement)."[17] In addition, one can only surmise that the high number of takes was in part due to the fact that Hitchcock and his technical staff were just getting to know each other's machinations, and that such a complicated movement, coming as it did on a Friday afternoon of the first week of shooting, might have stretched the crew to its limits. As we have seen from examining some of the other sequences, the crew became quite a bit more efficient as the production wore on.

Hitchcock devoted the last two takes of this day to scene #81, a fairly straightforward shot of Rusk and Babs arriving at the doorway of his flat.

He printed only the second take. The crew was dismissed at 6:30 P.M. after a day that had begun with a 7 A.M. call at the studio, then 8 A.M. on location at Covent Garden, and, most importantly, a 10:40 A.M. setup to begin the really difficult part of this sequence, scene #82.[18] This is the "backward tracking shot" itself, the glide out the door of Rusk's apartment after he leads Babs into it. One phrase from the script perfectly sets the tone of the moment:

> THE CAMERA, as if saying goodbye to Babs, retreats down the stairs and out through the front door.[19]

The phrase "as if saying goodbye to Babs" gives the scene its poignancy. Hitchcock and his technicians translated that into one of the most visually moving moments of pure cinema in the director's career. John Russell Taylor's description of the shot in the completed film concisely describes the moment: "as the murderer takes his next victim into his house, the camera pulls back from the stairs they have just ascended, out of the front door and back into the street as the sounds of busy Covent Garden, up to now tellingly suppressed, come flooding back on the sound track."[20]

Hitchcock began with the shot—scene #82 in the script—on the morning of that busy Friday, July 30. The complicated camera-tracking mechanism had been set up in the studio. He called for two different lenses to be used so that he could compare the results while screening the rushes over the weekend. The camera, as noted on the continuity sheet for the day, was a handheld (but here mounted on the tracking mechanism) Arriflex "running in reverse." The first attempt was with a 32-millimeter lens and required six takes before Hitchcock was satisfied. (He actually printed three of the six but noted that the first one was "too fast.") The camera crew then switched to a 25-millimeter lens (a wider angle of view) and took three takes, printing only the last. After these nine takes were completed, Hitchcock and the crew proceeded to the location at Covent Garden to film the completion of the shot, the part that leads us through the door and out to the busy street. The first take here was described as unacceptable because of "crowd action," the second take as well ("ditto" was recorded on the continuity sheet). Only takes #4 and 8 were printed, and Hitchcock turned his attention to the afternoon schedule, which included, as noted above, the long dialogue scene as Rusk and Babs walk through Covent Garden to his flat.

Hitchcock and the crew returned to the scene on Thursday, August 5. Six more takes were devoted that day to the opening section of the scene, where Rusk asks Babs if she has a place to stay. Hitchcock accepted the last three as suitable for printing. The same shot was taken seven more times on Friday, August 27, this time with the last four printed. Interestingly—and an apt demonstration of the complexity of such a project—one specific take, in this case #7, was devoted to a change in the dialogue for the television version of the film: Rusk had to say "dirty rat" instead of "bastard" in referring to Babs's boss.

The technically difficult and visually evocative last part of the scene was returned to by Hitchcock and his crew on Friday, September 10, at the end of the shooting day. This time, nine more takes were required before the crew was dismissed at 6:25 in the evening. Only two were printed. Apparently, Hitchcock was still not satisfied, and the crew was ordered to meet for a series of retakes on Sunday, September 12. This was highly unusual, as Hitchcock generally protected his weekends with a kind of insistent fervor. (In a letter to a relative written during the middle of October, Hitchcock explained why he had had no time to see her: "Life is just a matter of going from the hotel to the studio and back to the hotel during the week, and the weekends are spent resting as much as possible to be ready for the week ahead.")[21] Nevertheless, the call was for 6:30 at the studio, and dismissal was not until 5:30 P.M. Ten more takes were devoted to the part of the shot where a man with a sack of potatoes passes in front of the door to Rusk's apartment, thereby obscuring the cut. Five of the takes were printed, and the continuity sheet for the day listed one of them as "very good." In an interview the following year, after the film had been released, Hitchcock went into some detail in explaining this shot and how he had executed it:

> The overhead track extended a few feet in front of the door, and I had the façade of the building duplicated exactly in the studio. When the camera had pulled back to the end of its track, I had a man walk in front of the camera with a sack of potatoes over his shoulder. Here there was an imperceptible cut to the same man walking past the building on location. After that, I could pull back as far as I liked into Henrietta Street, and it looked like one continuous movement.[22]

All of the pieces of this complicated sequence had now been shot. In post-production, Hitchcock would put them together in such a way that one of his most successful uses of the moving camera would be the result. As the camera descends down the stairs and out of the apartment building, the viewer sits horrified in the knowledge of precisely what is now happening to Babs, even though not one part of the activity that actually occurs in

Rusk's flat is shown on the screen. It is yet another moment of pure cinema, and as with so many other of these moments, words are unnecessary, background music would be distracting, and ordinary theatrical emoting or literary repartée would undermine the subtle beauty of the movement, this time created by Hitchcock in the mind of each viewer. He thus plays upon this agonizing memory that the audience collectively holds, and the pacing of his camera movement leads us to reflect upon it in quiet horror.

The last example of Hitchcock's command of mise-en-scene in *Frenzy* can be appreciated by examining the "blank brick wall" scene. It is #34 in the script, and its transliteration from page to screen can be best approached by quoting from the script itself:

34 EXT. ALLEYWAY OUTSIDE MATRIMONIAL AGENCY—DAY
    We are in the main courtyard of the alleyway SHOOTING THROUGH the archway towards Oxford Street. Monica Barling detaches herself from the stream of pedestrians and turns into the alleyway. As she AP-PROACHES THE CAMERA, she sees something behind us, and WE CUT TO A TRACKING SHOT which represents her movements. WE SEE Blaney emerge from the doorway of the building, turn and go down the small alleyway. The CAMERA BECOMES OBJECTIVE again, and PANS Monica over to the entrance of the Matrimonial Agency as she continues to watch Blaney go down the alleyway. She goes inside and we wait below for her reaction. Imperceptibly, THE CAMERA RETREATS, giving us a wide view of the back end of the courtyard. People cross and recross in front of us, going about their business. After a reasonable pause, WE HEAR the SHRILLING SCREAM which tells us that Monica has discovered her dead employer. One or two people stop and look about them. Others ignore it, but even those who stop cannot tell where the scream is coming from, and after a pause, they too move on about their business.

As with the example from *Vertigo*, this rather bland description—while it contains all of the elements of the scene to be shot—nevertheless hardly renders a sense of what Hitchcock's visualization will eventually produce. For one thing, the scene as written gives no indication of the pacing of the events, and it is this pacing, masterfully orchestrated by the director, that will give the scene its power and its eerie moment—indeed, several moments, as we shall see—of concentrated anxiety.

Hitchcock and his crew undertook the shooting of this sequence for a first attempt on Wednesday, August 4. With a 7 A.M. call at the studio followed by an 8 A.M. call at the location and dismissal at 6 P.M., this was a fairly typical day on the production schedule. They achieved only eight setups, however, as the progress report noted that "rain and bad light held up shooting at various times during the day."[23] Altogether, three setups and seven takes were devoted to scene #34. Only two were printed. One of the takes that was rejected had this note attached to it on the continuity sheet: "reactions to scream too early." This was in fact the crucial matter in the orchestrating of this scene: the careful pacing of the movements, in this case, the movements of the characters counterbalanced by the moving—and eventual lack thereof—of the camera. In order to make more clear the complexity of the scene, it is useful to refer to the description of it that appears on the continuity sheet:

> Camera shooting from courtyard outside matrimonial agency onto Monica Barling as she walks thru alley from Oxford Street on her way back after lunch . . . camera tracks back in front of her . . . she looks ahead right . . . reacts as she sees Blaney O.S. leave the agency [O.S. means offscreen] . . . walks on passes close to camera looks off at Blaney walking away down narrow alley close to agency . . . camera pans her to entrance of matrimonial agency . . . she goes in . . . disappears . . . camera runs on . . . people walking towards camera react as Monica screams on finding Brenda's body. . . .

Once again, the description cannot capture the visual quality of the moment, but it should be evident that this is another fairly complicated moving camera sequence. What makes it unique, in my opinion, emerges from the phrase "camera runs on" in the continuity sheet. In the finished film, this moment seems excruciatingly long. Coming as it does after the brutal rape/murder scene, it serves as a kind of cinematic coup de grâce. As we watch it in the finished film, we see two brief exterior shots that establish that the murder victim's secretary, returning from lunch, sees Blaney exiting the office building. (The second shot is a POV—"point of view"— from her perspective so that the audience has no doubt that she sees him.) The camera then stops its pan as the secretary enters the building; the shot is focused on the blank wall of the building itself, the entrance door just on the left side of the frame. And here the camera sits, for an extraordinary twenty-three seconds, really an eternity in cinematic time. We watch this blank brick wall while we imagine what is happening inside: the secretary climbing the stairs as she does each day, probably twice a day. We imagine that she opens the door to the outer office, calling out to her boss that she has returned. Hearing no response, she no doubt enters the inner office, where she discovers the grotesque remains of her employer—and then she screams. Again, all of these events are quite literally constructed by the collective imagination of the audience, for what is on the screen in front of us is but a twenty-three-second shot of a blank brick wall, with some low street noise on the sound track, ambient atmospheric sound that is, on the twenty-fourth second, pierced by a scream. To call this indeed another of Hitchcock's moments of pure cinema seems exceedingly obvious. I would add that it is one of the richest moments in the entire film.

In his monograph on the shower scene in *Psycho*, Philip Skerry points out that "in film after film, Hitchcock meticulously crafts his spaces and places to position his camera in the most imaginative way to advance the narrative. . . ."[24] This is an apt description of how Hitchcock approached the filming of *Frenzy*. He had become by this time a true master of the art of the moving camera and of the craft of mise-en-scene, and his arrangement of these signature sequences provides ample evidence of his professional skill and creative energy.

Frenzy finally did wrap on October 26, when Hitchcock left London. The few remaining second-unit shots were completed by the end of that day by the assistant director. Postsynching—that is, dubbing by the actors of words that might have been lost in the filming process—began the next day. The original production schedule, dated June 17, had listed October 1 as the last day of shooting.[25] Bad weather and other technical problems had

Simple but exquisite example of mise-en-scene in *Frenzy. Photofest*

put the unit behind schedule, and they were also somewhat over budget. (The final year report from the studio listed the overage as $100,653, while the figure given at the end of the production period by project accountant Ron Allday was $64,118.)[26] Neither of these matters much bothered the veteran Hitchcock; he seemed sure that the film would make money. (As it turned out, he was right.)

The adventures of postproduction would now become the next challenge for Hitchcock and his assistants. Before leaving entirely the production period, however, some summary reflections are perhaps in order. Hitchcock spent over five months in London. The thirteen-week production schedule included a total of sixty-three shooting days. Three weekend days were part of this total, as well as six extended days. Also part of the total were six full nights of shooting, with the dismissal as late as 5:55 one morning and 5:10 A.M. on another. Hitchcock turned seventy-two on August 13, at the end of the third week of filming. It was, in short, a grueling shooting schedule, one that would tax any director, much less an overweight man of seventy-two. It was also a large-scale production, the sort where the director can be best likened to a general marshaling his troops as they enter into one battle against unpredictable elements after another. To cite but one example of the scale of the undertaking, on one of the call sheets for a day at the studio, the following note is appended: "Tea trolley for 70 people to be on 'D' Stage at 10 A.M. and 3:30 P.M." Simply managing tea for seventy people on a daily basis must have been a sizable undertaking. This was, as has been noted, a major studio production, and no detail was overlooked to guarantee that Hitchcock and his crew could proceed with each day's mission in comfort and with considerable support. Nevertheless, it had been an arduous undertaking, and it was a quite exhausted Alfred Hitchcock who at 1 P.M. on October 26, 1971, boarded TWA Flight #761 bound for Los Angeles. On October 29, Hitchcock sent a memo to Universal with this simple yet direct phrase: "Principal photography has been completed on FRENZY."[27]

Notes

1. Thomas Leitch suggests that Hitchcock had claimed this title by the time of his major British films. See Thomas Leitch, *The Encyclopedia of Alfred Hitchcock* (New York: Checkmark, 2002), xxii.

2. Robin Wood, *Hitchcock's Films Revisited*, rev. ed. (New York: Columbia University Press, 2002), 57–58.

3. François Truffaut, *Hitchcock*, rev. ed. (New York: Simon & Schuster/Touchstone, 1985), 214.

4. Leitch, *The Encyclopedia of Alfred Hitchcock*, 319.

5. In one of those odd bits of scholarly transgression, it has been reported numerous times that *Rope* consists of ten 8-minute shots OR eight 10-minute shots. Including the title shot, there are eleven shots in *Rope*, ranging from 1:52 to 10:08. [Title: 1:52; shot #1: 9:34; shot #2: 7:50; shot #3: 7:18; shot #4: 7:10; shot #5: 9:58; shot #6: 7:35; shot #7: 7:47; shot #8: 10:08; shot #9: 4:40; shot #10: 5:40.]

6. Pierre Boileau and Thomas Narcejac, *Sueurs froides* (Paris: Denoël, 1958), 56.

7. Truffaut, *Hitchcock*, 17.

8. Philip J. Skerry, *The Shower Scene in Hitchcock's* Psycho*: Creating Cinematic Suspense and Terror* (Lewiston, N.Y.: Edwin Mellen, 2005). See also Philip J. Skerry, *Psycho in the Shower: The History of Cinema's Most Famous Scene* (New York: Continuum, 2009).

9. Truffaut, *Hitchcock*, 73, and chapter 3 of the present study.

10. See Stefan Sharff, *The Elements of Cinema: Toward a Theory of Cinesthetic Impact* (New York: Columbia University Press, 1982), 107–18.

11. Skerry, *The Shower Scene in Hitchcock's* Psycho, 161.

12. According to Donald Spoto, Hitchcock told this story to "the press, colleagues, writers, and actors for decades." See Donald Spoto, *The Dark Side of Genius: The Life of Alfred Hitchcock* (Boston: Little, Brown, 1983), 16.

13. Spoto, *The Dark Side of Genius*, 514.

14. John Russell Taylor, *Hitch: The Life and Times of Alfred Hitchcock* (London: Faber and Faber, 1978), 285.

15. All references to the "script" in this chapter are to the June 3, 1971, "first revised screenplay" in *Frenzy* Folder #260 of the Alfred Hitchcock papers at the Margaret Herrick Library, Beverly Hills, California.

16. See the "continuity sheets," *Frenzy* Folders #277, 278, and 279 of the Alfred Hitchcock papers at the Margaret Herrick Library, Beverly Hills, California. All further references to the continuity sheets in this chapter will be to these folders.

17. Stefan Sharff, *Alfred Hitchcock's High Vernacular* (New York: Columbia University Press, 1991), 207–8.

18. See the "call sheets," *Frenzy* Folders #270 and 271 of the Alfred Hitchcock papers at the Margaret Herrick Library, Beverly Hills, California. All further references to the call sheets in this chapter will be to these folders.

19. *Frenzy* Folder #260 of the Alfred Hitchcock papers.

20. Taylor, *Hitch*, 285.

21. *Frenzy* Folder #297 of the Alfred Hitchcock papers.

22. Paul Sargent Clark, "Hitchcock's Finest Hour," *Today's Filmmaker* (November 1972): 42.

23. See the "daily progress reports," *Frenzy* Folder #283 of the Alfred Hitchcock papers at the Margaret Herrick Library, Beverly Hills, California. All further references to the progress reports in this chapter will be to this folder.

24. Skerry, *The Shower Scene in Hitchcock's* Psycho, 303.

25. See *Frenzy* Folder #334 of the Alfred Hitchcock papers.

26. See *Frenzy* Folder #311 of the Alfred Hitchcock papers.

27. *Frenzy* Folder #333 of the Alfred Hitchcock papers.

Brief Intertitle   10
Looking for a Lost Partner; or,
"Hitchcock in Love"

H ITCHCOCK SAT ALONE ON THE FLIGHT back to Los Angeles.
He had been examined one more time by Dr. Southward before
leaving Claridge's and had been given permission to undergo the
long flight. Alma was awaiting him at their Bel Air home to which she
had returned three weeks earlier in order to continue her rehabilitative
therapy. It is of course not recorded in the office files what thoughts might
have occupied Hitchcock as he endured the long journey home. The fact
that he was traveling alone, however, was unusual in and of itself, and he
certainly may have reminisced about the many challenges he had shared
with his lifelong collaborator.

Theirs had been a particularly effective partnership. They had met while
they were both working at London's Islington Studios, at the time overseen
by Famous Players-Lasky (the company that would become Paramount).[1]
By the time Hitchcock was hired there in 1921, Alma had been employed
as a "rewind girl" and then an editor for four years. Hitchcock had the
somewhat lower position as a graphic designer, his main function being
to design the title cards (the intertitles) that were inserted between scenes
when the visuals were not sufficient to advance the story. From this position
he worked himself up to what we would now call "art director," drawing
upon his talent for sketching and transforming that skill into the design-
ing of sets and the creating of film décor. Alma had meanwhile become a
highly valued assistant at the studio, having worked as an editor, a continuity writer, and a production manger. According to Hitchcock biographer
Patrick McGilligan, Hitchcock at that time was seen as a "lowly editorial
errand boy."[2] It is for this reason that Hitchcock did not speak at all to Alma

during his first few years at the studio. As his daughter puts it in her memoir of her mother, "It was unthinkable for a British man to admit that a woman had a better position, and Hitch waited to speak to her until he had a better job than she did."[3] The better job came about because Famous Players-Lasky did not last long in London, and Hitchcock himself managed to hold on to his position as the studio was cutting jobs; Alma Reville lost hers. Hitchcock moved up to the position of assistant director by 1923 and then called Reville and asked her if she would be interested in working with him—as the editor—on a film to be called *Woman to Woman*. She accepted, and they worked together for the next six decades. As their daughter later recalled, "Hitch and Alma were unstoppable. They were simply making one film after another. They would keep up that pace pretty much through the end of their long and successful lives and careers."[4]

It is difficult to quantify Alma's contributions to Hitchcock's successful career but far easier to qualify them. Biographer Patrick McGilligan puts it simply and directly: when Hitchcock found Alma, he found his soul mate, "a woman who made a greater contribution to his films than any other person."[5] The situation is complicated only due to the fact that the London and Hollywood film cultures are somewhat different. Working with Hitchcock in London, Alma (Reville) is credited for screenplay, continuity, or adaptation on sixteen of the films directed by her husband, including many that are considered to be among his crowning achievements in British cinema: *The Lodger*, *Murder*, *The Thirty-Nine Steps*, *Secret Agent*, *Sabotage*, *Young and Innocent*, and *The Lady Vanishes*. Once the couple moved to America, the union strictures and guild regulations often prevented Hitchcock from extending to Alma the formal credit she no doubt deserved on many of his projects. She did receive partial screenplay credit for *Suspicion* and *Shadow of a Doubt*, and adaptation credit for *The Paradine Case* and *Stage Fright*. After that film was released in 1950, Alma Reville's name never again appeared among the formal credits for any Hitchcock film. No one, however, who was involved in any significant way with any of these productions would doubt Alma's influence, and many memoirs from the period indicate as much. Veteran screenwriter Whitfield Cook, who wrote the screenplay for *Stage Fright* (Alma received credit for the adaptation), recalled years later that while Alma was not on set each day during a typical Hitchcock production, she "went to the dailies about every other day and would give her opinion to Hitch."[6] In addition to this, Alma played a significant informal role in the casting of a Hitchcock project, often sitting beside her husband while he viewed the screen tests. Her collaboration was said to be even more basic than that; according to their daughter, "whether it was in England or in America, each time my father received a book or a script to consider as a potential project,

Hitchcock and the two most important women in his life, daughter Pat on left, wife Alma on right. *Photofest*

he immediately gave it to my mother to read first. If she didn't like it, it was immediately rejected."[7] Peggy Robertson recalled in her 1995 interview with Barbara Hall of the Margaret Herrick Library that Alma's influence could extend to even the smallest detail. After viewing *Vertigo*, she told her husband how marvelous the picture was "as long as you get rid of that awful shot of Kim . . . the one where she runs across the square and you can see her fat legs." Hitchcock concluded from this one objection that Alma hated the film. "I loved it," Alma retorted. Hitchcock immediately ordered editor George Tomasini to remove one shot, causing Novak to seem, in Robertson's words, "to leap from one side of the square to the other." No one will notice, Hitchcock insisted, and Robertson claimed that no one ever did.[8] (It is certainly noticeable, although probably not on first viewing.)

Robertson told Pat Hitchcock that her parents "worked together like the two halves of an orange," and that seems to be as apt a metaphor for their sixty-year collaboration as any.[9] Of course, Pat Hitchcock wrote this memoir of her mother in part to make sure that proper credit was finally attributed. In her view, every Hitchcock production was a "Hitch and Alma" affair. She cites some powerful evidence to prove her point, perhaps none more subtle yet persuasive than a memo from the studio that pertained to the distribution of the final version of the script for *Marnie*. Listed among those to whom the script would be delivered were Mrs. Hitchcock, Mr. Hitchcock, and Peggy Robertson, Alma's name being first on the list.[10]

Hitchcock himself would no doubt have agreed with his daughter's attribution of credit. At the 1979 ceremony honoring him with the Life Achievement Award from the American Film Institute, Hitchcock poignantly paid tribute to the years of collaboration: "I beg permission to mention by name only four people who have given me the most affection, appreciation, and encouragement, and constant collaboration. The first of the four is a film editor, the second is a script writer, the third is the mother of my daughter, Pat, and the fourth is as fine a cook as ever performed miracles in a domestic kitchen, and their names are Alma Reville."[11]

Notes

1. The story of the Hitchcocks is told in all of the main biographies, of course, but more charmingly recounted in Pat Hitchcock O'Connell and Laurent Bouzereau, *Alma Hitchcock: The Woman behind the Man* (New York: Berkley, 2003).

2. Patrick McGilligan, *Alfred Hitchcock: A Life in Darkness and Light* (New York: HarperCollins, 2003), 53.

3. O'Connell and Bouzereau, *Alma Hitchcock*, 34.

4. O'Connell and Bouzereau, *Alma Hitchcock*, 67.

5. McGilligan, *Alfred Hitchcock*, 51.

6. Quoted in O'Connell and Bouzereau, *Alma Hitchcock*, 125.

7. O'Connell and Bouzereau, *Alma Hitchcock*, 102.

8. *An Oral History with Peggy Robertson.* Interviewed by Barbara Hall. (Academy of Motion Picture Arts and Sciences, Oral History Program, 2002), 171.

9. O'Connell and Bouzereau, *Alma Hitchcock*, 183.

10. O'Connell and Bouzereau, *Alma Hitchcock*, 196.

11. Quoted in Quentin Falk, *Mr. Hitchcock* (London: Haus, 2007), 151.

Adventures in Postproduction   11

HITCHCOCK'S LONGTIME (AND THEREBY TRUSTED) ASSISTANT, Peggy Robertson, left London for Los Angeles on Wednesday, November 10.[1] Altogether, she had been in the city for about a month longer than had Hitchcock (she arrived sooner and left later). The film itself was sent on the same flight. The cast and crew had been released, and now an entirely new group would assist Hitchcock in such matters as arranging the sound track, scoring the music, and most importantly, of course, editing the pieces of film together. That important function was put into the hands of John Jympson, a veteran capable "cutter," if not an especially inspired editor. He would be the third editor in as many films for Hitchcock, who was never able to find a suitable replacement for George Tomasini, who had edited every Hitchcock film from *Rear Window* through *Marnie*, with the exception of *The Trouble with Harry*. Tomasini died of a heart attack in 1964 at the age of fifty-five, and Hitchcock was simply not ever again to find a regular editor. This was indeed a part of the tragedy of Hitchcock's later years: his veteran crew was gradually diminished. He had, for example, worked with a quartet of colleagues for over a decade before Tomasini's early departure: Tomasini as editor, Robert Burks as director of photography, Edith Head as costume designer, and Bernard Herrmann as composer. (He was also able, during this same period, to call once again upon the talents of his favorite production designer, Robert Boyle, for *North by Northwest*, *The Birds*, and *Marnie*.) By the time of the shooting of *Frenzy*, Burks had also died (in a house fire), and Herrmann and Hitchcock were estranged. Edith Head remained a friend, but other commitments kept her from working on *Frenzy*. (Boyle survived them all, dying in 2010 at the age of one hundred.)

The term "postproduction" is somewhat of a misnomer in that a good deal of the work actually occurs during the production period itself. In addition to his duties as the overseer of the entire production process, Hitchcock had to screen the rushes and give directions to the editor and his staff as they prepared the "first assembly" of the film, that is, the initial attempt to put the film into the scene-by-scene order of the script. (Films are almost never shot in the order of the script; *Frenzy* was not an exception.)[2] Throughout the production, then, Hitchcock was making decisions regarding the assembly of the material; some of his decisions would invariably result in retakes on the set. He also had to oversee the dubbing and the introduction of sound effects. A memo from Peggy Robertson to the editing staff dated September 7, for example, lists several small changes—all having to do with the sound track—that "Mr. Hitchcock would like."[3] A much longer memo, dated October 14, contained six legal-sized pages of notes that Hitchcock had dictated to a staff secretary. One example offers some indication as to how closely attuned he was to every nuance of the film. Referring to the scene where Babs is in front of the pub and about to be addressed by Rusk, Hitchcock comments: "I would reduce the traffic noise for a moment so that the voice of Rusk startles all of us." That is indeed what occurs in the final cut of the film.

Back in Los Angeles, Hitchcock awaited the arrival of the film. When Peggy Robertson delivered it to the suite of offices on Thursday, November 11, he and editor Jympson spent the rest of the month laboring toward a version that would be complete enough for the composer—at this point Henry Mancini—to score the picture. After a screening on Friday, November 12, Hitchcock had further notes for Jympson—twenty-three of them in fact—including "put in a clock chiming two [A.M.] over Rusk with wheelbarrow" (referring to the scene where Rusk is disposing of the body into the potato truck). Other concerns had to do with problems with camera noise and dialogue that was "unclear and low." The penultimate note is labeled "per Pat and Peggy," referring to Patricia Hitchcock and Peggy Robertson and observes that "petite is not a correct description of Babs."[4] After another screening on November 26, Hitchcock dictated a document entitled "Final Dubbing Notes": it encompassed twelve pages, one page for each 35-millimeter reel of the film as it was now packaged. About the blank brick wall scene, Hitchcock noted: "We should hear the chatter from the two girls—but not very loud—otherwise, it will spoil the silence."[5] Several other staff members and Universal executives, including Lew Wasserman, saw the film and offered comments. It is not clear how many of these found Hitchcock receptive. One observation by Wasserman, however, provides an insight into his relationship with Hitchcock and his

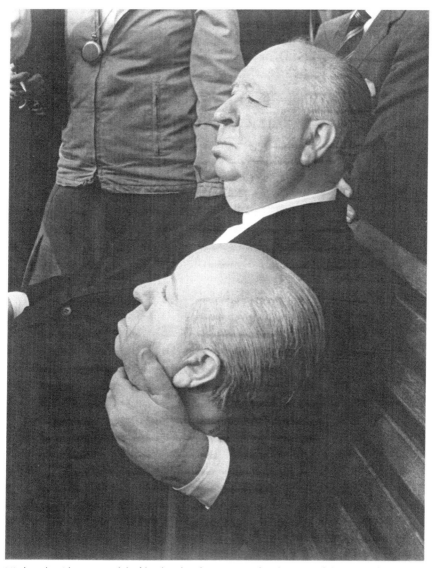

Hitchcock with wax model of his head as he oversees the shooting of the trailer for *Frenzy*. *Photofest*

own analytical approach to the project. He suggested that Hitchcock "take out one second after Monica enters Matrimonial Agency, before girls enter picture."[6] Wasserman was clearly aware of the power of that moment; he was no doubt merely trying to sharpen it. In a separate memo, Michael Ludmer, story editor at Universal, noted that "as Brenda lies dead on her chair toward the end of the scene, I spotted her breathing."[7]

In addition to overseeing the various aspects of postproduction, Hitchcock was kept busy by a constant barrage of requests to his office for interviews. The Universal executives encouraged him to meet with as many reporters and critics as he possibly could in order to publicize the upcoming release of the film. A partial list from the office files included scheduled meetings with film critic Aljean Harmetz on November 9, John Mahoney of *Performing Arts Magazine* on November 21, Bob Thomas of *Action* (the Director's Guild magazine) on November 22, and Ron Haver of the Los Angeles County Museum of Art (to discuss a Hitchcock retrospective that would conclude with a screening of *Frenzy*) on November 28.[8]

While all of this was going on, Hitchcock and his staff had to oversee preparations for the foreign-language versions of the film. Since *Frenzy* employed—by Hitchcock's insistence over Shaffer's occasional objections—dialogue that was especially provincial, even veteran translators had some problems rendering the expressions correctly. The French translator, Odette Ferry, had sent a query to the Hitchcock offices regarding some of these difficult expressions. Hitchcock himself sent her an answer to all six of the troublesome expressions that she had identified. For example, when Babs says "You can stuff your rotten job right up your jacksie," Hitchcock patiently explained that "again, this is street argot so the vulgarism for 'you can shove your rotten job right up your ass or behind, etc.' would have to be found." He also identified the prayer that Brenda so poignantly utters as she is under attack as being a section of Psalm 91.[9]

Editor Jympson took all of the notes dictated by Hitchcock and others with him when he returned to London on November 29. It was now his job to prepare a fine cut of the film so that the scoring could begin. More postsynching was scheduled for December 3, with the recording of the score itself, under the supervision of Henry Mancini, to commence on December 12. Mancini had been sent a copy of the final version of the *Frenzy* script on November 5 and had spent considerable time in Los Angeles and New York composing the score. Atypically, Hitchcock had apparently not been very specific about what he might have been seeking in a musical score, and Mancini took it upon himself to create something that was somewhat derivative of the work of Hitchcock's most accomplished previous composer, Bernard Herrmann, who is well known for his work on *Psycho* and *Vertigo* but who also received the music credit for *The Trouble with Harry*, *The Man Who Knew Too Much*, *The Wrong Man*, *North by Northwest*, and *Marnie*—in short, for all of the films of Hitchcock's most fertile period. This fruitful collaboration—one almost cannot think of *Vertigo*, for example, without recalling the lilting and elegant Herrmann score—ended bitterly on the ill-fated *Torn Curtain* project. Hitchcock bowed to studio pressure to dismiss Herrmann because the score he had produced for that project was not light enough and had, according to Hitchcock biographer Patrick McGilligan, "no apparent melody."[10] The Universal executives had hoped for something that might produce a pop hit song, perhaps sung by Julie Andrews. In retrospect, it is easy to see that this mission—tying a hit song to a movie—was one that was unsuited for either Herrmann or Hitchcock, but at the time, Hitchcock felt he had to at least try to assuage his studio employer. The two parted company in anger, and apparently were never to speak to each other again. Interestingly, when Hitchcock was still in the preproduction phase, working on the script with Anthony Shaffer, his office had received a letter (dated March 26, 1971) from Liz Keys of London Management offering him some assistance with the film score by informing him that "you will see that I represent two composers who have already worked with you, John Addison and Bernard Herrmann."[11] Apparently, not everyone had been informed of the breakup. The project that became *Torn Curtain* was responsible, then, for the loss of far more than the studio's investment. It was a failure on many levels, not the least of which was the unpleasant ending of one of the truly outstanding collaborations between director and composer in the history of cinema.

Thus when Hitchcock heard Mancini's score for the first time, he was none too pleased to note its resemblance to the work of Herrmann. He felt it was too heavy, too lugubrious. Mancini was dismissed, although not directly by Hitchcock, who hated this sort of confrontation. A studio executive conveyed the decision to Mancini, who later regretted that he had been given so few instructions by Hitchcock. Had he known, he insisted, that the director actually wanted to avoid the macabre in the score, "it might have been a different story."[12] Mancini had been paid a fee of $25,000 for the score, which now belonged to Universal.[13]

One of the many names of possible musicians that had been put forward during the preproduction period was that of the British composer Ron Goodwin. He was a veteran orchestrator familiar with a full range of genres, and his film credits include such respected pieces as the scores for *Where Eagles Dare* (1968) and *The Battle of Britain* (1969). Hitchcock gave him more specific instructions than he had given Mancini, telling him that he wanted "sparkling" music, not ponderous. Goodwin later recalled that Hitchcock wanted the music to in no way convey any hint of the horror that was to come.[14] Goodwin's score, while hardly the sort that would become (nor has it) a film music classic, is nevertheless adequate to its purpose, and more importantly, sufficiently responsive to Hitchcock's intent.

Hitchcock himself, accompanied by Alma, returned to London (via New York, where they stopped to see the Broadway play *Prisoner of Second Avenue*) on December 14. He was to stay but three days before departing for Paris and then a winter vacation in Marrakech. During the short stay, he made arrangements with Pinewood Studios to oversee the dubbing and scoring in early January. It was also during this brief stopover that he dismissed Mancini, who had arrived on December 12 and returned to Los Angeles on the eighteenth.

The Hitchcocks returned to London on New Year's Day, 1972. The next two weeks were scheduled in the studio for the final dubbing of *Frenzy*. The files for this period are filled with notes regarding this process, a generally tedious aspect of the postproduction period. The closing of doors, the ambient sound of traffic, the pouring of a glass of beer—all of this material must be carefully inserted into its proper spot, and Hitchcock was no less vigilant about these details than he had been about any others. By the end of the two weeks, the film seemed to be just about ready for scoring; the progress report for January 12 noted that the dubbing had been completed that day, and the running time was listed as one hour, fifty-five minutes, thirty-eight seconds.[15] Throughout this period, the requests for interviews continued, and Hitchcock met with, to name but two, David Brown of CBS News on January 10 and Jess Hoaglin of *Studio Magazine* on the following day.[16] The Hitchcocks left London on the weekend of January 15–16 and then spent two days at the St. Regis in New York before proceeding to Los Angeles on Wednesday, January 19. Remaining in London were Ron Goodwin with a hired orchestra and John Jympson and his editing staff. Their task was to align the music track to the picture track, using as their guide yet another voluminous series of notes left by the director. The cue sheet file alone contained thirty-eight pages of very detailed instructions.[17]

The music for the score was recorded over two evening sessions: Monday, January 31, from 8 to 11 P.M. and Tuesday, February 1, from 7:30 to 10 P.M. A third session was scheduled for Friday the fourth and took virtually the entire day. The next two weeks were spent laying the music track over the picture and synching everything up so that a final composite print (containing all of the elements, including, of course, the sound effects) could be struck. The schedule called for shipping this material to the Hitchcock offices on Wednesday, February 9, so that Hitchcock and his staff could screen it for final approval.[18] On that day, however, editor Jympson called the Hitchcock offices and claimed that the print was being shipped "under his protest." In his opinion, this particular print was "severe looking," with "the delicate shadings lost." He insisted that "no one else should see it until Mr. Hitchcock has seen it."[19]

The following day, a telex arrived from Bill Hill, the associate producer, with a rather disturbing message: "Technicolor informed me today that on their dye transfer system they cannot get closer to the quality of the work print owing to the way the film was lit. I pointed out that four months after completion of shooting was too BLANK late to tell us that. However, Technicolor Hollywood are alerted of our problems." Apparently, the Technicolor lab in Hollywood was able to make the color corrections, because the file contains no more information regarding a less-than-acceptable final print.[20]

The music score, too, was found to be acceptable by Hitchcock. He ordered no changes. A grateful Ron Goodwin wrote Hitchcock on February 18: "I really do appreciate your thoughtfulness and I am most happy to have won your approval."[21] Upon screening the composite print, Hitchcock did have some concerns and made yet another list of changes, most of them minor. A memo dated February 12 listed the changes reel by reel.[22] For example, in reel #1, Hitchcock wanted "more dialogue [added] to the end of the Minister's speech." In reel #2, "raise volume on word 'dandruff.'" In reel #4, "lose about 1½ feet from static shot of building before 2 girls appear and before scream." (Hitchcock was therefore still tinkering with the timing of the blank brick wall scene. This was indeed minor—yet precise—tinkering; since film is projected at ninety feet per minute, snipping off a foot and a half would amount to a cut of just about one second.) In reel #7, he wanted to rerecord one of Rusk's lines "in a lower and more sinister voice." (An important change; this is the line "Got a place to stay?") On reel #9, Hitchcock ordered several changes, all of them minor trims of individual shots. Finally, in reel #12, Hitchcock wanted the volume reduced in part of the prison hospital scene and the registered trademark logo added to the word "Universal" on the end titles. These changes were made, of course, and the material was scheduled to be deposited in the Universal Studios vault by the end of February. Postproduction on *Frenzy* was then complete.[23] The film was now ready to be scrutinized by the Universal executives who had, some grudgingly, approved the project in the first place.

The studio screenings at the end of the month resulted in virtually unanimous praise and enthusiasm, best summed up, perhaps, by the comment of veteran producer Norman Lloyd: "It's the picture of a young man."[24] Most important to Hitchcock, of course, was that his wife's health had improved enough for her to join him on the publicity tour that was to be his next challenge; he well knew, of course, that no matter the state of her health, Alma would not have wished to join him had she not herself approved of the finished product.

Notes

1. All travel dates—including those of Mr. and Mrs. Hitchcock—have been taken from the office diary kept at Universal; it can be found in *Frenzy* Folder #284 of the Alfred Hitchcock papers at the Margaret Herrick Library, Beverly Hills, California.

2. The assembly is followed by the "rough cut" of the film, then the "fine cut."

3. These and the following comments can be found in *Frenzy* Folder #285 of the Alfred Hitchcock papers.

4. See *Frenzy* Folder #298 of the Alfred Hitchcock papers.

5. *Frenzy* Folder #286 of the Alfred Hitchcock papers.

6. *Frenzy* Folder #285 of the Alfred Hitchcock papers.

7. *Frenzy* Folder #286 of the Alfred Hitchcock papers.

8. *Frenzy* Folder #299 of the Alfred Hitchcock papers.

9. *Frenzy* Folder #298 of the Alfred Hitchcock papers.

10. See Patrick McGilligan, *Alfred Hitchcock: A Life in Darkness and Light* (New York: HarperCollins, 2003), 674.

11. *Frenzy* Folder #282 of the Alfred Hitchcock papers.

12. McGilligan, *Alfred Hitchcock*, 710.

13. *Frenzy* Folder #307 of the Alfred Hitchcock papers.

14. Donald Spoto, *The Dark Side of Genius: The Life of Alfred Hitchcock* (Boston: Little, Brown, 1983), 516.

15. *Frenzy* Folder #286 of the Alfred Hitchcock papers.

16. *Frenzy* Folder #299 of the Alfred Hitchcock papers.

17. *Frenzy* Folder #305 of the Alfred Hitchcock papers.

18. The "Final Post Production Schedule" can be found in *Frenzy* Folder #310 of the Alfred Hitchcock papers.

19. *Frenzy* Folder #310 of the Alfred Hitchcock papers.

20. *Frenzy* Folder #306 of the Alfred Hitchcock papers.

21. Quoted in McGilligan, *Alfred Hitchcock*, 712.

22. *Frenzy* Folder #298 of the Alfred Hitchcock papers.

23. A sequence list of the completed film can be found in appendix D.

24. Quoted in McGilligan, *Alfred Hitchcock*, 712.

Releasing the Film
Creating a Frenzy around *Frenzy*

12

ALFRED JOSEPH HITCHCOCK, WHILE DESCRIBED by his closest friends as a shy man, was nonetheless a master of yet another medium, the much-maligned art of generating publicity. (His own daughter has called him "a born celebrity.")[1] Universal Studios, while certainly not responsible for the most creative contributions to the history of classic cinema, was nonetheless virtually unrivaled when it came to overseeing and trumpeting the release of a film that its executives deemed important. With *Frenzy*, Hitchcock's well-earned reputation as a raconteur meshed with Universal's well-organized publicity department to promote the film in every imaginable way. As one rather clever example of the Universal publicity-generating machine, journalists and other publicists who attended press screenings were sent a large envelope containing a rather bold necktie, with the word "Frenzy" emblazoned upon it. An accompanying note declared that "this necktie comes to you with the compliments of Alfred Hitchcock as a memento of his latest thriller, *Frenzy*."[2]

Alma's health had recovered sufficiently to allow her to accompany her husband on the de rigueur national publicity tour, which would take place during the spring and early summer of 1972. Hitchcock made himself available for interviews, and the media was clearly interested. There was open speculation, quite rampant, that this might indeed be the master's last film, and the press saw that as the story.[3] After all, no one had "officially" seen the actual film as yet. Word was leaking out, though, that Universal was quite happy with the work that had been completed by its veteran director, and that, in turn, made the actual release of the film a widely anticipated event.

The first stop on the official schedule was to be the Cannes Film Festival in May. *Frenzy* was scheduled to be shown out of competition. (This generally means that the festival committee has invited the studio to present the film but that it will not have to endure a competition with the official entries. It is considered an honor to be so invited.) Cannes Festival official Maurice Bessy asked Hitchcock's office to prepare a text of between five hundred and one thousand words "as an introduction to your film 'Frenzy.'"[4] Hitchcock was also invited to be the celebrity who would hand out the prizes to the official winners.

Before the international presentation at Cannes, however, there had been a few "private" screenings of the film. Whenever an important Hollywood film is about to be released, the studio often allows personal "sneak previews" for its upper-level executives and others "in the business" who are considered important enough for such treatment. As early as January, for example, a portion of the not-yet-completed film had been shown to fellow director Sidney Lumet. A telex from Peggy Robertson to associate producer Bill Hill gave Hitchcock's permission: "You can show Lumet murder of Brenda but no one else, repeat no one else, can accompany Lumet."[5] Universal executives Sid Sheinberg (at the time head of television production) and Jennings Lang (overseer of film production) were each granted private screenings at their homes; Sheinberg's took place on March 24 and Lang's on April 5.[6] While these screenings are indeed intended to be private, it has always been customary in Hollywood for the host of the screening to share the event with a few close friends and associates, each of whom is asked to be discreet about what was being screened. This in itself, in a society like Beverly Hills, for example, merely leads to more rumors about the film and about its potential at the box office. The "buzz" on *Frenzy* seemed to be almost entirely positive.

Another person who had an early look at the completed *Frenzy* was film historian Arthur Knight, whose book, *The Liveliest Art*, was one of the earliest comprehensive studies of the medium to have been published in the United States (the first edition came out in 1957). Knight was a professor of cinema at the University of Southern California and had been a longtime supporter of Hitchcock's work. In fact, he had been engaged by Hitchcock to write the official synopsis of the film for the studio press brochure. (He was paid $300 for this service.)[7] At the conclusion of the synopsis, Knight appended this note to Hitchcock himself: "In all seriousness, I feel that this is your best work—and your most authentically Hitchcockian—since *North by Northwest*, which has always been one of my great favorites." He then added that he would like to "induce you to come down to USC and introduce it at one of my Thursday night classes."[8] The office file indicates that Hitchcock accepted the invitation and screened *Frenzy* for a class of USC film students on April 27, 1972, making this particular group among the first to actually see the film in a public setting.

Before leaving on his publicity tour, Hitchcock was asked by Universal to record some radio and television advertising spots. This he did on April 13; each promo exhibited a bit of the Hitchcockian wry humor. One example has a man ordering a dozen ties from a store clerk. Hitchcock is standing in line behind the man and overhears the conversation as the clerk asks, "What kind?" The man replies, "Any kind will do—I want them for a friend of mine. . . ." Hitchcock then turns to face the camera and, with his signature deadpan expression, simply says, "He uses them to strangle women."[9]

The Hitchcocks left Los Angeles on May 6 for New York, where they stayed overnight at the St. Regis before departing the next day for Europe on board the liner *Michelangelo*.[10] (They attended the Broadway production of *Sugar* the one evening they were in New York.) During the crossing, many of Hitchcock's classic films were screened for the passengers, including *Rear Window*, *North by Northwest*, and *To Catch a Thief*. The series concluded with *Frenzy*, making this particular group of passengers the second audience to see the film publicly.

The ship sailed to Cannes, arriving on Monday, May 15. The couple was taken from the ship to the Carlton Hotel in order to rest for a few days before the screening of *Frenzy* on Friday evening, May 19. In those few days before the screening, Hitchcock met up with the young French director (and collaborator on the best-seller about Hitchcock's work) who had by now become a close friend, François Truffaut. Truffaut later recalled that Hitchcock looked "aged, tired, and tense" and that the director was worried about the upcoming screening of his film "very much like a young man about to take a school examination."[11] Hitchcock need not have been so concerned. The screening at Cannes turned out to be an enormous success, and the director was given a very warm standing ovation when he was introduced to the audience. Truffaut remarked that when he saw Hitchcock again, a week after the screening, "he looked fifteen years younger."[12]

Not only had the audience received the film enthusiastically but the reviews from the journalists and critics were universally positive. Odette Ferry, who often represented Hitchcock's interests in France, wrote that all the reviews were "wonderful in each paper whether it belongs to the rightist, the leftist or the centrist press."[13] (A writer and publicist, Ferry had, among other things, translated *Psycho*—the novel—into French.)

The reviewer for the flagship French newspaper *Le Monde* called the film "one of the best achievements by this director in a very long time."[14] The opening paragraph of a letter to Hitchcock from studio executive Jerry Evans summed up the festival screening: "I was delighted to hear about the wonderful reception which FRENZY received in Cannes."[15]

The London premiere—announced by the studio as the "world premiere"—was scheduled for Thursday, May 25. A separate press screening had been arranged for the previous Monday, May 22. The Hitchcocks themselves reached London on Sunday, May 21, after having spent Saturday at the palace in Monaco visiting with Prince Rainier and Princess Grace. Rested and in good spirits, Hitch and Alma—as they were known to old friends like Rainier and Grace—were now ready to spend the next month shepherding the film through its international premieres. On Friday the twenty-sixth, for example, they had lunch with the British Film Critics Circle. Perhaps more interesting for Hitchcock himself had been a lunch the previous day with the chief of the major crime team of Scotland Yard. (Hitchcock had made it a habit over the years to develop a relationship with Scotland Yard.)[16] The London reviews were also warm and appreciative, perhaps best characterized by an editorial in *Cinema TV Today*: "There is no more richly rewarding sight than the return of a Master to the city of his birth to make a movie after a long absence."[17] This was the general attitude expressed by the London press, although it was not as universal an endorsement of the film as the one Hitchcock had received from the French.

After London, the Hitchcocks flew to Paris for one night at the Plaza Athénée before a flight to New York on Saturday, June 3. Now, with the New York premieres of the film, the real test of its merits would commence. American audiences had not yet canonized Hitchcock the way the French had, and there was not in a New York City screening the allure of a film made by an artist returning to his home, as had been the case in London. In New York, Hitchcock would face the often capricious and at times even mean-spirited New York film critics circle. The official opening of the film was scheduled for June 21.

Before that, however, there was an exhausting round of appearances awaiting the director, beginning with a series of events at Columbia University. Hitchcock had been proposed for an honorary degree by Columbia film professor Stefan Sharff. The process for the granting of such honors at an Ivy League institution like Columbia is a long and involved one, but the correspondence indicates that Hitchcock had accepted the invitation in April.[18] The festivities began with a black-tie dinner at the campus residence of university president William McGill on Monday evening, June 5, followed the next day by a luncheon for the university alumni federation and then the official commencement exercises. Hitchcock was awarded a doctorate of humane letters by the university, and his well-practiced dour appearance was a big hit with the undergraduates and other guests at the formal ceremony.[19] Another luncheon—this time for the board of trustees—followed on Wednesday, June 7. Hitchcock and his wife were then able to rest up a bit before yet another appearance that would take place the following evening, Thursday, June 8.

This one was to be a true gala, Hitchcock-style. The entry on the office schedule sums it up: "Your private party—dinner at Cote Basque, screening of *Frenzy* and supper at '21.'"[20] Hitchcock had spared no expense—no doubt the studio's expense—for this event. He even chose the wines to be served to the three dozen guests: Montrachet Le Chevalier with the appetizer course and Chateau Haut-Brion 1964 or Chateau Latour 1964 with dinner. On the back of the invitations was the following bit of fashion advice: "La Cote Basque requests that ladies do not wear pants."[21] It was indeed a formal occasion, the launching of the publicity onslaught that would precede the opening of the film.

Answering questions about *Frenzy*: Alfred Hitchcock at Columbia University, June 1972 (Professor Stefan Sharff is on the left). *Raymond Foery*

Dining at places like La Cote Basque made up only part of Hitch-cock's schedule, of course. Universal made certain that such extravagances were repaid in kind by the number of appearances that Hitchcock was expected to make in order to promote the film. His schedule for but one week in June gives some indication of how busy he actually was. On Monday, June 5, for example, he met with Martha Deane of WOR Radio at 10 A.M., then had lunch with Richard Schickel of *Life* magazine, followed by a late-afternoon interview with Guy Flatley of the *New York Times*. Tuesday was devoted to the Columbia commencement activities, as noted, and Wednesday, June 7, began with a breakfast for the foreign press at the St. Regis Hotel (where the Hitchcocks were staying). Wednesday's afternoon meeting was with Earl Dowd of WOR Radio, and Thursday's lunch was with Gerald Clarke of *Time* magazine. Friday morning, June 9, the day after the gala at La Cote Basque, began early with a 7 A.M. appearance at the studios of the *Today* show, followed by a 10 A.M. interview back at the hotel with a representative of Andy Warhol's *Interview* magazine. The chores for the week ended with a 3 P.M. Friday afternoon interview with Mike Wallace of CBS. This sort of schedule continued throughout the following week, beginning with an appearance on the *Mike Douglas Show* in Philadelphia at 1 P.M. on Monday, June 12.[22] On June 13, the Hitchcocks were expected in Boston. They actually went directly there from Philadelphia, arriving in the late afternoon.

The Boston premiere was scheduled for Tuesday, June 20. That day had been officially declared as "Alfred Hitchcock Day" by Boston mayor Kevin White. There were the usual rounds of appearances, including an amusing one at the Harvard Drama Club where Hitchcock was made an honorary member. Hitchcock was apparently quite appreciative of this particular honor, for the last person to have received the awarded membership had been Noel Coward. The reception of the film in Boston was also generally positive—what can only be characterized as a decidedly "mixed" review appeared in the *Christian Science Monitor*—and the Hitchcocks proceeded immediately after the screening to New York, where *Frenzy* was to open the very next day.[23]

The New York critics were surprisingly receptive. Even those known for their disdain for the commercial cinema or their suspicion of the "auteur theory" welcomed the film as a distinctive work by a significant director. The tone was perhaps best captured by Jay Cocks in *Time* magazine, the headline of whose article simply declares that Hitchcock is "still the master."[24] Cocks begins with a brief description of the challenge the director had faced over the preceding several years: "In case there was any doubt, back in the dim days of *Marnie* and *Topaz*, Hitchcock is still in fine form."[25] Vincent Canby's headline in the *New York Times* echoes this sentiment: "Hitchcock in dazzling form," it declared.[26]

The ordeal of promoting the film was now coming to an end, and the Hitchcocks returned to the West Coast. Universal orchestrated a national opening over the next two weeks in order to build anticipation for the film in the minds of the millions who were purportedly waiting to see it. The studio was not wrong. *Frenzy* opened on June 21—the day of its New York "premiere"—in Philadelphia, Detroit, and other large cities, as well as in smaller ones like Providence, Rhode Island, and Hartford, Connecticut. On June 22, the release was wider, encompassing theaters in places like Saginaw, Michigan, and Tampa, Florida. Finally, by July 5, *Frenzy* was in theaters all across the United States.[27]

Meanwhile, back in Los Angeles, requests for screenings of the film from the Beverly Hills crowd were pouring into Universal's offices. In June alone, screenings were held (either at Universal or at the home of the viewer) for Mae West, Robert Wise, Ted Ashley (president of Warner Bros.), James Stewart, Lucille Ball, and John Wayne.[28] The film had opened in Los Angeles on June 28, once again to overwhelmingly positive reviews. Kevin Thomas in the *Los Angeles Times*, for example, calls *Frenzy* Hitchcock's "best picture in years" and claimed that the film had "all the marks of a work by a master at his craft and at his most assured."[29] Reviews of this sort simply contributed to the buzz around *Frenzy* and made the film one of the most popular to grace the private screening rooms in Beverly Hills during the summer of 1972. By the end of August, the film had been screened for Dean Martin, Kirk Douglas, and Barbra Streisand, to name but a few. Robert Evans wanted to see it over Labor Day weekend, as did Frank Sinatra. Requests continued into the fall, as more and more studio executives asked for screenings to be held at their offices or homes. A special screening was held for Academy members on September 30 and for the American Film Institute on October 2. The "season" ended with a showing for Disney Studios on October 31 and at the Motion Picture Home on November 3.[30]

By this time, Hitchcock was, according to biographer John Russell Taylor, "on a grueling tour of western Europe publicizing *Frenzy*."[31] He was, in short, drumming up even more business for Universal, enduring even more interviews, hosting even more dinners, while, of course, basking in the attention and the satisfaction that only an international success could bring him. *Frenzy* had indeed become precisely that.

Notes

1. See Pat Hitchcock O'Connell and Laurent Bouzereau, *Alma Hitchcock: The Woman behind the Man* (New York: Berkley, 2003), 3.

2. See *Frenzy* Folder #321 of the Alfred Hitchcock papers at the Margaret Herrick Library, Beverly Hills, California.

3. Patrick McGilligan, *Alfred Hitchcock: A Life in Darkness and Light* (New York: HarperCollins, 2003), 712.

4. *Frenzy* Folder #273 of the Alfred Hitchcock papers.

5. See *Frenzy* Folder #339 of the Alfred Hitchcock papers.

6. See *Frenzy* Folder #330 of the Alfred Hitchcock papers.

7. *Frenzy* Folder #300 of the Alfred Hitchcock papers.

8. *Frenzy* Folder #300 of the Alfred Hitchcock papers.

9. *Frenzy* Folder #338 of the Alfred Hitchcock papers.

10. For the Hitchcocks' travel schedule, see *Frenzy* Folder #298 of the Alfred Hitchcock papers.

11. François Truffaut, *Hitchcock*, rev. ed. (New York: Simon & Schuster/ Touchstone, 1985), 334.

12. François Truffaut, *Hitchcock*, 338.

13. *Frenzy* Folder #330 of the Alfred Hitchcock papers. The reviews are examined in some detail in the following chapter.

14. Jean de Baroncelli, "le cinema," *Le Monde*, 21–22 Mai 1972, 15.

15. See *Frenzy* Folder #320 of the Alfred Hitchcock papers.

16. For the Hitchcocks' travel schedule, see *Frenzy* Folder #298 of the Alfred Hitchcock papers.

17. Editorial: "Old Master 'Hitch,'" *Cinema TV Today*, 3 June 1972, 6. Reviews are examined in more detail in the following chapter.

18. See *Frenzy* Folder #298 of the Alfred Hitchcock papers.

19. The author of this study was in the audience that day.

20. See *Frenzy* Folder #298 of the Alfred Hitchcock papers.

21. *Frenzy* Folder #320 of the Alfred Hitchcock papers.

22. *Frenzy* Folder #298 of the Alfred Hitchcock papers.

23. See Louise Sweeney, "Foster and Finch in Hitchcock's 'Frenzy,'" *Christian Science Monitor*, 24 June 1972, 6.

24. Jay Cocks, "Still the Master," *Time* 99, no. 25 (19 June 1972): 70.

25. Cocks, "Still the Master," 70. (Of course, the days of *Marnie* are not now seen as having been so dim.)

26. Vincent Canby, "'Frenzy,' Hitchcock in Dazzling Form," *New York Times*, 22 June 1972, 48.

27. See *Frenzy* Folder #309 of the Alfred Hitchcock papers.

28. See *Frenzy* Folder #330 of the Alfred Hitchcock papers.

29. Kevin Thomas, "Hitchcock's Best Picture in Years—'Frenzy,'" *Los Angeles Times*, 25 June 1972, 22.

30. *Frenzy* Folder #330 of the Alfred Hitchcock papers.

31. John Russell Taylor, *Hitch: The Life and Times of Alfred Hitchcock* (London: Faber and Faber, 1978), 286.

Critical Acclaim and Box-Office Redemption

13

IN A MAY 2, 1972, MEMORANDUM to all Universal regional offices, Hitchcock assistant Peggy Robertson asked that "all reviews of *Frenzy* be sent to this office." She of course meant the Hitchcock suite of offices at Universal Studios. These clippings now occupy two full folders of the Hitchcock papers housed at the Margaret Herrick Library in Beverly Hills. The vast majority of the notices are positive evaluations of *Frenzy*.[1]

In what many refer to as the "authorized" biography (Hitchcock was still alive when it was written, and he and the author had long been friends as well as professional associates), John Russell Taylor notes the favorable reception that *Frenzy* received: "The press were unanimous in hailing it as a fantastic return to form, and with press and public alike it proved his most popular film since *Psycho*."[2] Taylor would have known a little something about these reviews, since he wrote one of them himself. His piece in the *Times* of London, under the headline "Hitchcock Magic Is Intact," concludes that *Frenzy* is an example of "a great director again making a film worthy of his great talents."[3] It was not, though, as if Taylor were simply promoting the work of a professional associate; he was rather joining so many others in their collective relief that Hitchcock had not made another *Torn Curtain* or *Topaz*. David Robinson, in the *Financial Times*, echoes Taylor's sentiment and celebrates the fact that Hitchcock remained "an artist who retains such freshness, vitality and magisterial control over his audience, after fifty years in pictures."[4] Another professional friend of the director, Arthur Knight, wrote a fine appreciation for *Saturday Review* in which he repeats publicly what he had intimated privately to Hitchcock: "The great thing is that everything works. For me, *Frenzy* is Hitchcock's best since *North by Northwest*, and *North by Northwest* I have always counted among my favorite Hitchcocks."[5] Vincent Canby in the *New York Times* writes that "'Frenzy' is Hitchcock in the dazzling, lucid form that is as much the meaning as the method of his films."[6]

This was the standard motif of so many of the reviews of *Frenzy* in the daily and weekly press: Hitchcock had made a great film, as he once did without fail, and it was a pleasure to be able to report this fact. Under the headline "The Return of Alfred the Great," Richard Schickel summarizes the widespread proclamation in his review for *Life* magazine: "After flat *Marnie*, mechanical *Torn Curtain*, diffuse *Topaz*, *Frenzy* is like a homecoming—not just to the London where Hitchcock began his career almost half a century ago, but to that country of the imagination which is uniquely his."[7] Gene Siskel says much the same thing in the *Chicago Tribune*: "Hitchcock, after a string of four indifferent films, is back providing grand entertainment."[8]

Many of the reviewers commented upon the screenplay. Siskel, for example, announces that "Alfred Hitchcock's latest film contains the one ingredient missing from most of today's movies: a good story."[9] Arthur Knight writes that the film "has been scripted with unflagging ingenuity by Anthony Shaffer."[10] A. D. Murphy, in *Variety*, simply and directly labels the script "finely-structured."[11] These remarks about the screenplay raise again, of course, the question as to the working relationship between Hitchcock and Shaffer and, beyond that, the proper attribution for the success of the project. One reviewer addresses it directly: "Hitchcock's scriptwriter was the noted author of 'Sleuth,' Anthony Shaffer. How did the two men work together? Hitchcock is always jealous of his authorship."[12] David Robinson addresses the same question, answering it himself:

> One of the mysteries of Hitchcock has always been his ability to work with quite different writers (they have included Thornton Wilder, Ben Hecht, Dorothy Parker; though at different times his loyalist collaborators have been his wife, Alma Reville, Charles Bennett, and John Michael Hayes) and yet remain solely and completely the *auteur* of all he does, so that it is possible to trace the same preoccupations and themes from the very start of his career in films. The screenplay of *Frenzy*, for instance, is credited to Anthony Shaffer, but at every point it is unmistakably Hitchcock's own.[13]

As we have seen, the collaboration between Hitchcock and Shaffer was quite pleasant and effective, certainly one of the least troubled of Hitchcock's career. There were easily enough accolades accorded the finished project to satisfy each of them, and nothing in the official records suggests either artist had any regrets. In fact, the opposite seems to be the case. Hitchcock would have worked with Shaffer again—on the project that became *Family Plot*—but it seems that the representatives of the two parties could not reach an agreement as to the terms of any contract. A cable from Hitchcock to Shaffer dated September 26, 1973, begins with "I was very upset that you were unable to do the next picture with me. It seems that the agent here could not get together with our front office." It continues with "I am not certain myself of the actual figures but there is no doubt that an impasse was reached." Hitchcock concluded, "Again I must repeat that it is a terrible shame that we aren't working together again" and signed "Love, Hitch."[14] In any case, the contributions of both the screenwriter and the director were each singled out for praise by a substantial number of reviewers.

But not all. *Frenzy* certainly had its share of detractors, and some of them were quite vitriolic. Gary Arnold, writing for the *Washington Post*, for example, begins this way: "The new Alfred Hitchcock thriller, 'Frenzy,' at the MacArthur, has a promising opening sequence and a witty curtain line, but the material in between is decidedly pedestrian." "The reviewers," he continues, "who've been hailing 'Frenzy' as a new classic and the triumphant return of the master of suspense are, to put it kindly, exaggerating the occasion."[15] Arnold reserves some of his most pointed remarks for the script, the very script that had been praised by so many: "Shaffer, who wrote 'Sleuth,' would appear to be a suitable collaborator, but 'Frenzy' is very shallow stuff: the dialogue is glib and overwritten . . . and there's precious little mystery, suspense or credibility in the mystery story."[16] His conclusion is sharp and a bit poignant: "It would be pleasant to greet 'Frenzy' as a triumphant comeback, but under the circumstances, it would be misleading."[17] Tim Dumont begins his *Hartford Courant* review with this comment: "Alfred Hitchcock's 'Frenzy,' sad to say, rests a bit too much on laurels and not enough on solid foundation."[18] He felt that the film was "as flat as forgotten ale from a combination of excess length and scanty suspense." He complains equally of Shaffer's contribution: "Nowhere in Anthony Shaffer's script is there the gut-stiffening tension of 'The Man Who Knew Too Much' or the breathless momentum of 'North by Northwest.'"[19] R. H. Gardner's review in the *Baltimore Sun* could be summarized by its headline: "Alfred Hitchcock's latest thriller less thrilling than funny."[20] Gardner calls *Frenzy* "a mediocre thriller but one that contains an inspired comic segment," and observes that Shaffer's screenplay was "hackneyed" and the plot was "crude."[21]

Even a relatively negative review, though, could contain some elements of praise for the film. Louise Sweeney, in the *Christian Science Moni-*

tor, concedes that "Hitchcock is such a brilliant director" but goes on to say that "it seems almost rude to point out that this new film is not in a class with the best of his films. It is no 'Suspicion' or 'Notorious.'" It is, though, she concludes, "unmistakably a movie, and one by a master technician."[22] Charles Champlin of the *Los Angeles Times* agrees that this was a movie, after all, for which audiences, in his words, were hungering. And this appetite led to some overestimation of the film: "That hunger is, I'd guess, the principal explanation for reviews which it seemed to me quite overlook or forgive an often unsatisfactory script, full of leaden exposition, particularly at the start, an unsympathetic early characterization from which the hero never recovers and some questionable explicitness of language, violence and nudity."[23]

It was this sort of critique of the film that was shared by some of *Frenzy*'s severest critics. Hitchcock's taking advantage of the looser production code that existed in the 1970s—as opposed to the 1950s, say—led to a good deal of criticism of what some saw as excessive violence or unnecessary nudity. As one critic puts it, "Fretful students of anti-social behavior contend that cinematic examples of sex and sadism spawn real-life examples of sex and sadism."[24] The most pointed attack along these lines was published in the *New York Times* under a July 30, 1972, headline that raised the question, "Does 'Frenzy' Degrade Women?"[25] The writer, a professor of English at a local New York City college, concludes that it—and many films like it—indeed did contribute to a pervasive fear that women have of being overcome by stronger, predatory males and that certain films can promote this sort of behavior: "It is quite possible a certain percentage of the movie audience is really titillated by the loving camera treatment of the murder, the lingering focus on the slowly expiring victim, the flashback strangulation, the frequent shots of nude dead female bodies."[26] Hitchcock defenders would, of course, question the phrase "loving treatment of the murder," but the point is one that has continued to be raised about the relationship of certain matters on the screen—sex and violence being the most obvious examples—to the reality of life off the screen. To what extent this question relates to Hitchcock's work and that work's relation in turn to women is a matter to which we shall return in chapter 15 of the present study.

The subject of negative reviews cannot be closed here without mention of one of the most negative of them all. The author of the original novel upon which *Frenzy* was based was less than pleased with the finished product. In a May 29, 1972, letter to the *Times* (of London), Arthur La Bern expresses his view:

Sir, I wish I could share John Russell Taylor's enthusiasm for Hitchcock's distasteful film, *Frenzy* (review, May 24). I endured 116 minutes of it at a press showing and it was, at least to me, a most painful experience.

I do speak with some authority on this subject. It so happens that I am the author of the novel, *Goodbye Piccadilly, Farewell Leicester Square*, on which the film was based.

Mr. Hitchcock employed Mr. Shaffer to adapt my book for the screen, apparently because of the latter's successful stage play, *Sleuth*. The result on the screen is appalling.

The dialogue is a curious amalgam of an old Aldwych farce, *Dixon of Dock Green* and that almost forgotten *No Hiding Place*. I would like to ask Mr. Hitchcock and Mr. Shaffer what happened between book and script to the authentic London characters I created.

Finally: I wish to disassociate myself with Mr. Shaffer's grotesque misrepresentation of Scotland Yard offices.

Yours, etc,

ARTHUR LA BERN

The reviews that accompanied the opening of the film across the United States were followed in turn by longer, more reflective analyses of the work. Richard Schickel, who had already reviewed the film (favorably) for *Life* magazine, was given the opportunity to write a longer piece for the Sunday magazine published by the *New York Times*. In it he relates *Frenzy* to Hitchcock's dark vision of the world. Hitchcock, Schickel believes, viewed our world—not just his world—as "essentially a less reasonable place than nice people like to think, a place where we live under constant threat of the dark forces breaking through and disrupting the careful order of our days."[27] Hitchcock himself was nothing if not about order; a man of habits, he would return year after year to the same hotel suites as he traveled the globe, and, as we have seen, eat the same spartan lunch every day in his office bungalow. Hitchcock himself, then, wanted simply to be shielded from those forces of the real world that caused him anxiety, and he therefore created in his films characters who shared his "precious little faith in the systems we erect in hopes of keeping the absurd at bay. On the contrary, he sees them partaking of the very thing they are supposed to protect us from."[28] Hence we have the wrong-man theme; hence we have, in the case *of Frenzy*, Richard Blaney.

Penelope Gilliatt wrote of Hitchcock's career in her piece for the *New Yorker*. She appreciates the humor of *Frenzy* and compares it in that vein to *The Trouble with Harry*, a 1955 film that Hitchcock always felt had failed because the American audiences were not able to appreciate the touches of

British humor in it. Gilliatt touches on form and style as well, noting that in any Hitchcock film, *Frenzy* being no exception, "the camera is often used subjectively as a character in the story." "One would never find," she continues, "Hitchcock putting the camera in one of those impossible positions behind the steering wheel of a car or below the waste catch of a washbasin."[29] Joy Gould Boyum echoes this theme—that is, that *Frenzy* is really quintessential Hitchcock—in the *Wall Street Journal*: "If Alfred Hitchcock does have the genius his followers claim for him, it lies above all—as 'Frenzy' reminds us—in his extraordinary ability to put his formulas to work again and again without ever allowing even those of us most familiar with them to escape their power."[30]

Perhaps the most appreciative of reviews—certainly the sweetest—was written by François Truffaut for *Paris Match*. Quoting one of Hitchcock's favorite phrases, Truffaut reminds his readers that many directors made films that were slices of life, while Hitchcock always insisted that his work was more like a "piece of cake." With *Frenzy*, Truffaut writes, Hitchcock had created "a home-made cake baked by a gastronomic septuagenarian who nevertheless remained the 'young boy director' of his early London period."[31]

Hitchcock was no doubt pleased with the reviews, certainly with the majority of them. He was never too happy with the daily and weekly critics in any case, often complaining that they were not truly "perceptive" about film. "Some of them," he was quoted on more than one occasion, "tend to judge a picture on its content. But content isn't everything. It's treatment, style and the handling of it that creates an emotion in the audience."[32] At least, he might have concluded about a number of the reviews of *Frenzy*, the critics in this case seemed just as interested in form as they were in content. He said as much in one interview: "I'm not concerned about issues . . . but in pure cinema. And the critics seem to realize that is what this film is about."[33]

For Hitchcock, of course, reviews only mattered in their relationship to the audience. For him, the value of a positive review was certainly not in its appeal to his vanity; it was in its ability to bring more patrons into the theaters where his film might be currently playing. He was quoted in an interview as believing that "the two cardinal sins a director can commit are creative self-indulgence and movies that don't make money."[34] Indeed it can be said that the former inevitably leads to the latter, in Hitchcock's estimation. With *Frenzy*, Hitchcock achieved that rare combination—although not as rare for him as for some other directors—of a critical and a popular success. The box-office reports sent back to Universal were wildly beyond what even the most optimistic of the executives could have predicted.

One reviewer comments upon "the long lines in London" where *Frenzy* was "playing to standing room only" audiences.[35] This was accurate; *Variety* reported that *Frenzy* broke the opening week record at the Paramount Theater in London that had been set by *Love Story*. The gross receipts were $27,823 for that first week.[36] The *Hollywood Reporter* reported a strong second week as well: receipts totaled $22,276.[37] The news was just as good coming out of the New York area; the *Hollywood Reporter* put the gross receipt figure at "more than $50,000 in the first day" at various New York theaters, including "a $4,708 gross at the Murray Hill Theatre, a house record; $4,322 at the Palace; and $3,350 at the Symphony, also a house record."[38] The same sort of report came out of Los Angles, and after the first few weeks of screenings, *Variety* summed up the financial situation of *Frenzy*'s initial release:

> Alfred Hitchcock's "Frenzy" has broken both the general-release and hard-ticket box-office records at Pacific Cinerama Dome Theatre in Hollywood with a first week gross of $58,302 for the week ended July 4. In New York, "Frenzy" reports more than $1 million from its first two weeks in 38 Showcase Theatres. In Paris, now at 21 theatres, "Frenzy" has posted a four-week mark of $348,235 and at an exclusive engagement at London's Paramount Theatre has racked up $83,371 after five weeks.

By the end of 1972, *Frenzy* was listed in *Variety* as among the "50 top-grossing films" at #33 with a total box-office return of $4,809,694.[39] It was eventually to become the most financially successful of any of Hitchcock's projects for Universal—even outgrossing *Psycho*—a detail that no doubt pleased Lew Wasserman and rewarded the risk he had taken with his old friend Hitch.[40] Also by December, *Frenzy* was appearing on a number of "Ten Best" lists put out by film critics across the country. Most notably, it was one of the ten chosen by Vincent Canby of the *New York Times*. Canby's year-end summary of Hitchcock's achievement was glowing: "For the 73-year-old director, the mastery of style and the perfection of technique are the expressions of a passion that might prompt other men to seek cancer cures, or to construct completely non-utilitarian towers out of pieces of broken glass and bottle tops."[41] Canby's list came out in the New Year's Eve edition of the *Times*. A mere two years before this, we should note, Alfred Hitchcock had placed a call to playwright Anthony Shaffer to ask him if he might be interested in becoming involved in Hitchcock's next project.

Notes

1. *Frenzy* Folders #325 and 326 of the Alfred Hitchcock papers at the Margaret Herrick Library, Beverly Hills, California.

2. John Russell Taylor, *Hitch: The Life and Times of Alfred Hitchcock* (London: Faber and Faber, 1978), 285.

3. John Russell Taylor, "Hitchcock Magic Is Intact," *London Times*, 23 May 1972, 15.

4. David Robinson, "Old Master," *Financial Times*, 26 May 1972, 3.

5. Arthur Knight, "Whodunit Didn't," *Saturday Review*, 24 June 1972, 74.

6. Vincent Canby, "'Frenzy,' Hitchcock in Dazzling Form," *New York Times*, 22 June 1972, 48.

7. Richard Schickel, "The Return of Alfred the Great," *Life* 72, no. 21 (2 June 1972): 25.

8. Gene Siskel, "'Frenzy': Hitchcock Returns in Style," *Chicago Tribune*, 14 July 1972, B1.

9. Siskel, "'Frenzy,'" B1.

10. Knight, "Whodunit Didn't," 74.

11. A. D. Murphy, "*Frenzy*," *Variety*, 31 May 1972, 6.

12. David Elliott, "Frenzy over 'Frenzy': His Best or Worst?" *Chicago Daily News*, 1 August 1972, 11.

13. Robinson, "Old Master," 3.

14. *Family Plot* Folder #200 of the Alfred Hitchcock papers.

15. Gary Arnold, "'Frenzy': The Thrill Is Gone," *Washington Post*, 23 June 1972, B1.

16. Arnold, "'Frenzy.'"

17. Arnold, "'Frenzy.'"

18. Tim Dumont, "'Frenzy' Focuses on Sex Slayings," *Hartford Courant*, 23 June 1972, 28.

19. Dumont, "'Frenzy.'"

20. R. H. Gardner, "Alfred Hitchcock's Latest Thriller Less Thrilling Than Funny," *Baltimore Sun*, 26 June 1972, B1.

21. Gardner, "Alfred Hitchcock's Latest," B1.

22. Louise Sweeney, "Foster and Finch in Hitchcock's 'Frenzy,'" *Christian Science Monitor*, 24 June 1972, 6.

23. Charles Champlin, "Hitchcock's Special Place," *Los Angeles Times*, 14 July 1972, F1.

24. Guy Flatley, "'I Tried to Be Discreet with That Nude Corpse,'" *New York Times*, 18 June 1972, D13.

25. Victoria Sullivan, "Does 'Frenzy' Degrade Women?," *New York Times*, 30 July 1972, D9.

26. Sullivan, "Does 'Frenzy' Degrade Women?," D9.

27. Richard Schickel, "We're Living in a Hitchcock World, All Right," *New York Times Magazine*, 29 October 1972, SM40.

28. Schickel, "We're Living in a Hitchcock World, All Right," SM46.

29. Penelope Gilliatt, "The Current Cinema," *New Yorker*, 24 June 1972, 52.

30. Joy Gould Boyum, "Alfred Hitchcock's Pleasurable Horrors," *Wall Street Journal*, 30 June 1972, 12.

31. François Truffaut, "Un Gâteau Hitchcock Fait à la Maison," *Paris Match* no. 1205 (10 June 1972): 83. (Translation R. Foery)

32. Digby Diehl, "Q & A Alfred Hitchcock," *Los Angeles Times*, 25 June 1972, W20.

33. Elliott, "Frenzy over 'Frenzy,'" 11.

34. Kevin Kelly, "Fright Power Is His," *Boston Globe*, 18 June 1972, 70.

35. Rex Reed, "Oh, What a Lovely Murder," *Washington Post*, 11 June 1972, F1.

36. *Variety*, 1 June 1972, 3.

37. *Hollywood Reporter*, 15 June 1972, 3.

38. *Hollywood Reporter*, 23 June 1972, 3.

39. *Variety*, 6 December 1972, 9.

40. Thomas Leitch, *The Encyclopedia of Alfred Hitchcock* (New York: Checkmark, 2002), 113. According to Ken Mogg, the cost to produce *Frenzy* was about $2.5 million, and the worldwide gross became $16 million. See Ken Mogg, *The Alfred Hitchcock Story* (London: Titan, 1999), 179.

41. Vincent Canby, "Critic's Choice—Ten Best Films of '72," *New York Times*, 31 December 1972, D1.

The Response from the Academy   **14**

I N HIS WELL-RESEARCHED (AND WITTY) ENCYCLOPEDIA, Thomas Leitch refers to the monumental amount of scholarship that surrounds the work of the director in question as the "Hitchcock industry."[1] He rightly claims that "Hitchcock has been by far the most analyzed filmmaker in the world."[2] Once the supercharged hyperbole that surrounded the release of *Frenzy* had died down a bit—certainly by the end of 1972—the scholars who were an ongoing part of that particular industry to which Leitch referred were ready to weigh in with their evaluations of the film. There were, for example, some reconsiderations of *Frenzy* and how it related to Hitchcock's other work. In *Time Out*, a London journal, John Du Cane begins his examination of the film with the declaration that "we don't feel we gave 'Frenzy' the coverage it deserved when it first opened."[3] Du Cane goes on to claim that what "gives the film its particular strength and subtlety" is a "process of inversion" by which he means that Hitchcock sets up "one group of norms while simultaneously turning those norms outside in." Humor is one of the examples that Du Cane mentions: "the inversion of the serious into the humorous"; he claims that the power of the film comes from the fact that the audience is continually "suspended between the two extremes."[4] In a similar vein, Jean-Loup Bourget, writing in the French journal *Positif*, notes that *Frenzy* was simply "superb" and had been "an unequaled pleasure" to watch.[5] This view is echoed by Albert Johnson in *Film Quarterly*: "It would not be possible for Alfred Hitchcock to restrain his sense of humor." Johnson praises the film as "packed with some of the best facial expressions, subtle delivery of lines and superb comic timing to be found in Hitchcock since Radford and Wayne in *The*

Lady Vanishes." He concludes that *Frenzy* marked a "return to the realm he commanded for so long: the fears and excitement felt when viewing and hearing the stories of a diabolical narrator."[6]

Longer, more analytical pieces followed as the major journals added their commentary on the film. One of the most hallowed in the history of film scholarship has been the publication of the British Film Institute, *Sight and Sound.* Joseph Sgammato wrote a long examination of *Frenzy* for the summer 1973 issue. His essay opens with an astute analysis of what Hitchcock's audience had come to expect when they attended a Hitchcock film. "I will show you what you want to see, says Hitchcock, but you must admit that you want to see it. I will cast an evil spell here in the darkness, says our not-so-benevolent Prospero, but you must share the burden of guilt with me."[7] "Much of the vitality of *Frenzy*," Sgammato continues, "results from this implied relationship between director and audience. Hitchcock plays with our anticipation, showing us sometimes too little, sometimes too much of what we expect to see, but in every case drawing our somewhat ruffled attention to the expectations themselves." While Sgammato did not mention the term "inversion" in his analysis, much of what he wrote did suggest an affinity with the remarks of Du Cane. "Hitchcock plays slyly with the expectation the audience brings to the film," Sgammato continues a few paragraphs later in his essay, for "every moment of conventional, open shock we are permitted to feel is accompanied by a feeling of unconventional, hidden delight." Sgammato concludes his analysis with a superb comparison of *Frenzy* to some of Hitchcock's previous work: "The difference between *Frenzy* and other Hitchcock pictures is that in this latest work the uncannily supple Hitchcock camera—at once ironic Virgil and wide-eyed Dante—reminds us of our taste for the pleasures of the inferno with more insistence, and with perhaps a darker and more severe humour, than ever before."[8] The felicitous phrase—"the uncannily supple Hitchcock camera"—would no doubt have pleased the master if indeed he ever read the piece (and on this score there is evidence neither to affirm nor deny).

The "Hitchcock industry" to which Leitch referred had been largely instituted by the translation into English of the Truffaut book (*Hitchcock/Truffaut*) in 1967, but it had been given its original scholarly impetus by the 1965 publication of the first version of *Hitchcock's Films* by Robin Wood. The expanded revised edition came out in 1969, and these two texts formed the basis of what was soon to become a full examination of Hitchcock's career by the burgeoning community of academic film scholars in both Britain and the United States.[9] (The French had far earlier developed an appreciation for Hitchcock; Eric Rohmer and Claude Chabrol had published their groundbreaking study of Hitchcock's work in 1957.)[10] By the time of the 1989 publication of what was by then entitled *Hitchcock's Films Revisited*, Robin Wood—later to be called the "dean" of Hitchcock criticism—was able to include his remarks concerning *Frenzy*. They were, however, few. Wood clearly saw *Frenzy* as an apt metaphor for Hitchcock's view of the world: "The film's crucial thematic opposition is between characters who never come together until the very end of the film; . . . an opposition that can stand as part paradigm, part parody, of the Hitchcock view of life."[11] He then adds very little to this declaration (although he did acknowledge that *Frenzy* was "much the most satisfying" of the three films Hitchcock made between *Marnie* and *Family Plot*). In terms of Hitchcock's later work—arbitrarily considered to be everything after *The Birds*—Wood far preferred *Marnie*.

Other scholars gave the film more attention. As early as 1974, a mere two years after the release of the film itself, another one of the early book-length analyses of Hitchcock's entire career was published. Pointedly entitled *The Strange Case of Alfred Hitchcock*, it was British scholar Raymond Durgnat's attempt to resolve what he saw as a series of contradictions in Hitchcock's cumulative work. After announcing that his intention is to occupy a position between the poles of Hitchcock as master entertainer and Hitchcock as profound moralist, Durgnat summarizes his approach as follows:

> Not the least of the fascinations which Hitchcock exerts is this mixture of contrarieties: the Symbolism whose emotional key-signature is a delicious fear is also the *petit bourgeois* shopkeeper out of Orwell or Mass observation, whose stock-in-trade is Suspense. A precise moralist encounters an indulgent sybarite. The Calvinist God becomes an amiable Sade. A *petit maitre* of the realistic vignette is also a master of escapist melodrama; and an aesthetic virtuoso is also a Hollywood conservative.[12]

This uneasiness occurs, Durgnat asserts, in *Frenzy*:

> The dramatic tone possesses a similar sense of flux. As intimately as Hitch observes the sexual aspects of the rape, so his camera stresses the violence of strangling which the victim's reactions soft-pedal. That discrepancy contributes to the film's at times almost inconsequential air, its bizarre good humour, mixed with the coolness of its none the less quite assured moral judgments.[13]

This identification of the bipolar affinities of so much of Hitchcock's work is, of course, a theme with which any Hitchcock scholar is by now familiar. Durgnat was one of the first to acknowledge this as a recurring pattern in the director's career and one of the first to include *Frenzy* as part of that pattern.

Hitchcock's death in 1980 spawned the predictable collection of picture books and reminiscences, of course, but it also signaled the commencement of full examinations of the total career of the director who had by then been roundly acclaimed as one of cinema's legitimate pioneers. Among the earliest and most rigorous of these was a study written by Harvard-trained William Rothman. Entitled *Hitchcock: The Murderous Gaze*, its publication in 1982 added further legitimatization to the notion that scholarship in the area of Hitchcock's work in cinema could be accepted by the Academy. Rothman examined only five films (*The Lodger, Murder!, The Thirty-Nine Steps, Shadow of a Doubt,* and *Psycho*), but he did so in such a thorough and rigorous manner that he set a standard for the scholarship that was to follow. His eloquence is worth quoting: "What separates these films is also what joins them: a body of work that movingly stands in for an entire human life, even as it traverses and sums up the history of an art."[14]

While only partially devoted to Hitchcock's work, John Belton's 1983 *Cinema Stylists* did contain some astute commentary on *Frenzy*. Indeed, his summation of the Hitchcock mission—and its subsequent result—in the film is lucid and illuminating: "In *Frenzy*, Hitchcock carefully calculates his effects and then, as in the potato-truck sequence, brilliantly pushes them beyond traditional aesthetic limits. As a result, *Frenzy*'s horror is more grotesque than that in any other Hitchcock film; its humor blacker and more perverse."[15] Donald Spoto's *The Dark Side of Genius* was also published in 1983, and his view of the film certainly echoes Belton's, as we have seen in previous chapters of the present study.[16]

A richer appreciation of *Frenzy* can be found in yet another volume that focused on but three of Hitchcock's films. Stefan Sharff's *Alfred Hitchcock's High Vernacular*, published in 1991, examined *Notorious, Family Plot,* and *Frenzy* (interestingly in that order). Sharff's detailed investigation of *Frenzy* was literally a shot-by-shot analysis of the film, the most complete dissection of the work to be published, before or since. (Sharff did the same—that is, complete shot-by-shot analyses—for both *Notorious* and *Family Plot* as well.) While this laborious research project—one of the very few of its kind—may finally have interested only the most dedicated film analysts, Sharff's conclusions revealed important structural aspects of the film. For example, he uniquely tied the much-celebrated reverse tracking shot out of Rusk's flat to the structure of the film as a whole. Calling Hitchcock's general use of transitions "elegant," Sharff noted this one:

> After the long duration dolly shot retreating from Rusk's stairway into the street, a technical tour de force, there follows a shot of Inspector Oxford entering his apartment and walking toward the camera in the same direction as the dolly in the previous scene. This transition has a touch of irony in it, since we know that the first dolly shot signifies the rape and murder of poor Babs, while the inspector's walk reflects his mistaken assurance that Blaney is the guilty man.[17]

Sharff's shot-by-shot analysis of the rape/murder sequence, the creation of which was examined in chapter 8 of this volume, is a model of careful structural analysis. His appreciation for the complex intermixing of elements of both mise-en-scene and montage in this scene led Sharff to declare that despite the fact that he found it "awkward to use superlatives here as not appropriate in such a gruesome part of the drama," he must nevertheless "state that the scene is, without question, a masterpiece."[18] This kind of close attention to detail suggested to Sharff that virtually nothing in a Hitchcock film was ever left to chance and that even the seemingly most minor matter was attended to with consummate skill. Sharff's concluding summary of Hitchcock's mastery of cinematic form is eloquent:

> Therefore it should be repeated over and over that his most important pattern is this precision enhanced by a scrupulous attention to details. Adherence to a proper cinema-specific grammar is not enough; Hitchcock's form is the sum total of his superb syntax, his originality, and most of all his exactitude.[19]

As if addressing those critics of the genre in which he worked throughout his career, Sharff proclaims that Hitchcock "throws light upon what amounts to base life and turns it into these exquisite masterpieces."[20]

David Sterritt's *The Films of Alfred Hitchcock*, published in 1993, acknowledges both the power and the prohibitive qualities of *Frenzy*. While Sterritt's attention was primarily devoted to six films—*Blackmail, Shadow of a Doubt, The Wrong Man, Vertigo, Psycho*, and *The Birds*—he did perceive the duality within *Frenzy*, identifying it as "among the works that present Hitchcock's personality at its most gleeful and its most sinister—pulling off one macabre jest after another, yet revealing an undercurrent of convulsive gloom just beneath the queasily entertaining surface."[21] A similar comment was made by Thomas Leitch in a collection of essays that he published a decade before his encyclopedia. Entitled *Find the Director and Other Hitch-*

cock Games, Leitch examined the director's purportedly perverse playful side. About *Frenzy*, he notes that the film "makes the audience laugh but makes them ashamed for laughing, simultaneously allowing and condemning the release it encourages."[22]

While the two decades following the death of Hitchcock saw a steady stream of books, articles, and retrospectives of the master's works at selected international film festivals, the centenary of his birth in 1999 provided an impetus for even further examination of the totality of his career and its place within the firmament of cinematic luminaries. An international conference on Hitchcock—one of the few such academic gatherings that included both significant Hitchcock players (like Janet Leigh) and well-known Hitchcock scholars (like Robin Wood)—was sponsored in October 1999 by the Cinema Studies program at New York University. Held in Manhattan, with screenings of several Hitchcock classics at the Director's Guild Theater just down the street from Carnegie Hall, it was a festive and at the same time serious occasion. Those who had known and worked with Hitchcock—screenwriters Joseph Stefano and Evan Hunter, to name two—gave presentations that alternated with papers delivered by a significant number of scholars in attendance. Interestingly, there was not much said about *Frenzy*. The focus of attention during the proceedings tended to fall upon the recognized classics: *Rear Window*, *Vertigo*, *Psycho*, *The Birds*, *Marnie*, among others. A collection of essays—suitably entitled *Alfred Hitchcock Centenary Essays*—was published as an accompaniment to the conference (or as a direct result of it). Edited by conference director Richard Allen (with S. Ishii Gonzalès), the volume represented an impressive array of the spectrum of Hitchcock scholarship. It included essays by William Rothman, Raymond Bellour, Lesley Brill, Susan White, James Naremore, and others whose names would have been easily recognized by fellow scholars in the field. Not one article, however, was on *Frenzy*, and the film received but scant mention in the volume.[23] It was clearly not yet one of the "recognized classics," and if it were ever to be included in that grouping remained to be seen.

Ken Mogg's "definitive illustrated history of the master of suspense"— so read the declaration of his editor—was published in 1999. Entitled *The Alfred Hitchcock Story*, it was a lavishly illustrated edited volume, containing essays by Hitchcock scholars and critics like Dan Auiler (who had published a study of *Vertigo* in 1998 and *Hitchcock's Notebooks* the following year) and Steven DeRosa (who would publish *Writing with Hitchcock* in 2001), among others. Mogg wrote the essays on the individual films himself, and his view of *Frenzy* was at odds with that of Donald Spoto, whom he quoted. He claims that Spoto's conclusion that the film was "devoid of any positive feeling" is misleading. Rather, "*Frenzy* is a perfect illustration of Hitchcock's (and Schopenhauer's) idea that 'everything's perverted in a different way,' and that ultimately all is One. The film's imagery, like Dickens's depiction of London in *Our Mutual Friend*, reminds us that everything comes to dust."[24] "In turn," Mogg continues, "the lesson taught by *The Birds* (and again by Schopenhauer), that 'catastrophe surrounds us all,' is very much what *Frenzy* implies."[25] Mogg's contribution to the Hitchcock scholarship industry has continued far beyond the publication of this particular study. He created a web presence for Hitchcock aficionados called "The MacGuffin" in 1995 (and previous to that a journal of the same name in 1990). The MacGuffin continues to serve as an extremely useful international forum for the exchange of notes and commentary—and recent scholarship—on Hitchcock's work and the legacy of that work.

Leitch's *The Encyclopedia of Alfred Hitchcock* was published in 2002, one of the first major contributions to the Hitchcock industry of the new century. Leitch's entry on *Frenzy* was concise and balanced. Citing the fact that the censoring of scenes that would have been once considered extremely salacious was no longer occurring in the early 1970s, Leitch claims that Hitchcock was "finally able to film a rape and murder with no external constraints" and thereby "turned the event into the most repulsive scene of his career."[26] This freedom of expression, argues Leitch, served to produce "in many respects the ultimate Hitchcock film—the film *The Lodger* might have been if not for the constraints of censorship." "If *Frenzy* is Hitchcock with the gloves off," Leitch concludes, "it has made thousands of viewers thankful for gloves."[27]

Among those thousands were a number of articulate feminist scholars who argued that *Frenzy* raised serious questions about Hitchcock's relationship to women.

Notes

1. Thomas Leitch, *The Encyclopedia of Alfred Hitchcock* (New York: Checkmark, 2002), xxv–xxvii.
2. Leitch, *Encyclopedia*, xxvii.
3. John Du Cane, "Hitchcock Inverts," *Time Out*, 11 August 1972, 43.
4. Du Cane, "Hitchcock Inverts," 43.
5. Jean-Loup Bourget, "Le Dernier Carré?," *Positif* 149 (April 1973): 2.
6. Albert Johnson, "*Frenzy*," *Film Quarterly* 26, no. 1 (Autumn 1972): 60.
7. Joseph Sgammato, "The Discreet Qualms of the Bourgeoisie: Hitchcock's 'Frenzy.'" *Sight and Sound* 42, no. 3 (Summer 1973): 135.

THE RESPONSE FROM THE ACADEMY   135

8. Sgammato, "The Discreet Qualms of the Bourgeoisie," 137.

9. See François Truffaut, *Hitchcock* (New York: Simon and Schuster, 1967) and Robin Wood, *Hitchcock's Films* (London: A. S. Barnes, 1969).

10. Eric Rohmer and Claude Chabrol, *Hitchcock* (Paris: Editions Universitaires, 1957).

11. Robin Wood, *Hitchcock's Films Revisited* (New York: Columbia University Press, 1989), 225. For the "dean" remark, see Greg Garrett, "Hitchcock's Women on Hitchcock: A Panel Discussion with Janet Leigh, Tippi Hedren, Karen Black, Suzanne Pleshette, and Eva Marie Saint," *Literature/Film Quarterly* 27, no. 2 (Spring 1999): 78.

12. Raymond Durgnat, *The Strange Case of Alfred Hitchcock* (London: Faber and Faber, 1974), 61.

13. Durgnat, *The Strange Case of Alfred Hitchcock*, 399.

14. William Rothman, *Hitchcock: The Murderous Gaze* (Cambridge: Harvard University Press, 1982), 3.

15. John Belton, *Cinema Stylists* (Metuchen, N.J.: Scarecrow Press, 1983), 70.

16. See chapter 8. See also Donald Spoto, *The Dark Side of Genius: The Life of Alfred Hitchcock* (Boston: Little, Brown, 1983).

17. Stefan Sharff, *Alfred Hitchcock's High Vernacular: Theory and Practice* (New York: Columbia University Press, 1991), 242.

18. Sharff, *Alfred Hitchcock's High Vernacular*, 185.

19. Sharff, *Alfred Hitchcock's High Vernacular*, 244.

20. Sharff, *Alfred Hitchcock's High Vernacular*, 245.

21. David Sterritt, *The Films of Alfred Hitchcock* (Cambridge: Cambridge University Press, 1993), 16.

22. Thomas Leitch, *Find the Director and Other Hitchcock Games* (Athens: University of Georgia Press, 1991), 250.

23. Richard Allen and S. Ishii Gonzalès, *Alfred Hitchcock Centenary Essays* (London: British Film Institute, 1999).

24. Ken Mogg, *The Alfred Hitchcock Story* (London: Titan, 1999), 179.

25. Mogg, *The Alfred Hitchcock Story*, 179.

26. Thomas Leitch, *The Encyclopedia of Alfred Hitchcock* (New York: Checkmark, 2002), 113.

27. Leitch, *The Encyclopedia of Alfred Hitchcock*, 115.

Hitchcock and Women,
Hitch and His Women

15

THE HEADLINE ALONE SIGNALED CONTROVERSY: "Does 'Frenzy' Degrade Women?" The question was asked by Professor Victoria Sullivan in the July 30, 1972, issue of the *New York Times* and was answered by the author in the affirmative. (See chapter 13 of the present study.) Sullivan's attack on the film contains an explicit complaint about its visual effectiveness: "I suspect that films like *Frenzy* may be sicker and more pernicious than your cheapie hum-drum porno flick, because they are slicker, more artistically compelling versions of sado-masochistic fantasies. . . ."[1] Just about one month later, it was announced by the National Organization of Women that *Frenzy* was to be awarded one of eight "Keep Her in Her Place" awards as part of the third annual celebration of Women's Rights Day in New York City. Other awardees included film critic John Simon for "continual reference to the physical attributes of actresses rather than to their acting abilities."[2] Neither Hitchcock nor Universal Studios responded to the award, nor was it ever physically presented to the director.

The controversy over *Frenzy* and its relationship to the notion of a patriarchal complicity in the degradation of women was played out in more detail and with more cogency in the academic journals than in the popular press. Robin Wood himself acknowledged the dilemma in an eloquent 1983 article in which he pointedly asks the question "Can Hitchcock be saved for feminism?"[3] Not surprisingly, Wood insists that Hitchcock could, especially if we were to pay closer attention to his sympathetic portrayals of women in *Rear Window* and *Vertigo*. Jeanne Thomas Allen, in a 1985 piece for *Film Quarterly*, responds to Wood's contention as she examines the question of the representation of violence to women in the film.[4] Surprised that there had been up to that point "no extended analysis of *Frenzy*," Allen lays out her mission: "I will argue here that *Frenzy* is not only centered on the victimization of women, projecting a point of view in which women's welfare and safety are negated, but that its black humor despairingly demonstrates the dread of vulnerability which men project upon women, sharing their fear and confirming men's need for control and dominance."[5] Allen goes on to illustrate her point with a detailed examination of the rape/murder scene in *Frenzy*. Her approach involves looking at the scene in terms of "its critical location in the narrative structure of the film, its own internal structure, and then individual dimensions of its style (dialogue, behavior, lighting, point of view)."[6] Perhaps the most telling argument came from Hitchcock's use of the latter, that is, point of view. Allen notes that throughout most of the disturbing scene, the camera's point of view was objective, not favoring the position of either character. But during the murder itself, Allen asserts, "the camera assumes classic point-of-view shots several times from Rusk's position." "Point of view is nowhere so strong in this whole segment as during the murder," Allen continues. "Several extreme close-ups of her face accentuate this, but the closest shot of the entire film is of Brenda's eyes darting back and forth in the final moments of strangulation just before they are still in death (freeze frame)."[7] For Allen, this brutal scene was merely symptomatic of Hitchcock's general approach. "Misogyny is evident in the film beyond its physical violence to women," she concludes. "*Frenzy* is unremittingly anti-female in its characterization of women. . . . With the possible exception of Babs, women in *Frenzy* are overbearing, hostile and suspicious."[8]

Other scholars examined *Frenzy*—and indeed, many of Hitchcock's films—in this hardly flattering light. The most accomplished was Tania Modleski, whose cleverly entitled *The Women Who Knew Too Much* articulates the argumentation in clearly delineated prose. Her introduction to the second edition of the text, published in 2005 (the first edition was 1988), carefully summarizes many if not all of the positions that had been taken up to that time on the subject of Hitchcock and the feminist response. Entitled "Hitchcock and Feminist Film Theory," the essay could be read as a virtual tour through the impressive amount of serious scholarship that addressed this question during the latter quarter of the twentieth century. While it is far beyond the scope of the present study to undertake a thorough examination of the topic covered so well by Modleski in her introduction, a few landmarks ought to be identified. Modleski herself acknowledges the scope of what might be called a subfield of cinema studies: "It is nevertheless somewhat surprising to reflect on the extent to which feminists have found themselves compelled, intrigued, infuriated, and inspired by Hitchcock's works."[9] Modleski cites in her introduction such important feminist critics as Laura Mulvey, Teresa de Lauretis, E. Ann Kaplan, Mary Ann Doane, Linda Williams, B. Ruby Rich, Janet Bergstrom, Kaja Silverman, Gaylyn Studlar, and Julia Kristeva in her insistence that sexual difference plays a major role—if not *the* major role—in the manner by which certain aspects of that spectacle called cinema are individually appropriated. Modleski uses *Psycho* to make her concluding observation, but she could have easily substituted *Frenzy*: "For example, male critics frequently point to *Psycho* as a film that punishes audiences for their illicit voyeuristic desires, but they ignore the fact that within the film not only are women objects of the male gaze, they are also recipients of most of the punishment."[10]

Modleski devotes an entire chapter to *Frenzy*. Her observations are both illuminating and, in my view, conclusive. She first correctly characterizes the work of Donald Spoto as having as his central mission the conception of Hitchcock as "something of a dirty old man." "The way the biographer [Spoto] tells it," Modleski continues, "Hitchcock's career can be seen as one long frustrating bout with cinematic impotence until he managed finally to achieve full orgasmic satisfaction with *Frenzy*."[11] Rejecting the simplistic nature of this approach, Modleski calls for a more nuanced view of Hitchcock as a male director. For example, Modleski agrees with Allen's analysis regarding the use of point-of-view shots during the rape/murder sequence: "While critics have frequently noted Hitchcock's detachment in this late film, evidenced in his sparing use of point-of-view shots, it is important to note that this particular sequence employs several point-of-view shots, drawing us into an immediate experience of the man's grotesque encounter with death."[12] But she disagrees with Allen's characterization of the female characters, and on this issue sides with Robin Wood's contention that "the main female characters are more sympathetic than anyone else in the film."[13] In her concluding pages, Modleski summarizes the balanced position she had so forthrightly articulated, rejecting in turn both Spoto's and Allen's characterizations:

> It seems to me more useful, however, to consider *Frenzy* not simply as the reflection of the dirty mind of a frustrated old man nor even of a new "freedom" in sexual mores, but rather as a cultural response to women's demands for sexual and social liberation, demands that were, after all, at their height in 1972 when *Frenzy* was made.

A few paragraphs later, she adds:

> This is not to say that the film endorses all the violence it portrays, despite feminist analyses of *Frenzy* that assume Hitchcock's total approbation of his villain's behavior. I have argued in previous chapters that Hitchcock's fear and loathing of women is accompanied by a lucid understanding of—and even sympathy for—women's problems in patriarchy.[14]

The subject of Hitchcock's presumed "fear and loathing of women" was at the core of Donald Spoto's portrait of his "dark side."[15] Indeed, Spoto painted such a grim picture of the master director that it has come to occupy an equal place in the cultural landscape just next to the portrait Hitchcock himself so meticulously created over the years, especially during his period as host of a weekly television series. It has been left to later commentators, especially family members and those who worked closely with him, to counteract the impression created by Spoto. During his lifetime, Hitchcock almost never responded to this kind of criticism, although he did on occasion make a general point about the social responsibilities of any artist and indeed had a few words to say about the construction of *Frenzy*. Regarding the film itself, Hitchcock responded during at least two interviews to specific questions regarding the level of brutality in the film. It was his claim, for example, that he (and Shaffer) "cleaned up" the original La Bern story.[16] Indeed they did, somewhat. As one commentator recalls, "In the book the murderer is exposed because he left a fingerprint on a potato he had stuffed up his victim's genitals."[17] Hitchcock and Shaffer left out that particular detail in their version of the plot. When asked about the rape/murder scene by the film critic of *Newsweek* during the period when Hitchcock was promoting the opening of the film, he responded that "you need a frank approach to that rape scene." Had he not been so frank, Hitchcock continued, "something very crucial would have been lost: you would never have seen the killer at work."[18] For Hitchcock, then, the matter was simply one of technique: "You can't get the audience to participate in a scene," he went on to say, "unless you bring them very close to the action."[19] For some, of course, *Frenzy* brought them too close, and the man who directed their vision was the "dirty old man" of the Spoto portrait.[20]

According to Peggy Robertson, Hitchcock's personal and professional assistant, this particularly unflattering portrait that Spoto drew of the man for whom she worked for so many years is not an image she recognized. When asked that very question by Barbara Hall for the Academy Oral

History Program, she replied quite directly that Spoto's characterization "wasn't the Hitch that I knew."[21] Hall pressed Robertson on the specific subject of Hitchcock and women by telling her that "some people have gone so far as to say that he hates his women characters." Robertson was quick with her reply:

> Well, they must be half-blind, I think, if they say that he hated women, because Grace Kelly has never been so great as she was in the Hitchcock pictures. Ingrid Bergman was at her most glamorous with him. His daughter Pat . . . I don't see how you can say, or they can say, that he was hard on women. He was very good with women. Women always wanted to be in his pictures.[22]

This is a factor that other scholars have taken into consideration. Susan Jhirad, writing in *Cineaste*, while acknowledging that "it is important not to ignore the distorted view of women in his films," declares that the positive side, "both on and off the screen, was his respect for them as working partners."[23] Peggy Robertson was one of those working partners, of course, as was, most importantly, Alma Reville. Joan Harrison came over from England on the very ship that brought the Hitchcocks and worked for him for many years, eventually serving as the producer of his television series. When Peggy Robertson died in 1998, her obituary in the *Manchester Guardian* included this sentence: "Despite Alfred Hitchcock's reputation as a misogynist, the three most important people in his life were his screenwriter-wife Alma Reville, screenwriter-producer Joan Harrison, and his personal assistant and script supervisor, Peggy Robertson."[24] Robertson, it should be added, was not unaware of the power of Hitchcock's imagery. In a note from London to a colleague back at the Universal offices in Hollywood, she recounted her experiences with the rape/murder scene: "We've finished the rape and murder of Brenda sequence and it is absolutely terrifying! I've seen the rushes three times now and am still absolutely petrified."[25]

In the memoir that she wrote about her mother's life and work, Patricia Hitchcock O'Connell, the only child of Hitchcock and Alma, tried to adjust what she certainly felt was a misconception about her father. As if rebutting the characterizations of Spoto and some others, O'Connell echoes the sentiment expressed by Robertson: "At work, Daddy also surrounded himself with women: Joan Harrison, collaborator on many of the scripts and producer of the television show *Alfred Hitchcock Presents*; his personal assistant, Peggy Robertson; his secretary, Carol Stevens; and his costume designer, Edith Head."[26] To support her corrective portraiture, O'Connell quotes Jay Presson Allen, who had received screenplay credit for *Marnie*: "Hitch loved to work with women. He felt that with women, he didn't have to waste any energy on control. And he liked women; he surrounded himself with women."[27] While the phrase "he didn't have to waste any energy on control" can certainly be read as not quite supporting the position the loving daughter was making in this case, it is clear from what memoirs we do have that virtually all of the women who worked for and with Hitchcock had found the experience to be professionally satisfying.

One example of this can be found in the transcript of a panel discussion that took place in 1997 as the Hitchcock centenary approached. Brought together were Janet Leigh, Tippi Hedren, Karen Black, Suzanne Pleshette, and Eva Marie Saint. The transcript was published in a 1999 issue of *Literature/Film Quarterly*. The panel discussion was moderated by Greg Garrett, who also edited the transcript. His opening was direct: "Hitchcock has often been described as a misogynist, and certainly some of the characters portrayed by you ladies suffered the ultimate fate in Hitchcock's films."[28] None of the actresses rose to that bait. In fact, all of them, including Tippi

Hitchcock on the set of *To Catch a Thief* with his dear friend Grace Kelly and his best friend Alma Reville. *Photofest*

Hedren (who had been, according to Spoto, the most mistreated of any of Hitchcock's performers), had but kind words regarding the master and his methods. Karen Black (who appeared in Hitchcock's last film, *Family Plot*) was the most demonstrative in responding to what she claimed as a false characterization of Hitchcock: "I think whoever said he was a misogynist is a very silly, mistaken person."[29] Tippi Hedren went to some lengths to clear up a misconception regarding a doll sent to her daughter by Hitchcock. Apparently it had been sent in a small pine box, which some took as a threatening gesture by the director to his actress. Hedren rejected this analysis: "This was not an intentional thing for Hitch to hurt my daughter. . . . It was supposed to be a very, very kind of wonderful, thoughtful gift."[30]

Alfred Hitchcock was an extremely complicated man. There is perhaps no way to definitively separate the Hitchcock whose films can surely be interpreted as containing some brutal elements—most especially toward women—from the "Hitch" who surrounded himself in both his personal and his professional life with strong, supportive women. Perhaps he was what Paula Marantz Cohen concludes in her examination of some of his central themes, *Alfred Hitchcock: The Legacy of Victorianism*: "One might say that he spent his career juggling the two faces of Victorianism: the feminine legacy of feeling and imagination associated with the domestic novel and the masculine legacy of law and hierarchy—the world of the schoolyard—associated with dominant institutions and values."[31] Ignored on the schoolyard as the overweight boy from a middle-class upbringing, Hitchcock learned to translate those twin Victorian fascinations with romantic love on the one side and Jack-the-Ripper-like crime stories on the other into a professional legacy that continues to disturb us. With *Frenzy*, those twin obsessions are exemplified in a cinematically superb manner by a charming couple dining each evening in their simple home as they calmly discuss the voracious sexual appetite of a rapist/murderer still on the loose in old London. This is Hitchcock with all of his contradictions in evidence.

Notes

1. Victoria Sullivan, "Does 'Frenzy' Degrade Women?" *New York Times*, 30 July 1972, D9.

2. Laurie Johnston, "Women's Group to Observe Rights Day Here Today," *New York Times*, 25 August 1972, 40.

3. Robin Wood, "Fear of Spying," *American Film* 9, no. 2 (November 1983): 28–35.

4. Jeanne Thomas Allen, "The Representation of Violence to Women: Hitchcock's 'Frenzy,'" *Film Quarterly* 38, no. 3 (Spring 1985): 30–38.

5. Allen, "The Representation of Violence to Women," 30.

6. Allen, "The Representation of Violence to Women," 32.

7. Allen, "The Representation of Violence to Women," 35.

8. Allen, "The Representation of Violence to Women," 36.

9. Tania Modleski, *The Women Who Knew Too Much*, 2nd ed. (New York: Routledge, 2005), 1.

10. Modleski, *The Women Who Knew Too Much*, 13.

11. Modleski, *The Women Who Knew Too Much*, 104.

12. Modleski, *The Women Who Knew Too Much*, 110.

13. Modleski, *The Women Who Knew Too Much*, 107.

14. Modleski, *The Women Who Knew Too Much*, 112–13. Slight correction: *Frenzy* was shot in 1971, not 1972. It was released in 1972.

15. See Donald Spoto, *The Dark Side of Genius: The Life of Alfred Hitchcock* (Boston: Little, Brown, 1983).

16. Recalled in Patrick McGilligan, *Alfred Hitchcock: A Life in Darkness and Light* (New York: HarperCollins, 2003), 701.

17. Leland A. Poague, "The Detective in Hitchcock's *Frenzy*: His Ancestors and Significance," *Journal of Popular Film and Television* 2, no. 1 (1973): 54.

18. Paul D. Zimmerman, "Return of the Master," *Newsweek*, 26 June 1972, 83.

19. Zimmerman, "Return of the Master," 83.

20. Spoto wrote another work on the subject, this one an examination of Hitchcock's relationships with some of his most famous stars, like Madeleine Carroll, Ingrid Bergman, Grace Kelly, Kim Novak, and, most problematical, Tippi Hedren. See Donald Spoto, *Spellbound by Beauty: Alfred Hitchcock and His Leading Ladies* (New York: Harmony Books, 2008).

21. *An Oral History with Peggy Robertson*. Interviewed by Barbara Hall. (Academy of Motion Picture Arts and Sciences, Oral History Program, 2002), 383.

22. *An Oral History with Peggy Robertson*, 354.

23. Susan Jhirad, "Hitchcock's Women," *Cineaste* 13, no. 4 (Autumn 1984): 33.

24. Ronald Bergan, "Obituary: Peggy Robertson; Smoothing Out the Hitch," *Guardian*, 16 February 1998, 13.

25. *Frenzy* Folder #327 of the Alfred Hitchcock papers at the Margaret Herrick Library, Beverly Hills, California.

26. Pat Hitchcock O'Connell and Laurent Bouzereau, *Alma Hitchcock: The Woman behind the Man* (New York: Berkley, 2003), 5.

27. O'Connell and Bouzereau, *Alma Hitchcock*, 193.

28. Greg Garrett, "Hitchcock's Women on Hitchcock: A Panel Discussion with Janet Leigh, Tippi Hedren, Karen Black, Suzanne Pleshette, and Eva Marie Saint," *Literature/Film Quarterly* 27, no 2 (Spring 1999): 79.

29. Garrett, "Hitchcock's Women on Hitchcock," 81.

30. Garrett, "Hitchcock's Women on Hitchcock," 88.

31. Paula Marantz Cohen, *Alfred Hitchcock: The Legacy of Victorianism* (Lexington: The University Press of Kentucky, 1995), 3.

Forty Years Later   16

SIGHT AND SOUND, THE RENOWNED JOURNAL of the British Film
Institute, conducts a poll every ten years to arrive at a list of "the ten
best films ever made." From 1952 through 1982, the poll queries
were sent to a select group of international film critics. In 1992, a separate
"director's poll" was added, and this practice has continued through the
most recent poll, 2002. It probably would come as no surprise to most film
aficionados that in all of the recent polls, *Citizen Kane* has retained its top
spot, having first claimed that position in the 1962 poll.[1] In the 2002 poll,
however, *Vertigo* was listed as number two in the critic's poll and at number eight in the director's poll. It had made its first appearance at number
eight in the critic's poll of 1982, no doubt as a posthumous acknowledgment of a director's masterpiece, Hitchcock having died in 1980. Around
the time of the centenary celebrations and various reconsiderations of the
Hitchcock oeuvre in 1999, *Sight and Sound* commissioned a special poll
that asked critics to rank Hitchcock's top ten films. The resulting list is
an interesting one: Number one was *Psycho*, followed in order by *Vertigo*,
Notorious, *The Birds*, *North by Northwest*, *Shadow of a Doubt*, *Foreign Cor-
respondent*, *Frenzy*, *The Lady Vanishes*, and *Marnie*.[2] All polls are subject
to contemporaneous whim, of course, and the fact that *Frenzy* made this
particular list while *Rear Window* did not is merely evidence of the whimsy
inherent in the process.

The same can be said regarding published opinions. For example, as
recently as 2008, a reviewer for the *San Jose Mercury News*, in an article recalling that *Vertigo* had been released fifty years previously, lists Hitchcock's
top five films as *Psycho*, *The Birds*, *North by Northwest*, *Rear Window*, and

Frenzy.[3] Despite the presence of the aforementioned whimsical fluctuation in such matters, it should be noted with interest that *Frenzy* continued to be quite highly regarded so many years after Hitchcock's death and even that many more years after it had been originally released. This must be seen as a testament to the film's ability to sustain continued viewings, surely the only real criteria for greatness in any work of art. Ironically, this sort of validation of *Frenzy* came but a few years after the publication of a book that had claimed just the opposite fate for the film. Robert Kapsis maintains in his 1992 study, *Hitchcock: The Making of a Reputation*, that "the film has not fared well over time."[4] Kapsis offers no personal support for this position, although he does announce that "neither Robin Wood nor William Rothman, for example, rank *Frenzy* among Hitchcock's major achievements."[5]

Other scholars have attested that *Frenzy* does indeed sustain repeated viewings. For example, in a thoughtful analysis published in the 2004 *Hitchcock Past and Future*, Adam Lowenstein chose to regard *Frenzy* as "something closer to the culmination of Hitchcock's project of manipulating the very senses of his spectators, rather than a regrettable aberration from his signature style."[6] He found the uneasy feeling one might have after viewing *Frenzy* to be an intentional concoction by Hitchcock: "Other Hitchcock films ignore the taboo on violating audience sympathies (*Psycho*, of course, most famously), but *Frenzy* lays bare what had been present in Hitchcock's work all along—the interdependence of horror and suspense rather than their mutual exclusivity." *Frenzy* succeeds in part, Lowenstein continues, because it "posits forewarning in terms of audience expectations gleaned from Hitchcock's previous films as well as from his reputation as the master of suspense."[7] Lowenstein concludes that *Frenzy* represented, then, an advancing achievement for Hitchcock in that it demanded "that viewers redefine their ways of seeing Hitchcock, of perceiving his films between showing and suggesting, between suspense and horror."[8]

Stefan Sharff, whose shot-by-shot analysis of *Frenzy* represents a major contribution to film scholarship (see chapter 14), offered high praise for the film and for its place within not only the genre so often associated with Hitchcock but within the larger context of what Hitchcock himself would have called "pure cinema": "*Frenzy*, seemingly a film within the genre, is, in fact, ascending to a finesse and ambivalence that satirizes and questions the rationale of the genre. Most importantly, Hitchcock's exquisite film language reaches here such heights of expressiveness that it becomes a showcase for cinema art."[9] Sharff viewed *Frenzy*, then, not as merely a return to previous form but, echoing Lowenstein to some extent, as a master work by a master craftsman, one still operating at the height of his creative powers.

Frenzy was released as a DVD in 2001. Included with the film itself was a documentary about the production that had been made the previous year by Laurent Bouzereau, who has produced literally dozens of these "back story features" over the past three decades (dating to the Criterion laser disc release of Brian De Palma's *Carrie* in 1976).[10] Interviewed thirty years after the shooting of *Frenzy*, the participants in the production seemed to have had by this time only fond memories of the occasionally arduous process and would seem, by virtue of their comments, to agree with Sharff's description of the film as a master work directed by a veteran fully in control of both the set and of his own artistic vision. This is an important detail in the saga of *Frenzy* if only because it serves as a public corrective to the impression given by Donald Spoto in his conception of the dark side of Hitchcock's career. For example, Spoto claims that after Alma's stroke in June, Hitchcock became "disinterested in his work."[11] None of the principals seem to recall this. By contrast, each of the main actors commented upon how carefully arranged everything was on the set and how avidly Hitchcock oversaw the production. Anna Massey (who had played Babs) recalled that Hitchcock had "made a lovely atmosphere on the set." "It was good fun," she continued, "good ironic fun."[12] Jon Finch (Blaney) commented that Hitchcock good-naturedly accepted small script changes from him but eventually told him that "while I said you could make alterations, I didn't say you could rewrite the whole script."[13] Perhaps most significant were the recollections of Anthony Shaffer, the screenwriter (who died shortly after this interview). As reported by the Hitchcock biographers, this particular collaboration seems to have gone swimmingly. Shaffer verified this; he had only positive responses as he recalled the interesting challenges he had faced in working with the most famous director in the world. For Shaffer, the project had been an enormous professional success, and the fact that it had also become a commercial success made him quite happy, he said, for Hitchcock. "It put him back on his pedestal again," Shaffer concluded, "where he remains to this day."[14]

The ultimate evaluation of *Frenzy*, is, of course, directly related to the ultimate evaluation of Alfred Joseph Hitchcock as an important artist. The age in which we now live has certainly not been without its revisionist approaches to Hitchcock's career. In part as a reaction to the lionizing that came on the heels of Truffaut's series of interviews and Robin Wood's classic study, what followed over the next several decades has been a series of examinations that sought to place Hitchcock within a historical context that regarded him on the one hand as merely an accomplished entertainer, and on the other as one of the great artists of the twentieth century. Truffaut and Wood obviously put Hitchcock next to, say, Picasso or Stravinsky. Others were not so certain.

Two articles, published a decade apart, give a sense of the misgivings expressed by those who would not make Hitchcock the equal of either a Picasso or a Stravinsky. Writing for the *London Spectator* in 1997, Michael Harrington asks in his title, "Is Hitchcock's reputation deserved?" "No," is Harrington's reply to his own question: "The truth about Alfred Hitchcock is that he was a light entertainer of great professional skill and a splendid joker."[15] Hitchcock, Harrington goes on to write, "never produced work of the originality, depth and power required for the title of 'genius,' nor is it clear that the films he made should be attributed to him in the exclusive way that, say, the Sherlock Holmes stories can be attributed to Conan Doyle or *Saint Joan* to George Bernard Shaw."[16]

Terry Teachout, a drama critic for the *Wall Street Journal*, wrote an article for *Commentary* in 2009 under the title "The Trouble with Alfred Hitchcock." For Teachout, the trouble was simply that Hitchcock was overrated, that Hitchcock's elevation to the status of great artist had more to do with the politics of criticism than with artistic evaluation. Teachout asks: "Is its [Hitchcock's work] current critical standing a reflection of the postmodern tendency to treat pop culture as though it were comparable in significance to high art?"[17] Claiming that "after *Psycho* he lost his touch," Teachout finds fault with many of the films that have been called masterpieces by others, like *Notorious, Strangers on a Train, Rear Window,* and *Vertigo* (although these were at least better than Hitchcock's others, Teachout acknowledges), and his example of a fully realized project rests solely on *North by Northwest,* where Hitchcock "comes closest to creating a perfect work of art."[18] All this suggested to Teachout that Hitchcock, "far from being a great creative artist, was actually a minor master who succeeded in creating only one fully realized masterpiece."[19] An eloquent reply to Teachout was published a few months later by *Commentary*. Michael Lewis argues that it was hardly proper to compare Hitchcock's work to that of an artist from a different medium, like, say, Noel Coward. "One does not judge a film by the same standards that one does a play, an opera, or a novel," Lewis insists. "Film is a visual medium, and its expressive instruments are composition (the way figures and objects are disposed in the picture plane) and momentum (the way that images change to establish rhythm and tempo)."[20]

These are, then, the parameters of the current state of Alfred Hitchcock's reputation. In many ways, the discussion recalls Robin Wood's apt comparison of so many years ago. He viewed Hitchcock as much of an exemplar of our age as Shakespeare was of his own. Wood saw the limits of such an evaluation but found it useful in placing Hitchcock within a recognized historical context. "One does not want to deny Shakespeare his imperfections, or Hitchcock his," Wood wisely counsels. "Indeed," he continues, "a strong objection to much current French exegesis of Hitchcock, as to so much current critical work on Shakespeare, is that the writers tend to start from the assumption that their hero can do no wrong, and quite fail to make necessary discriminations between different works, or admit occasional failures of realization within works."[21] Wood addressed the concern (later expressed by critics like Harrington and Teachout) regarding Hitchcock's relationship to popular art forms. The same argument, Wood insists, had been used periodically to discredit Shakespeare: "If we somehow removed all trace of 'popular' appeal from Shakespeare and Hitchcock, then we would have lost Shakespeare and Hitchcock."[22]

Hitchcock, then, like Shakespeare, was a popular artist. He was, too, I would argue, an artist whose popularity did not come at the cost of a strong, sometimes fierce personal vision. Like Shakespeare, Hitchcock was a master of his craft. Just as Shakespeare knew how to mount a production of one of his plays, Hitchcock knew how to organize and conduct the production of one of his scenarios. In most cases, he had quite literally cowritten the script, a significant contribution for which he never claimed official credit. Like Shakespeare, Hitchcock created works that we now regard as masterpieces and others that we relegate to a second rank. For Shakespeare, we easily count *Hamlet* and *Macbeth* among the masterpieces; for Hitchcock *Rear Window* and *Vertigo*. With Shakespeare, the ultimate evaluation of *Pericles*, for example, might raise some critical debate; with Hitchcock, as we have seen, it might well be *Frenzy*.

What can be said about *Frenzy*, I have become convinced (after two summers with the Hitchcock papers in Beverly Hills and a year and a half of writing this text), is the following: It is, like so many of the grand Hitchcocks, extremely well written, which is to say, well structured. The collaboration between director and screenwriter worked so well that the result satisfied those members of the audience who would come to a film to hear sparkling dialogue (as in, say *North by Northwest*) and those who came to experience one or another "Hitchcock moment." There is very little spare material in *Frenzy*, very little that an overeager producer might have been tempted to trim. The film moves with a pace that recalls the snappy delivery of some of the earlier pieces from Hitchcock's British period (like *The Lady Vanishes*, for example).

The mise-en-scene is inspired and exquisite. The film has the look, even the "feel" (if such a thing is possible) of the gritty London streets that Hitchcock endeavored to capture. It is quite a different world from the Nice of *To Catch a Thief*, the San Francisco of *Vertigo*, or even the London of *Dial M for Murder*. *Frenzy*'s London is the London of Hitchcock's father, of the stalls of Covent Garden, the narrow streets of the old parts of the city, the lively capital without the tourists. Even the interiors ring true. The office of the matrimonial agency is a period piece in and of itself. The small flat occupied by the Oxfords is probably not so different from the one in which young Hitchcock grew up. And Rusk's flat was based on one that is actually there, above a storied book publisher. The overseeing of the camera movement—perhaps the most essential part of mise-en-scene—was exceptionally well done. Again and again, Hitchcock directed his crew to attempt elaborate setups, marvelously flowing shots, and complex interactions between the movement of the camera and the organized pacing of the actors. Very few of the scenes suggested "photographs of people talking"; rather, they were usually punctuated with a subtle camera movement that brought to life the interplay that had been articulated by the dialogue.

The same can be said for the editing. Hitchcock's ability to orchestrate a scene through absolutely precise cutting is evident in virtually all of *Frenzy*. The celebrated (and notorious) scenes have been examined in this study (see chapter 8, for example), but it should be added here that there are no embarrassing gaffes in *Frenzy*, no poorly edited sequences. Rather there is a crispness that suggests the studied attention of a master cutter, a craftsman who knew precisely when the shot should end and when the short insert might be needed. These are matters that are the result of years and years of experience. The placing together of individual pieces of celluloid in an order that creates something that is more than the sum of those pieces is what Hitchcock so often called "pure cinema." In *Frenzy*, there are several examples of pure cinema, I have contended, and they have each been examined in this study.

During the 1979 tribute to Hitchcock by the American Film Institute, legendary actor James Stewart used the old line about Hitchcock and cattle ("What he said," Stewart drawled, "is that actors should be treated like cattle.") It got a good laugh. The fact is, as I have suggested earlier in this study (chapter 6), that Hitchcock was an extraordinary director of actors, that he pulled from each of them some of their finest performances. (In addition to Stewart, Cary Grant, Henry Fonda, Anthony Perkins, and Ingrid Bergman were all there at the AFI dinner to agree with this assessment.)[23] In *Frenzy*, there is not a poorly acted moment. Hitchcock spent weeks assembling his cast, examining literally hundreds of hours of film material,

scheduling dozens of interviews, conducting many screen tests before settling on a cast that turned out to be virtually flawless. His direction was
direct and straightforward, as it always was. He corrected an actor only if
something seemed false in the performance. Apparently, there were very
few false notes in *Frenzy*. The recollections from the actors all attest to the
fact that Hitchcock was generally satisfied with their performances. As are
we, forty years later.

Barry Foster recalled that Hitchcock really gave him but one very specific
bit of advice on his performance. At the end of the film, when Rusk realizes
that the detective has caught him red-handed, Foster's instinct was to lower
his head, as if in shame. Hitchcock said that he wouldn't do it that way.
"Don't drop your head," Hitchcock advised Foster. "That's the last thing a
serial murderer is going to do—as it were, admit defeat. Drop the trunk, but
don't drop your head."[24] Foster followed the director's suggestion, and the
closing scene ends with the ideal touch of Hitchcockian irony.

The archival evidence, coupled with a careful analysis of the work, reveals, then, that *Frenzy* is a well-written, impeccably constructed film that
was shot and edited with unerring precision by a master director who, at the
age of seventy-two, managed to elicit marvelously effective performances
from his well-chosen cast. It is also a film that reveals the director's darkest
vision of the world. It is a Hitchcockian world, all right, as Richard Schickel
called it in 1972, and if anything, it is darker now than it was then. *Frenzy*
is perhaps not an easy film to love, in that the audience finds the main character to be unpleasant and surly, while the physical abuse exhibited by the
villain is uncomfortably repellent. Yet it is an easy film to admire in that it
is the work of one of the enduring masters of a medium not yet a century
and a quarter old. Debates will continue over Hitchcock's position in what
Andrew Sarris once called the "pantheon" of great film directors. (In 2002,
MovieMaker magazine named Hitchcock the "most influential director of all
time," ranking him ahead of D. W. Griffith and Orson Welles.)[25] Debates
will continue over the number of masterpieces produced by any great artist,
Hitchcock among them. What there should be no debate over is the assertion that *Frenzy* is indeed the last masterpiece of one of the great pioneers
and one of the foremost innovators in the history of the medium.

Notes

1. See *Sight and Sound* "Top Ten Poll" at http://www.bfi.org.uk/sightand
sound/topten/.

2. Paul McCann, "'Psycho' Given a Curtain Call as Best Hitchcock Movie,"
Independent (UK), 6 August 1999, 1.

3. Richard Scheinin, "'Vertigo' 50 Years Later and What Hitchcock Saw," *San Jose Mercury News*, 20 November 2008, 10.

4. Robert Kapsis, *Hitchcock: The Making of a Reputation* (Chicago: University of Chicago Press, 1992), 146.

5. Kapsis, *Hitchcock*, 146.

6. Adam Lowenstein, "The Master, the Maniac, and *Frenzy*," in *Hitchcock Past and Future*, ed. Richard Allen and Sam Ishii-Gonzalès (London: Routledge, 2004), 180.

7. Lowenstein, "The Master, the Maniac, and *Frenzy*," 186.

8. Lowenstein, "The Master, the Maniac, and *Frenzy*," 190.

9. Stefan Sharff, *Alfred Hitchcock's High Vernacular: Theory and Practice* (New York: Columbia University Press, 1991), 168.

10. Laurent Bouzereau, "The Story of Frenzy," *Frenzy*, directed by Alfred Hitchcock (Universal City, Calif.: Universal Pictures Limited, 2001), DVD.

11. Donald Spoto, *The Dark Side of Genius: The Life of Alfred Hitchcock* (Boston: Little, Brown, 1983), 512.

12. Bouzereau, "The Story of Frenzy," 1:30.

13. Bouzereau, "The Story of Frenzy," 24:46.

14. Bouzereau, "The Story of Frenzy," 43:20.

15. Michael Harrington, "Is Hitchcock's Reputation Deserved?," *London Spectator*, 10 May 1997, 44.

16. Harrington, "Is Hitchcock's Reputation Deserved?," 44.

17. Terry Teachout, "The Trouble with Alfred Hitchcock," *Commentary* 127, no. 2 (February 2009): 43–46.

18. Teachout, "The Trouble with Alfred Hitchcock," 45.

19. Teachout, "The Trouble with Alfred Hitchcock," 46.

20. Michael J. Lewis, "Letter to the Editor," *Commentary* 127, no. 5 (May 2009): 12.

21. Robin Wood, *Hitchcock's Films Revisited*, rev. ed. (New York: Columbia University Press, 2002), 57–58.

22. Wood, *Hitchcock's Films Revisited*, 58.

23. "AFI Salute to Alfred Hitchcock," *Frenzy* and *Family Plot*, *Alfred Hitchcock Masterpiece Collection* (Universal City, Calif.: Universal Studios, 2005), DVD Bonus Disc.

24. Bouzereau, "The Story of Frenzy," 40:05.

25. Jennifer M. Wood, "The 25 Most Influential Directors of All Time," *MovieMaker* 47 (Summer 2002): 54–59.

Postscript
Becoming Sir Alfred

ALFRED HITCHCOCK NEVER WON an Academy Award as Best Director. He was nominated for five different films and lost each time. Perhaps more surprising, Hitchcock never won a Director's Guild of America Award either, despite nominations for eight different films. (Two films, each now considered among his classics, brought nominations for each award: *Rear Window* and *Psycho*.)

He was honored by the British Society for Film and Television Arts in 1971, during which time he was preparing the script for *Frenzy*. The Royal Family was represented at the ceremony by Princess Anne, who personally awarded Hitchcock an honorary membership in the newly formed society. This public acknowledgment by the Royal Family of the importance of Hitchcock to the British film industry might very well have been a significant marker along the path to his eventual knighthood. This can only be speculated upon, of course, since the British Royal Family is famously guarded about the process it undertakes toward granting public honors. Twice a year, once on the day designated the Queen's birthday (oddly enough, it is not really her birthday that day) and again at each New Year, Her Majesty's government publishes a list of those to be honored at that time. There are many different ranks in the British system, the highest of which is the "Order of Merit."[1] Knighthood, however, remains the most well known of the designations, if only because it is accompanied by permission to forever thereafter use the term "Sir" for gentlemen and "Dame" for gentlewomen.

When Hitchcock's knighthood was announced on December 31, 1979, there was some commentary that suggested that the honor was by

Hitchcock receiving the Irving G. Thalberg Award from Robert Wise at the Academy Awards ceremony, April 10, 1968. He never received an Oscar as Best Director. His words upon receiving this honorary award were "Thank you." He then turned and walked offstage. *Photofest*

then long overdue. One newspaper headline proclaimed as much; under a banner announcing "an overdue knighthood for Hitch," the *Baltimore Sun* noted that Hitchcock had been awarded the Legion of Honor by France in 1977 and that he might well have been proposed for the knighthood earlier but that palace infighting had prevented the title from being granted.[2]

This, too, was speculation. What we do know now—thanks to a cache of once-secret government documents obtained by the *Sunday Times* in 2003—is that Hitchcock was among a rather wide-ranging group (some three hundred in all) who had turned down proffered honors from Her Majesty's government at one time or other. In Hitchcock's case, it was the offer in 1962 of a CBE (Commander of the British Empire, often referred to as "Companion" of the British Empire), an award that is not considered a knighthood. Why he turned it down is not clear, but when he was offered the more prestigious "Knight Commander of the British Empire" at the end of 1979, the then eighty-year-old quietly accepted. That particular order comes with permission to use the term "Sir," although technically that would not have been entirely proper, since Hitchcock had been an American citizen for over two decades by then, and the title is generally reserved exclusively to British citizens. That minor detail, of course, prevented virtually no one from addressing Hitchcock as "Sir Alfred" during his last few months on earth.

According to an official Universal Studios biography of the director, published three years after Hitchcock's death (and thus intended by the studio to be the "last word" on their famous business partner), "of the honors he received, the one Hitchcock must have most cherished was the knighthood bestowed upon him in January 1980 by Her Majesty Queen Elizabeth II."[3] What Hitchcock actually thought of all this remains, too, a matter of speculation. By this time he was too frail to even make the trip to London, and the award was presented to him in his Universal bungalow by the British consul general. On the general subject of such matters, though, Hitchcock had conveyed his feelings to an interviewer back in 1971 while on the set of *Frenzy*. Speaking to Charles Champlin of the *Los Angeles Times*, who had been visiting the set to observe Hitchcock at work, the director was asked how England might have changed since he had lived there. "They say the class system is going, but I wonder," he mused to Champlin. "As long as you have titles, you have the class thing, don't you? I mean, I've never really understood titles. You become Sir George. But who ever really calls you Sir George? Waiters in good restaurants and your servants at home. To your friends, you're still good old Stinky."[4]

Irreverent as always, Hitchcock, I would like to think, rather enjoyed the irony that he would leave this world as not merely Hollywood royalty but as a recognized knight commander of his former empire. I would end the speculation around this topic with but one more postulate: Hitchcock's success in directing *Frenzy* at the age of seventy-two contributed mightily to his consideration just a few years later by the myriad forces surrounding the British Crown. In directing *Frenzy*, he was, then, becoming Sir Alfred.

Notes

1. Stanley Martin, *The Order of Merit: One Hundred Years of Matchless Honour* (London: I. B. Tauris, 2007).

2. "An Overdue Knighthood for Hitch," *Baltimore Sun*, 4 January 1980, B3.

3. "Sir Alfred Hitchcock Biography," *Universal News*, 17 August 1983, 13.

4. Charles Champlin, "What's It All About, Alfie?" *Los Angeles Times*, 2 June 1971, F1.

Appendix A:
Frenzy Cast and Crew

Cast

Richard Blaney	Jon Finch
Robert Rusk	Barry Foster
Brenda Blaney	Barbara Leigh-Hunt
Babs Milligan	Anna Massey
Chief Inspector Oxford	Alec McCowen
Mrs. Oxford	Vivien Merchant
Hetty Porter	Billie Whitelaw
Johnny Porter	Clive Swift
Felix Forsythe	Bernard Cribbins
Sergeant Spearman	Michael Bates
Monica Barling	Jean Marsh
Sir George	John Boxer
Mrs. Davison	Madge Ryan
Neville Salt	George Tovey
Gladys	Elsie Randolph
Hotel Porter	Jimmy Gardner
Solicitor in Pub	Gerald Sim
Doctor in Pub	Noel Johnson

Crew

Directed by	Alfred Hitchcock
Screenplay by	Anthony Shaffer
	From the novel *Goodbye Piccadilly, Farewell Leicester Square* by Arthur La Bern
Music Composed and Conducted by	Ron Goodwin
Associate Producer	William Hill
Director of Photography	Gil Taylor
Film Editor	John Jympson
Assistant Director	Colin M. Brewer
Production Manager	Brian Burgess
Art Director	Bob Laing
Production Designer	Syd Cain
Set Dresser	Simon Wakefield
Hairdresser	Pat McDermott
Makeup Artist	Harry Frampton
Visual Effects	Albert Whitlock
Casting	Sally Nicholl
Assistant to Mr. Hitchcock	Peggy Robertson
Wardrobe Supervisor	Dulcie Midwinter
Sound Editor	Rusty Coppleman
Sound Recordist	Gordon K. McCallum
Sound Mixer	Peter Handford
Continuity	Angela Martelli
Camera Operator	Paul Wilson

Appendix B:
Frenzy Scene List

The script from June 3 (with changes through July 9), 1971.
The script itself is copyrighted and cannot be reproduced here.
What follows is a listing of the scenes.

1 EXT. AERIAL VIEW—LONDON—DAY
2 CLOSE SHOT of the MINISTER OF HEALTH.
   2A <u>C.S. of MINISTER and the MAYOR</u>.
3 INT. RICHARD BLANEY'S BEDROOM IN THE GLOBE—
   DAY
4 INT. STAIRCASE, THE GLOBE—DAY
5 INT. THE SALOON BAR OF THE GLOBE—DAY

   INSERT A
     WE CUT to a CLOSE UP in which we note that he has only two
   pounds left.
     FULL SHOT
     He replaces his wallet, screws the two notes up into little paper balls and
   flicks them down the bar towards Forsythe with his middle finger.

  6 INT. DOWNSTAIRS HALLWAY AT GLOBE—DAY
  7 INT. SALOON BAR—GLOBE—DAY
  8 EXT. GLOBE—DAY
  9 EXT. COVENT GARDEN—DAY
10 EXT. COVENT GARDEN, EASTERN COLONNADE—DAY
11 EXT. COVENT GARDEN, SOUTHERN COLONNADE—DAY

INSERT B
WE CUT to an EXTREME CLOSE UP of the paper to see the horse's name, and also note that in the Stop Press column there is a freshly printed brief account of the new Necktie Murder. It is headed: New Victim for "Necktie Murderer," and goes on—"A young woman, believed to be the fourth victim of the strangler, was found floating this morning in the River Thames near Westminster Bridge. As before the tie which strangled her had been left round her neck."
FULL SHOT
Rusk takes no notice of the item.

12 EXT. NELL OF OLD DRURY PUB, DRURY LANE—DAY
13 INT. NELL OF OLD DRURY PUB—DAY
14 EXT. RUSK'S APARTMENT, HENRIETTA STREET—DAY
15 EXT. HENRIETTA STREET—DAY
16 EXT. OXFORD STREET—DAY
17 EXT. ALLEYWAY OUTSIDE MATRIMONIAL AGENCY—DAY
18 INT. STAIRS LEADING FROM STREET TO MATRIMONIAL AGENCY ON FIRST FLOOR—DAY
19 INT. OUTER OFFICE OF MATRIMONIAL OFFICE—DAY
20 INT. STAIRS LEADING FROM MATRIMONIAL AGENCY TO STREET—DAY
21 INT. OUTER OFFICE MATRIMONIAL AGENCY—DAY
22 INT. INNER OFFICE MATRIMONIAL AGENCY—DAY
23 INT. OUTER OFFICE MATRIMONIAL AGENCY—DAY
24 INT. INNER OFFICE MATRIMONIAL AGENCY—DAY
25 INT. DINING ROOM—WOMEN'S CLUB—NIGHT

INSERT C
A CLOSE UP of Blaney's hand as it grips his brandy glass. He crashes it, and blood covers his palm.
FULL SHOT
A waitress who has been hovering near, half listening to the conversation, MOVES FORWARD to pick up the pieces.
                         BRENDA
         (hissing)
Now look what you've done.
The furious Blaney directs a look of rage at his wife. The waitress, picking up the pieces of glass from the table, intercepts the look.
                        WAITRESS
Oh sir, let me help.

BLANEY

Leave me alone.

The waitress HURRIES AWAY, half scared. There is a silence between them. The room resumes its chatter. Blaney's look of rage fades, and is replaced by a look of conciliation.

26 INT. LOBBY OF WOMEN'S CLUB—NIGHT
27 EXT. STREET OUTSIDE WOMEN'S CLUB—NIGHT
28 EXT. MEWS, BRENDA BLANEY'S HOUSE—NIGHT
29 INT. DORMITORY IN SALVATION ARMY HOSTEL—NIGHT
30 INT. INNER OFFICE, MATRIMONIAL AGENCY—DAY
31 INT. HALLWAY BOTTOM OF STAIRS OUTSIDE
      MATRIMONIAL AGENCY—DAY
32 EXT. ALLEYWAY OUTSIDE MATRIMONIAL AGENCY—DAY
33 INT. HALLWAY BOTTOM OF STAIRS OUTSIDE
      MATRIMONIAL AGENCY—DAY
34 EXT. ALLEYWAY OUTSIDE MATRIMONIAL AGENCY—DAY
35 INT. TELEPHONE BOX IN CROWDED STREET—DAY
36 INT. BAR AT GLOBE PUB—DAY
37 INT. PHONE BOOTH—DAY
38 INT. BAR OF GLOBE PUB—DAY
39 INT. PHONE BOOTH—DAY
40 INT. SALOON BAR GLOBE PUB—DAY
41 INT. MATRIMONIAL AGENCY OUTER OFFICE—DAY
42 INT. INNER OFFICE MATRIMONIAL AGENCY—DAY
43 INT. OUTER OFFICE MATRIMONIAL AGENCY—DAY
44 EXT. LEICESTER SQUARE—DAY
45 INT. TAXI CAB—DAY
46 EXT. STREET OUTSIDE COBURG HOTEL BAYSWATER—
      DAY
47 INT. LOBBY COBURG HOTEL—DAY
48 INT. COBURG HOTEL, LANDING AT TOP OF STAIRS AND
      CORRIDOR—DAY
49 INT. HOTEL BEDROOM, COBURG HOTEL—DAY
50 INT. CORRIDOR, COBURG HOTEL—DAY
51 INT. BEDROOM AT COBURG HOTEL—DAY
52 EXT. HENRIETTA STREET OUTSIDE RUSK'S
      APARTMENT—NIGHT.
      [Here is an added scene of Rusk explaining to a cop about a girl run-
      ning from his apartment. It is later dropped.]

53 INT. BEDROOM AT COBURG HOTEL—EARLY MORNING
54 INT. LOBBY OF THE COBURG HOTEL—MORNING
55 EXT. BAYSWATER ROAD COBURG HOTEL—DAY
56 INT. LOBBY COBURG HOTEL—DAY
57 INT. LANDING AND CORRIDOR AT COBURG HOTEL—
     DAY
58 EXT. BACK OF COBURG HOTEL—DAY
59 EXT. HYDE PARK NEAR THE HILTON HOTEL—DAY
     <u>INSERT D</u>
     HETTY PORTER, a striking looking lady of thirty-five or there-
     abouts stares down into the park with compulsive interest.
60 EXT. HYDE PARK NEAR HILTON HOTEL—DAY
61 INT. LIVING ROOM OF SUITE, HILTON HOTEL—DAY
62 INT. DOOR FROM BACKSTAIRS LEADING INTO
     CORRIDOR, HILTON HOTEL—DAY
63 INT. CORRIDOR, HILTON HOTEL—DAY
64 INT. LIVING ROOM OF SUITE IN HILTON HOTEL—DAY
65 EXT. NEW SCOTLAND YARD—DAY
66 INT. INSP. OXFORD'S OFFICE—NEW SCOTLAND YARD—
     DAY
67 INT. INSP. OXFORD'S OFFICE—DAY
68 INT. BAR OF THE GLOBE PUB—DAY
69 INT. OXFORD'S OFFICE—SCOTLAND YARD—DAY
70 INT. BAR OF THE GLOBE PUB—DAY
71 INT. OXFORD'S OFFICE—SCOTLAND YARD—DAY
72 INT. BAR OF THE GLOBE PUB—DAY
73 INT. OXFORD'S OFFICE—SCOTLAND YARD—DAY
74 INT. BAR OF THE GLOBE PUB—DAY
75 INT. OXFORD'S OFFICE—SCOTLAND YARD—DAY
76 INT. BAR OF THE GLOBE PUB—DAY
77 INT. THE PRIVATE BAR OF THE GLOBE PUB—DAY
78 INT. SALOON BAR, THE GLOBE—DAY
79 EXT. THE STREET OUTSIDE THE GLOBE PUB—DAY
80 EXT. SOUTHERN SIDE OF COVENT GARDEN MARKET—
     DAY
81 EXT. RUSK'S HOUSE IN HENRIETTA STREET—DAY
82 INT. THE STAIRS LEADING UP TO RUSK'S APARTMENT—
     DAY

83 EXT. HENRIETTA STREET OUTSIDE RUSK'S APARTMENT—DAY
The CAMERA continues its retreat across the street outside Rusk's house and comes to rest holding the whole building in a longish shot.

84 EXT. ASHLEY GARDENS ALONGSIDE WESTMINSTER CATHEDRAL—EVENING

85 INT. APARTMENT BLOCK, ASHLEY GARDENS, CORRIDOR—EVENING

86 INT. HALLWAY, OXFORD'S APARTMENT—EVENING

87 INT. LIVING ROOM/DINING ROOM—OXFORD'S APARTMENT—EVENING

88 INT. KITCHEN—OXFORD'S APARTMENT—EVENING

89 INT. DINING AREA/LIVING ROOM—OXFORD'S APARTMENT—EVENING

90 EXT. COVENT GARDEN—NIGHT

91 INT. HALLWAY AND STAIRS LEADING UP TO RUSK'S APARTMENT—NIGHT

92 INT. RUSK'S APARTMENT—NIGHT

93 DELETED

94 INT. RUSK'S APARTMENT—NIGHT

95 INT. RUSK'S APARTMENT—DAY

96 INT. RUSK'S APARTMENT—NIGHT

97 INT. STAIRS OUTSIDE RUSK'S APARTMENT—NIGHT

98 EXT. COVENT GARDEN—NIGHT

99 INT. TRUCK UNDER TARPAULIN—NIGHT

100 INT. TRUCK DRIVER'S CABIN—NIGHT

101 INT. TRUCK UNDER TARPAULIN—NIGHT

102 EXT. DUAL CARRIAGEWAY OUTSIDE LONDON—NIGHT

103 INT. THE TRUCK UNDER THE TARPAULIN—NIGHT

104 EXT. THE ROAD—NIGHT

105 INT. THE TRUCK UNDER THE TARPAULIN—NIGHT

106 EXT. THE M.1 MOTORWAY—NIGHT

107 INT. THE TRUCK UNDER THE TARPAULIN—NIGHT

108 EXT. ALL NIGHT CAFÉ ON THE M.1 MOTORWAY—NIGHT

109 INT. MEN'S TOILET OUTSIDE BUSY BEE CAFÉ—NIGHT

110 CAR PARK AT BUSY BEE CAFÉ AND M.1 MOTORWAY—NIGHT

111 INT. MEN'S TOILET—NIGHT
112 EXT. BUSY BEE CAR PARK—NIGHT
113 INT. BUSY BEE CAFÉ—NIGHT
114 EXT. THE M.1 MOTORWAY—NIGHT
115 EXT. HUMP-BACKED BRIDGE LEADING TO A
     SECONDARY ROAD
116 EXT. HILL ROAD IN THE COUNTRY—NIGHT
117 EXT. A SIDE ROAD AT RIGHT ANGLES TO THE HILL
     ROAD—NIGHT
118 INT. POLICE CAR—NIGHT
119 INT. DRIVER'S CABIN OF TRUCK
120 EXT. HILL ROAD—NIGHT
121 INT. THE LIVING ROOM OF THE PORTER'S SUITE IN
     THE HILTON HOTEL—MORNING
122 EXT. COVENT GARDEN MARKET—DAY
123 EXT. BARTLETT'S FRUIT STALL ON THE SOUTHERN
     COLONNADE—DAY—INT. RUSK'S FRUIT SHOP,
     COVENT GARDEN—DAY
124 EXT. RUSK'S SHOP, COVENT GARDEN—DAY
125 INT. RUSK'S SHOP, COVENT GARDEN—DAY
126 EXT. RUSK'S SHOP, COVENT GARDEN—DAY
127 INT. HALLWAY, RUSK'S OUTSIDE APARTMENT—DAY
128 EXT. SOUTHAMPTON STREET AND HENRIETTA
     STREET—DAY
129 INT. HALLWAY OUTSIDE RUSK'S APARTMENT—DAY
130 INT. RUSK'S APARTMENT—DAY
131 INT. HALLWAY OUTSIDE RUSK'S APARTMENT—DAY
132 EXT. COVENT GARDEN OUTSIDE RUSK'S HOUSE—DAY
133 EXT. COVENT GARDEN, NEAR THE FRONT OF THE
     INIGO JONES CHURCH—DAY
134 INT. C.I.D. ROOM, BOW STREET POLICE STATION—DAY
135 INT. CORRIDOR OUTSIDE THE DOORS OF NUMBER
     ONE COURT, THE OLD BAILEY—AND INSIDE NUMBER
     ONE COURT—DAY
136 INT. THE CORRIDOR UNDER THE COURT LEADING
     TO THE CELLS—DAY
137 INT. THE TEMPORARY CELL AT THE OLD BAILEY—DAY
138 INT. NUMBER ONE COURT, OLD BAILEY—DAY
139 INT. WORMWOOD SCRUBS PRISON—GALLERY—NIGHT
     (MATTE)

140 INT. WORMWOOD SCRUBS PRISON—GROUND
     FLOOR—NIGHT
141 EXT. WORMWOOD SCRUBS PRISON—NIGHT
142 EXT. UNLOADING BAY OUTSIDE HOSPITAL—NIGHT
143 INT. OXFORD'S OFFICE—SCOTLAND YARD—DAY
144 INT. TAXI CAB IN COVENT GARDEN MARKET—DAY
145 INT. OUTER OFFICE OF BLANEY MATRIMONIAL
     AGENCY—DAY
146 INT. THE LIVING ROOM /DINING AREA OF OXFORD'S
     APARTMENT—EVENING
147 INT. KITCHEN OF OXFORD'S APARTMENT—EVENING
148 INT. LIVING ROOM/DINING AREA OF OXFORD'S
     APARTMENT—EVENING
149 INT. HALLWAY, OXFORD'S APARTMENT—EVENING
150 INT. LIVING ROOM/DINING ROOM, OXFORD'S
     APARTMENT—EVENING
151 INT. HOSPITAL WARD—NIGHT
     <u>INSERT E</u>

C.S. of remains of pills in bottle
A HIGH SHOT of the ward SHOWS a crowd of milling nurses, interns
and prisoners gathered round the sleeping guard. Some are attempting to
raise him from the floor. In all the commotion, we scarcely notice Blaney
slipping out of the ward. The guard is carried through the door. The prisoners crowd forward.

152 INT. CORRIDOR OF HOSPITAL—NIGHT
153 DELETED
154 EXT. HOSPITAL CAR PARK AND MAIN ROAD—NIGHT
155 EXT. THE ROAD OUTSIDE WORMWOOD SCRUBS
     PRISON—NIGHT
156 INT. LIVING ROOM/DINING ROOM OF OXFORD'S
     APARTMENT—NIGHT
157 EXT. COVENT GARDEN, WESTERN SIDE—NIGHT
158 INT. CAR, COVENT GARDEN—NIGHT
159 EXT. COVENT GARDEN MARKET, WESTERN SIDE—
     NIGHT
160 EXT. COVENT GARDEN, WESTERN SIDE—NIGHT
161 INT. HALLWAY AND STAIRS OF RUSK'S BUILDING—
     NIGHT
162 INT. RUSK'S APARTMENT—NIGHT

CONCLUDES WITH:

OXFORD

Good evening, Mr. Rusk. . . . You don't have your tie on.

THE CAMERA ZOOMS IN to an EXTREME CLOSE UP of Rusk's horrified face. Instinctively, his eyes flick directly to the body. The trunk drops to the floor with a crash and his mouth opens wide; but no sound comes.

Appendix C:
The Entire Continuity
Sheet for September 8, 1971

321. Sep 8

sc 30

MS down onto carpet in front of door . . . Brenda (double) comes in from right . . . Rusk's (double) right hand catches her right ankle . . . and she falls to the ground on her face . . . he drops her ankle . . . starts to move past her . . .

Two takes, second printed

322. Sep 8

sc 30

CS Rusk's right hand catching Brenda's right ankle to make her fall to the ground. (Doubles)

Two takes, both printed

323. Sep 8

sc 30

Camera shooting from low angle onto Rusk as he drops Brenda's right ankle comes forward . . . pulls her up out of shot . . .

One take, printed

W.T. 323X covers sound of Brenda's fall and Rusk's movements. [W.T. = "wild track"]

324. Sep 8

sc 30

Low side angle onto Rusk and Brenda as he pulls her up into shot and throws her back into arm chair . . . pan with her

One take

W.T. 324X covers dialogue . . .

325. Sep 8

sc 30

Camera starts on Rusk standing centre of office . . . pan him down to Brenda in arm chair . . . her head falls over onto chair arm so that we are shooting past her head onto him

Dialogue: "Leave me alone, please" to "I told you I've locked the outside door. We won't be disturbed."

One take

326. Sep 8

sc 30

MCS . . . side angle Brenda on right head over arm of chair . . . Rusk on left lying on top of her . . .

One take

327. Sep 8

sc 30

Camera shooting close down onto Brenda's head over arm of chair . . . over Rusk's head bending down over her . . .

One take

328. Sep 8

sc 30

Side angle MCS onto Brenda's head over arm of chair . . . Rusk lying on top of her . . . focus is on Brenda's hand as she points . . .

One take

329. Sep 8

sc 30

Camera starts n Rusk standing left of window . . . pan right with him as he moves forward and leans over Brenda lying over chair . . .

NB. This TV alternative is to cut out Rusk pulling her down onto the ground.

330. Sep 8

sc 30

MCS shooting down onto back of Brenda's head on arm of chair Rusk lying on top of her . . . His right hand goes to her right shoulder (preparing to rip her dress) . . .

One take

331. Sep 8

sc 30

Low angle onto Brenda's legs with Rusk's between them . . . Brenda's legs kicking during struggle . . . various sizes

One take

332. Sep 8

sc 30

CS Rusk's right hand fumbling at Brenda's dress on her r. shoulder . . . tearing it apart and the brassiere . . .

Two takes, second printed

333. Sep 8

sc 30

CS Rusk's right hand tearing down Brenda's tights . . . (Double)

One take

334. Sep 8

sc 30

CS Rusk kneeling . . . facing camera right . . . finishing tearing Brenda's dress O.S . . .

Two takes, second printed

335. Sep 8

sc 30

CS Brenda sitting in arm chair . . . head against back of chair. Brenda: Thou shalt not be afraid . . . thru in all thy ways . . ."

Three takes, last printed

336. Sep 8

sc 30

High angle above Brenda sitting back in chair onto Rusk who moves closer to her . . .

One take

337. Sep 8

sc 30

CS Brenda's (Double's) exposed left breast . . . her left hand pulls bra up
to cover it . . . and shoulder strap back onto shoulder . . .

Note: "NB. The idea was to put this in after Brenda says: 'Deny me you?'
I think."

Two takes, second printed

338. Sep 8

sc 30

CS Brenda's head against back of chair . . . shoulders bare . . .

Rusk: O.S. Lovely, . . . lovely . . . lovely . . . She turns her head . . . Please
don't deny me.

Brenda: Deny you? . . . His hands go round her throat . . . then he draws
back . . .

Rusk: O.S. You bitch . . .

Seven takes, 6 and 7 printed

Appendix D:
Frenzy Final List of Sequences

1) CREDITS—Tower Bridge.
2) MINISTER addressing crowd.
3) Discovery of body.
4) Introduction of BLANEY in bedroom. He descends to GLOBE saloon Bar. Argument with FORSYTHE . . . BABS defends BLANEY . . . BLANEY exits Globe.
5) BABS follows BLANEY outside . . . "What are you going to do?" She returns into GLOBE after FORSYTHE.
6) BLANEY walks through Covent Garden to:
7) HARTLETTS. Introduction of RUSK . . . "Take some grapes."
8) POLICEMAN comes to RUSK . . . BLANEY has vanished.
9) BLANEY enters Nell of Old Drury . . . discussion between DOCTOR and SOLICITOR . . . BLANEY argues with BARMAN.
10) BLANEY walking along Henrietta Street, is introduced to RUSK's MUM at window.
11) BLANEY walks on—squashes grapes.
12) Oxford Street to Matrimonial Agency. MONICA talking to Mrs. DAVISON and Mr. SALT
13) BLANEY demands to see BRENDA.
14) BRENDA talks to BLANEY in her office . . . lets MONICA go . . . BRENDA and BLANEY make dinner date.
15) BRENDA and BLANEY at Women's Club—BLANEY breaks glass during argument.
16) Lobby of Women's Club. BRENDA slips money in his coat.

17) Arrival of taxi at BRENDA's Mews Flat. They enter after dismissing taxi.

18) Salvation Army.

19) RUSK enters Matrimonial Agency—rapes and murders BRENDA. Exits after eating apple.

20) RUSK crosses alleyway.

21) BLANEY enters alleyway, upstairs, tries locked door and exits.

22) MONICA crossing alleyway, see BLANEY, enters door. Hold on doorway—screams.

23) Telephone box—BLANEY calls BABS. FORSYTHE answers . . . BABS grabs phone . . . They arrive to meet in Leicester Square. FORSYTHE reproves her . . . customer holds out rotten egg.

24) Matrimonial Agency. Photographers, etc., OXFORD enters and talks to weeping MONICA, who describes BLANEY—discover missing money—identify face powder.

25) BLANEY awaiting BABS in Leicester Square. Her taxi arrives—he jumps in and it drives off to the Coburg Hotel.

26) Arrival at Coburg Hotel—pay taxi—register with Receptionist—go up elevator with BERTIE—enter room—BLANEY in doorway—takes off dirty clothes and sends them to cleaners.

27) Early morning—BABS awakens—goes to bathroom—PAN DOWN to newspaper.

28) BERTIE and GLADYS read newspaper—summon Police, who arrive—all go upstairs to empty Cupid Room—look down fire escape.

29) BLANEY explaining to BABS on park bench—interrupted by PORTER's shout.

30) Zoom up to Hetty.

31) BABS, BLANEY, PORTER go furtively upstairs into suite.

32) HETTY accuses BLANEY—BABS exits.

33) New Scotland Yard sign.

34) OXFORD's office—eating breakfast—talks to SPEARMAN about psychopath killers—FORSYTHE phones him re describing BLANEY and BABS.

35) BABS returns to Globe—row with FORSYTHE—she quits.

36) FORSYTHE returns to Bar where RUSK and JIM are discussing potato problems.

37) Outside Globe RUSK rises behind her and they walk through glassed in flower market where he offers her his place to stay. "Your whole life ahead of you."

38) They cross Henrietta Street—go up RUSK's stairs—"My type of woman"—closes door. CAMERA RETREATS downstairs—out into street—screech of brakes.

39) OXFORD enters his apartment—"Soupe de Poisson" while he tells Mrs. OXFORD of evidence against BLANEY—"Caille aus raisins."

40) Night. RUSK wheels barrow with sack—unloads sack onto truck. Returns to his apartment—he drinks—eats pork pie—misses pin—searches for it—FLASHBACK—rushes out.

41) RUSK is trapped on truck, which moves off. Can't find pin. Potatoes spill. Car stops truck. RUSK finds pin—cannot alight. Truck arrives at café and DRIVER goes in. RUSK hides in men's room. Truck Driver drives off.

42) Police car spot legs and give chase. Body falls into road. POLICEMEN and TRUCK DRIVER gather round.

43) Hilton Hotel. HETTY awakens BLANEY with news of BABS' murder—argument and BLANEY leaves.

44) Police melee at Covent Garden.

45) FORSYTHE talks to RUSK outside the shop then exits.

46) RUSK enters shops and discovers hidden BLANEY. RUSK exits with BLANEY's bag and goes to his apartment.

47) BLANEY walks down street and enters RUSK's apartment. RUSK exits.

48) POLICEMEN rush in and arrest BLANEY—downstairs.

49) POLICEMAN and RUSK watch BLANEY being taken away.

50) Bow Street Station. OXFORD enters and charges BLANEY, who calls out, "It's Rusk."

51) Old Bailey. BLANEY sentenced and taken down to cells. OXFORD sitting in empty courtroom.

52) Ext. Covent Garden—taxi with OXFORD and PHOTO-GRAPHER—RUSK is pointed out.

53) Matrimonial Agency—OXFORD and MONICA discuss Mr. Robinson.

54) EXT. WORMWOOD SCRUBBS.

55) INT. WORMWOOD SCRUBBS—BLANEY, after giving a look, throws himself downstairs.

56) Ambulance takes him to hospital.

57) OXFORD's apartment – pig's trotters (pied de porc). SPEARMAN enters with clothes brush.

58) Hospital Ward—BLANEY escapes down corridor—takes lever from trunk of car—starts car—drives off.

59) OXFORD hears of BLANEY's escape and exits.

60) OXFORD and SPEARMAN in car re "suicide attempt."

61) BLANEY walks up street, up RUSK's stairs, across room and brings down lever on blonde head—girl's arm with bangles falls out. OXFORD arrives—looks—hears sound of trunk—motions silence—RUSK enters with trunk—looks to BLANEY and OXFORD—lets trunk fall . . . Cast Credits over trunk.

Works Cited

"AFI Salute to Alfred Hitchcock." *Frenzy* and *Family Plot*. DVD Bonus Disc, *Alfred Hitchcock Masterpiece Collection*. Universal City, Calif.: Universal Studios, 2005.

Allen, Jeanne Thomas. "The Representation of Violence to Women: Hitchcock's 'Frenzy.'" *Film Quarterly* 38, no. 3 (Spring 1985): 30–38.

Allen, Richard, and S. Ishii Gonzalès. *Alfred Hitchcock Centenary Essays*. London: British Film Institute, 1999.

"An Overdue Knighthood for Hitch." *Baltimore Sun*, 4 January 1980, B3.

Arnold, Gary. "'Frenzy': The Thrill Is Gone." *Washington Post*, 23 June 1972, B1.

Auiler, Dan. *Hitchcock's Notebooks: An Authorized and Illustrated Look inside the Creative Mind of Alfred Hitchcock*. New York: Avon, 1999.

Barr, Charles. *Vertigo*. London: British Film Institute, 2002.

Beck, Marilyn. "'Frenzy' to Continue Hitchcock Tradition." *Hartford Courant*, 24 March 1971, 18.

Belton, John. *Cinema Stylists*. Metuchen, N.J.: Scarecrow Press, 1983.

Bergan, Ronald. "Obituary: Peggy Robertson; Smoothing Out the Hitch." *Guardian*, 16 February 1998, 13.

Bogdanovich, Peter. "Period Piece." *New York Magazine*, 25 February 1974, 64.

Boileau, Pierre, and Thomas Narcejac. *Sueurs froides*. Paris: Denoël, 1958.

Bourget, Jean-Loup. "Le Dernier Carré?" *Positif* 149 (April 1973): 1–13.

Bouzereau, Laurent. *Hitchcock: Piece by Piece*. New York: Abrams, 2010.

———. "The Story of Frenzy." *Frenzy*. DVD. Directed by Alfred Hitchcock. Universal City, Calif.: Universal Pictures Limited, 2001.

Boyum, Joy Gould. "Alfred Hitchcock's Pleasurable Horrors." *Wall Street Journal*, 30 June 1972, 12.

Bruck, Connie. *When Hollywood Had a King*. New York: Random House, 2003.

Canby, Vincent. "Critic's Choice—Ten Best Films of '72." *New York Times*, 31 December 1972, D1–9.

_____. "'Frenzy,' Hitchcock in Dazzling Form." *New York Times*, 22 June 1972, 48.

Champlin, Charles. "Hitchcock's Special Place." *Los Angeles Times*, 14 July 1972, F1.

_____. "What's It All About, Alfie?" *Los Angeles Times*, 2 June 1971, F1.

Clark, Paul Sargent. "Hitchcock's Finest Hour." *Today's Filmmaker* (November 1972): 42.

Cocks, Jay. "Still the Master." *Time* 99, no. 25 (19 June 1972): 70.

Cohen, Paula Marantz. *Alfred Hitchcock: The Legacy of Victorianism.* Lexington: University Press of Kentucky, 1995.

Coleman, Herbert. *The Man Who Knew Hitchcock.* Lanham, Md.: Scarecrow Press, 2007.

de Baroncelli, Jean. "le cinema." *Le Monde*, 21–22 Mai 1972, 15.

DeRosa, Steven. *Writing with Hitchcock: The Collaboration of Alfred Hitchcock and John Michael Hayes.* New York: Faber and Faber, 2001.

Diehl, Digby. "Q & A Alfred Hitchcock." *Los Angeles Times*, 25 June 1972, W20.

Du Cane, John. "Hitchcock Inverts." *Time Out*, 11 August 1972, 43.

Dumont, Tim. "'Frenzy' Focuses on Sex Slayings." *Hartford Courant*, 23 June 1972, 28.

Durgnat, Raymond. *The Strange Case of Alfred Hitchcock.* London: Faber and Faber, 1974.

Elliott, David. "Frenzy over 'Frenzy': His Best or Worst?" *Chicago Daily News*, 1 August 1972, 11.

Evening Standard, 12 July 1971, 8.

Falk, Quentin. *Mr. Hitchcock.* London: Haus, 2007.

Family Plot Folder #200 of the Alfred Hitchcock papers at the Margaret Herrick Library of the Academy of Motion Picture Arts and Sciences, Beverly Hills, California.

Flatley, Guy. "'I Tried to Be Discreet with That Nude Corpse.'" *New York Times*, 18 June 1972, D13.

Frenzy Folders #241 through #345 of the Alfred Hitchcock papers at the Margaret Herrick Library of the Academy of Motion Picture Arts and Sciences, Beverly Hills, California.

Gardner, R. H. "Alfred Hitchcock's Latest Thriller Less Thrilling Than Funny." *Baltimore Sun*, 26 June 1972, B1.

Garrett, Greg. "Hitchcock's Women on Hitchcock: A Panel Discussion with Janet Leigh, Tippi Hedren, Karen Black, Suzanne Pleshette, and Eva Marie Saint." *Literature/Film Quarterly* 27, no. 2 (Spring 1999): 78–89.

Gilliatt, Penelope. "The Current Cinema." *New Yorker*, 24 June 1972, 51–52.

Gottlieb, Sidney, ed. *Hitchcock on Hitchcock.* Berkeley: University of California Press, 1995.

Hall, Barbara. *An Oral History with Peggy Robertson.* Academy of Motion Picture Arts and Sciences, Oral History Program, 2002.

Harrington, Michael. "Is Hitchcock's Reputation Deserved?" *London Spectator*, 10 May 1997, 44–46.

"Hitch." *Take One* 1, no. 1 (September/October 1966): 14–17.

Hitchcock, Alfred. "Close Your Eyes and Visualize!" *Stage* 13 (July 1936): 52–53.

_____. "Life among the Stars." *News Chronicle*, 1–5 March 1937. Quoted in *Hitchcock on Hitchcock*, edited by Sidney Gottlieb. Berkeley: University of California Press,1995.

Hollywood Reporter, 15–23 June 1972.

Hotchner, A. E. *Doris Day: Her Own Story*. New York: William Morrow, 1975.

Jhirad, Susan. "Hitchcock's Women." *Cineaste* 13, no. 4 (Autumn 1984): 31–33.

Johnson, Albert. "*Frenzy*." *Film Quarterly* 26, no. 1 (Autumn 1972): 58–60.

Johnston, Laurie. "Women's Group to Observe Rights Day Here Today." *New York Times*, 25 August 1972, 40.

Kapsis, Robert. *Hitchcock: The Making of a Reputation*. Chicago: University of Chicago Press, 1992.

Kelly, Kevin. "Fright Power Is His." *Boston Globe*, 18 June 1972, 69–70.

Knight, Arthur. "Whodunit Didn't." *Saturday Review*, 24 June 1972, 74.

Krohn, Bill. *Hitchcock at Work*. London: Phaidon, 2000.

La Bern, Arthur. *Goodbye Piccadilly, Farewell, Leicester Square*. New York: Stein and Day, 1967.

LaValley, Albert, ed. *Focus on Hitchcock*. Englewood Cliffs, N.J.: Prentice-Hall, 1972.

Leff, Leonard J. *Hitchcock with Selznick: The Rich and Strange Collaboration of Alfred Hitchcock and David O. Selznick in Hollywood*. New York: Weidenfeld & Nicholson, 1987.

Leitch, Thomas. *The Encyclopedia of Alfred Hitchcock*. New York: Checkmark, 2002.

_____. *Find the Director and Other Hitchcock Games*. Athens: University of Georgia Press, 1991.

_____. "The Hitchcock Moment." *Hitchcock Annual* 6 (1997–1998): 19–39.

Lewis, Michael J. "Letter to the Editor," *Commentary* 127, no. 5 (May 2009): 12.

Lowenstein, Adam. "The Master, the Maniac, and *Frenzy*." In *Hitchcock Past and Future*, edited by Richard Allen and Sam Ishii-Gonzalès. London: Routledge, 2004.

Martin, Stanley. *The Order of Merit: One Hundred Years of Matchless Honour*. London: I. B. Tauris, 2007.

McCann, Paul. "'Psycho' Given a Curtain Call as Best Hitchcock Movie." *Independent* (UK), 6 August 1999, 1.

McDougal, Dennis. *The Last Mogul: Lew Wasserman, MCA, and the Hidden History of Hollywood*. New York: Crown, 1998.

McGilligan, Patrick. *Alfred Hitchcock: A Life in Darkness and Light*. New York: HarperCollins, 2003.

Modleski, Tania. *The Women Who Knew Too Much.* 2nd ed. New York: Routledge, 2005.

Mogg, Ken. *The Alfred Hitchcock Story.* London: Titan, 1999.

——. *The Alfred Hitchcock Story.* Rev. ed. London: Titan, 2008.

Murphy, A. D. "*Frenzy.*" *Variety,* 31 May 1972, 6.

O'Connell, Pat Hitchcock, and Laurent Bouzereau. *Alma Hitchcock: The Woman behind the Man.* New York: Berkley, 2003.

"Old Master 'Hitch,'" *Cinema TV Today.* 3 June 1972, 6.

Poague, Leland A. "The Detective in Hitchcock's *Frenzy*: His Ancestors and Significance." *Journal of Popular Film and Television* 2, no. 1 (1973): 47–58.

Pudovkin, Vsevolod. *Film Technique and Film Acting.* London: Vision Press, 1958.

Rebello, Stephen. *Alfred Hitchcock and the Making of* Psycho. New York: St. Martin's, 1990.

Reed, Rex. "Oh, What a Lovely Murder." *Washington Post,* 11 June 1972, F1–5.

Robinson, David. "Old Master." *Financial Times,* 26 May 1972, 3.

Rohmer, Eric, and Claude Chabrol. *Hitchcock.* Paris: Editions Universitaires, 1957.

Rothman, William. *Hitchcock: The Murderous Gaze.* Cambridge: Harvard University Press, 1982.

Scheinin, Richard. "'Vertigo' 50 Years Later and What Hitchcock Saw." *San Jose Mercury News,* 20 November 2008, 10–11.

Schickel, Richard. "The Return of Alfred the Great." *Life* 72, no. 21 (2 June 1972): 25.

——. "We're Living in a Hitchcock World, All Right." *New York Times Magazine,* 29 October 1972, SM40, SM46.

Sgammato, Joseph. "The Discreet Qualms of the Bourgeoisie: Hitchcock's 'Frenzy.'" *Sight and Sound* 42, no. 3 (Summer 1973): 134–37.

Shaffer, Anthony. *So What Did You Expect?* London: Picador, 2001.

Sharff, Stefan. *Alfred Hitchcock's High Vernacular: Theory and Practice.* New York: Columbia University Press, 1991.

——. *The Elements of Cinema: Toward a Theory of Cinesthetic Impact.* New York: Columbia University Press, 1982.

Sharp, Kathleen. *Mr. and Mrs. Hollywood: Edie and Lew Wasserman and Their Entertainment Empire.* New York: Carroll and Graf, 2003.

Sight and Sound. "Top Ten Poll" at http://www.bfi.org.uk/sightandsound/topten/.

"Sir Alfred Hitchcock Biography." *Universal News,* 17 August 1983, 13.

Siskel, Gene. "'Frenzy': Hitchcock Returns in Style." *Chicago Tribune,* 14 July 1972, B1.

Skerry, Philip J. *Psycho in the Shower: The History of Cinema's Most Famous Scene.* New York: Continuum, 2009.

——. *The Shower Scene in Hitchcock's* Psycho: *Creating Cinematic Suspense and Terror.* Lewiston, N.Y.: Edwin Mellen, 2005.

Spoto, Donald. *The Dark Side of Genius: The Life of Alfred Hitchcock.* Boston: Little, Brown, 1983.

_____. *Spellbound by Beauty: Alfred Hitchcock and His Leading Ladies*. New York: Harmony Books, 2008.

Sterritt, David. *The Films of Alfred Hitchcock*. Cambridge: Cambridge University Press, 1993.

Sullivan, Victoria. "Does 'Frenzy' Degrade Women?" *New York Times*, 30 July 1972, D9.

Sweeney, Louise. "Foster and Finch in Hitchcock's 'Frenzy.'" *Christian Science Monitor*, 24 June 1972, 6.

Taylor, John Russell. *Hitch: The Life and Times of Alfred Hitchcock*. London: Faber and Faber, 1978.

_____. "Hitchcock Magic Is Intact." *London Times*, 23 May 1972, 15.

Teachout, Terry. "The Trouble with Alfred Hitchcock," *Commentary* 127, no. 2 (February 2009): 43–46.

Thomas, Kevin. "Hitchcock's Best Picture in Years—'Frenzy.'" *Los Angeles Times*, 25 June 1972, 22.

Truffaut, François. *Hitchcock*. New York: Simon and Schuster, 1967.

_____. *Hitchcock*. Rev. ed. New York: Simon & Schuster/Touchstone, 1985.

_____. "Un Gâteau Hitchcock Fait à la Maison." *Paris Match*, no. 1205 (10 June 1972): 83.

Variety, 1 June–6 December 1972.

Williams, J. Danvers. "What I'd Do to the Stars: An Interview with Alfred Hitchcock." *Film Weekly*, 4 March 1939, 12.

Wood, Jennifer M. "The 25 Most Influential Directors of All Time." *MovieMaker* 47 (Summer 2002): 54–59.

Wood, Robin. "Fear of Spying." *American Film* 9, no. 2 (November 1983): 28–35.

_____. *Hitchcock's Films*. London: A. S. Barnes, 1969.

_____. *Hitchcock's Films Revisited*. New York: Columbia University Press, 1989.

_____. *Hitchcock's Films Revisited*. Rev. ed. New York: Columbia University Press, 2002.

Zimmerman, Paul D. "Return of the Master." *Newsweek*, 26 June 1972, 83–84.

Index

Note: Page numbers in italics refer to photographs.

About the Author

Raymond Foery has been teaching at the college level for over forty years and is currently professor of communications at Quinnipiac University, where he founded the media production program, presently incorporated into the department of Film, Video, and Interactive Media. After receiving his undergraduate degree in philosophy and literature from Notre Dame, he went on to study film at Columbia University, where he wrote his dissertation on Louis Lumière and the invention of cinema. It was at Columbia that he initially became an admirer of the work of Alfred Hitchcock, an interest that has led to several presentations at the annual Popular Culture Association conference. At Quinnipiac, he continues to teach an annual senior seminar on Hitchcock. His other research interests include international and independent cinema, including the American avant-garde, and the process by which novels or plays are translated into works of cinema. Before coming to Quinnipiac, he taught at Bard and at Dartmouth, where he was a director of the film studies program. He also founded and edited a New York arts journal, the *Downtown Review*, and directed an independent film and video foundation in Vermont. He has recently written a chapter on Clint Eastwood's film *The Bridges of Madison County* for *Clint Eastwood, Actor and Director* and will have a chapter on *Invictus* in the forthcoming *Clint Eastwood: Further Reflections*.

Professor Foery resides in Hamden with his wife and their two part-Siamese cats, Cheddar and Brie. He has three children and two marvelous grandchildren.